MY LIFE

ISADORA DUNCAN

From a photograph by Arnold Genthe

My Life

by

ISADORA DUNCAN

LIVERIGHT

NEW YORK

LIST OF ILLUSTRATIONS

Isadora Duncan   *Frontispiece*
From a photograph by Arnold Genthe

FACING PAGE

Isadora Duncan (1898)   24
Two photographs by Jacob Schloss

Isadora Duncan   56
As the First Fairy in "Midsummer Night's Dream"

Raymond Duncan   172

Isadora Duncan with Her Pupils   180
From a photograph by Paul Berger

Edward Gordon Craig   188

Isadora Duncan   212
Photograph by Arnold Genthe

Isadora Duncan (Paris)   244

Isadora Duncan with Her Two Children   280

Isadora Duncan at the Acropolis   356

INTRODUCTORY

I CONFESS that when it was first proposed to me I had a terror of writing this book. Not that my life has not been more interesting than any novel and more adventurous than any cinema and, if really well written, would not be an epoch-making recital, but there's the rub—the writing of it!

It has taken me years of struggle, hard work and research to learn to make one simple gesture, and I know enough about the Art of writing to realise that it would take me again just so many years of concentrated effort to write one simple, beautiful sentence. How often have I contended that although one man might toil to the Equator and have tremendous exploits with lions and tigers, and try to write about it, yet fail, whereas another, who never left his verandah, might write of the killing of tigers in their jungles in a way to make his readers feel that he was actually there, until they can suffer his agony and apprehension, smell lions and hear the fearful approach of the rattle-snake. Nothing seems to exist save in the imagination, and all the marvellous things that have happened to me may lose their savour because I do not possess the pen of a Cervantes or even of a Casanova.

Then another thing. How can we write the truth about ourselves? Do we even know it? There is the vision our friends have of us; the vision we have of ourselves, and the vision our lover has of us. Also the vision our enemies have of us—and all these visions are different. I have good reason to know this, because I have had served to me with my morning coffee newspaper criticisms that declared I was beautiful as a goddess, and that I was a genius, and hardly had I finished smiling contentedly over this, than I picked up the next paper and read that I was without any talent, badly shaped and a perfect harpy.

I soon gave up reading criticisms of my work. I could not stipulate that I should only be given the good ones, and the bad were too depressing and provocatively homicidal. There was a critic in Berlin who pursued me with insults. Among other things he said that I was profoundly unmusical. One day I wrote imploring him to come and see me and I would convince him of his errors. He came and as he sat there, across the tea-table, I harangued him for an hour and a half about my theories of visional movement created from music. I noticed that he seemed most prosaic and stolid, but what was my uproarious dismay when he produced from his pocket a deafaphone and informed me he was quite deaf and even with his instrument could hardly hear the orchestra; although he sat in the first row of the stalls! This was the man whose views on myself had kept me awake at night!

So, if at each point of view others see in us a different person how are we to find in ourselves yet another personality of whom to write in this book? Is it to be the Chaste Madonna, or the Messalina, or the Magdalen, or the Blue Stocking? Where can I find the woman of all these adventures? It seems to me there was not one, but hundreds—and my soul soaring aloft, not really affected by any of them.

It has been well said that the first essential in writing about anything is that the writer should have no experience of the matter. To write of what one has actually experienced in words, is to find that they become most evasive. Memories are less tangible than dreams. Indeed, many dreams I have had seem more vivid than my actual memories. Life is a dream, and it is well that it is so, or who could survive some of its experiences? Such, for instance, as the sinking of the *Lusitania*. An experience like that should leave forever an expression of horror upon the faces of the men and women who went through it, whereas we meet them everywhere smiling and happy. It is only in romances that people undergo a sudden metamorphosis. In real life, even after the most terrible experiences, the main character remains exactly the same. Witness the number of Russian princes who, after losing everything they possessed, can be seen any evening at Montmartre supping as gaily as ever with chorus girls, just as they did before the war.

Any woman or man who would write the truth of their lives would write a great work. But no one has dared to write the truth of their lives. Jean-Jacques Rousseau made this supreme sacrifice for Humanity—to unveil the truth of his soul, his most intimate actions and thoughts. The result is a great book. Walt Whitman gave his truth to America. At one time his book was forbidden to the mails as an "immoral book." This term seems absurd to us now. No woman has ever told the whole truth of her life. The autobiographies of most famous women are a series of accounts of the outward existence, of petty details and anecdotes which give no realisation of their real life. For the great moments of joy or agony they remain strangely silent.

My Art is just an effort to express the truth of my Being in gesture and movement. It has taken me long years to find even one absolutely true movement. Words have a different meaning. Before the public which has thronged my representations I have had no hesitation. I have given them the most secret impulses of my soul. From the first I have only danced my life. As a child I danced the spontaneous joy of growing things. As an adolescent, I danced with joy turning to apprehension of the first realisation of tragic undercurrents; apprehension of the pitiless brutality and crushing progress of life.

When I was sixteen I danced before an audience without music. At the end some one suddenly cried from the audience, "It is Death and the Maiden," and the dance was always afterwards called "Death and the Maiden." But that was not my intention, I was only endeavouring to express my first knowledge of the underlying tragedy in all seemingly joyous manifestation. The dance, according to my comprehension, should have been called "Life and the Maiden."

Later on I danced my struggle with this same life, which the audience had called death, and my wresting from it its ephemeral joys.

Nothing is further from the actual truth of a personality than the hero or heroine of the average cinema play or novel. Endowed generally with all the virtues, it would be impossible for them to commit a wrong action. Nobility, courage, fortitude, etc. . . . etc. . . .; for *him*. Purity, sweet temper, etc. . . . for *her*. All the meaner qualities and sins for the villain of the plot and for the "Bad Woman," whereas in reality we know that no one is either good or bad. We may not all break the Ten Commandments, but we are certainly all capable of it. Within us lurks the breaker of all laws, ready to spring out at the first real opportunity. Virtuous people are simply those who have either not been tempted sufficiently, because they live in a vegetative state, or because their purposes are so concentrated in one direction that they have not had the leisure to glance around them.

I once saw a wonderful film called "The Rail." The theme was that the lives of human beings are all as the engine running on a set track. And if the engine jumps the track or finds an insurmountable object in its way, there comes disaster. Happy those drivers who, seeing a steep descent before them, are not inspired with a diabolical impulse to take off all brakes and dash to destruction.

I have sometimes been asked whether I consider love higher than art, and I have replied that I cannot separate them, for the artist is the only lover, he alone has the pure vision of beauty, and love is the vision of the soul when it is permitted to gaze upon immortal beauty.

Perhaps one of the most wonderful personalities of our times is Gabriel d'Annunzio, and yet he is small and, except when his face lights up, can hardly be called beautiful. But when he talks to one he loves, he is transformed to the likeness of Phœbus Apollo himself, and he has won the love of some of the greatest and most beautiful women of the day. When D'Annunzio loves a woman, he lifts her spirit from this earth to the divine region where Beatrice moves and shines. In turn he transforms each woman to a part of the divine essence, he carries her aloft until she believes herself really with Beatrice, of whom Dante has sung in immortal strophes. There was an epoch in Paris when the cult of D'Annunzio rose to such a height that he was loved by all the most famous beauties. At that time he flung over each favourite in turn a shining veil. She rose above the heads of ordinary mortals and walked surrounded by a strange radiance. But when the caprice of the poet ended, this veil vanished, the radiance was eclipsed, and the woman turned again to common clay. She herself did not know what had happened to her, but she was conscious of a sudden descent to earth, and looking back to the transformation of herself when adored by D'Annunzio, she realised that in all her life she would never again find this genius of love. Lamenting her fate, she became more and more desolate, until people, looking at her, said, "How could D'Annunzio love this commonplace and red-eyed woman?" So great a lover was Gabriel d'Annunzio

that he could transform the most commonplace mortal to
the momentary appearance of a celestial being.

Only one woman in the life of the poet withstood this test.
She was the re-incarnation of the divine Beatrice herself,
and over her D'Annunzio needed to throw no veil. For I
have always believed that Eleanore Duse was the actual
Beatrice of Dante re-incarnated in our days, and so before
her D'Annunzio could only fall upon his knees in adoration,
which was the unique and beatific experience of his life. In
all other women he found the material which he himself
transmitted; only Eleanore soared above him, revealing to
him the divine inspiration.

How little do people know of the power of subtle flattery!
To hear oneself praised with that magic peculiar to
D'Annunzio is, I imagine, something like the experience of
Eve when she heard the voice of the serpent in Paradise.
D'Annunzio can make any woman feel that she is the centre
of the universe.

I remember a wonderful walk I had with him in the Forêt.
We stopped in our walk and there was silence. Then
D'Annunzio exclaimed, "Oh, Isadora, it is only possible to
be alone with you in Nature. All other women destroy the
landscape, you alone become part of it." (Could any woman
resist such homage?) "You are part of the trees, the sky,
you are the dominating goddess of Nature."

That was the genius of D'Annunzio. He made each
woman feel she was a goddess in a different domain.

Lying here on my bed at the Negresco, I try to analyse
this thing that they call memory. I feel the heat of the
sun of the Midi. I hear the voices of children playing in a
neighbouring park. I feel the warmth of my own body. I
look down on my bare legs—stretching them out. The softness of my breasts, my arms that are never still but con-

tinually waving about in soft undulations, and I realise that for twelve years I have been weary, this breast has harboured a never-ending ache, these hands before me have been marked with sorrow, and when I am alone these eyes are seldom dry. The tears have flowed for twelve years, since that day, twelve years ago, when, lying on another couch, I was suddenly awakened by a great cry and, turning, saw L. like a man wounded: "The children have been killed."

I remember a strange illness came upon me, only in my throat I felt a burning as if I had swallowed some live coals. But I could not understand. I spoke to him very softly; I tried to calm him; I told him it could not be true. Then other people came, but I could not conceive what had happened. Then entered a man with a dark beard. I was told he was a Doctor. "It is not true," he said, "I will save them."

I believed him. I wanted to go with him but people held me back. I know since that this was because they did not wish me to know that there was indeed no hope. They feared the shock would make me insane, but I was, at that time, lifted to a state of exaltation. I saw every one about me weeping, but I did not weep. On the contrary I felt an immense desire to console every one. Looking back, it is difficult for me to understand my strange state of mind. Was it that I was really in a state of clairvoyance, and that I knew that death does not exist—that those two little cold images of wax were not my children, but merely their cast-off garments? That the souls of my children lived on in radiance, but always lived? Only twice comes that cry of the mother which one hears as without one's self—at Birth and at Death—for when I felt in mine those little cold hands that would never again press mine in return I heard my cries—the same cries as I had heard at their births. Why the same—since one is the cry of supreme joy and the other of Sorrow? I do not know why but I know they are the same. Is it that in all the Universe there is **but** one Great Cry containing Sorrow, Joy, Ecstasy, Agony, the Mother Cry of Creation?

MY LIFE

CHAPTER ONE

THE character of a child is already plain, even in its mother's womb. Before I was born my mother was in great agony of spirit and in a tragic situation. She could take no food except iced oysters and iced champagne. If people ask me when I began to dance I reply, "In my mother's womb, probably as a result of the oysters and champagne—the food of Aphrodite."

My mother was going through such a tragic experience at this time that she often said, "This child that will be born will surely not be normal," and she expected a monster. And in fact from the moment I was born it seemed that I began to agitate my arms and legs in such a fury that my mother cried, "You see I was quite right, the child is a maniac!" But later on, placed in a baby jumper in the centre of the table I was the amusement of the entire family and friends, dancing to any music that was played.

My first memory is of a fire. I remember being thrown into the arms of a policeman from an upper window. I must have been about two or three years old, but I distinctly remember the comforting feeling, among all the excitement—the screams and the flames—of the security of the policeman and my little arms round his neck. He must have been an Irishman. I hear my mother cry in frenzy, "My boys, my boys," and see her held back by the crowd from entering the building in which she imagined my two brothers had been left. Afterwards I remember finding the two boys sitting on the floor of a bar-room, putting on their shoes and stockings, and then the inside of a carriage, and then sitting on a counter drinking hot chocolate.

I was born by the sea, and I have noticed that all the great events of my life have taken place by the sea. My first idea of movement, of the dance, certainly came from the rhythm of the waves. I was born under the star of Aphrodite, Aphrodite who was also born on the sea, and when her star is in the ascendant, events are always propitious to me. At these epochs life flows lightly and I am able to create. I have also noticed that the disappearance of this star is usually followed by disaster for me. The science of astrology has not perhaps the importance to-day that it had in the time of the ancient Egyptians or of the Chaldeans, but it is certain that our psychic life is under the influence of the planets, and if parents understood this they would study the stars in the creation of more beautiful children.

I believe, too, that it must make a great difference to a child's life whether it is born by the sea or in the mountains. The sea has always drawn me to it, whereas in the mountains I have a vague feeling of discomfort and a desire to fly. They always give me an impression of being a prisoner to the earth. Looking up at their tops, I do not feel the admiration of the general tourist, but only a desire to leap over them and escape. My life and my art were born of the sea.

I have to be thankful that when we were young my mother was poor. She could not afford servants or governesses for her children, and it is to this fact that I owe the spontaneous life which I had the opportunity to express as a child and never lost. My mother was a musician and taught music for a living and as she gave her lessons at the houses of her pupils she was away from home all day and for many hours in the evening. When I could escape from the prison of school, I was free. I could wander alone by the sea and follow my own fantasies. How I pity the children I see constantly attended by nurses and governesses, constantly protected and taken care of and smartly dressed. What chance of life have they? My mother was too busy to think of any dangers which might befall her children, and therefore my two brothers and I were free to follow our own vagabond impulses, which sometimes led us into adventures which, had our mother known of them, would have driven her wild with anxiety. Fortunately she was blissfully unconscious. I say fortunately for me, for it is certainly to this wild untrammelled life of my childhood that I owe the inspiration of the dance I created, which was but the expression of freedom. I was never subjected to the continual "don'ts" which it seems to me make children's lives a misery.

I went to the public school at the early age of five. I think my mother prevaricated about my age. It was necessary to have some place to leave me. I believe that whatever one is to do in one's after life is clearly expressed as a baby. I was already a dancer and a revolutionist. My mother, who had been baptised and raised in an Irish Catholic family, was a devout Catholic up to the time when she discovered that my father was not that model of perfection she had always thought him to be. She divorced him and left with her four children to face the world. From that time her faith in the Catholic religion revolted violently to definite atheism, and she became a follower of Bob Ingersoll, whose works she used to read to us.

Among other things, she decided that all sentimentality was nonsense, and when I was quite a baby she revealed to us the secret of Santa Claus, with the result that at a school festival for Christmas, when the teacher was distributing candies and cakes and said, "See, children, what Santa Claus has brought you," I rose and solemnly replied, "I don't believe you, there is no such thing as Santa Claus." The teacher was considerably ruffled. "Candies are only for little girls who believe in Santa Claus," she said. "Then I don't want your candy," said I. The teacher unwisely flew into a temper and, to make an example of me, ordered me to come forward and sit on the floor. I came forward, and, turning to the class, I made the first of my famous speeches. "I don't believe lies," I shouted. "My mother told me she is too poor to be Santa Claus; it is only the rich mothers who can pretend to be Santa Claus and give presents."

At this the teacher caught hold of me and endeavoured to sit me down upon the floor, but I stiffened my legs and held on to her, and she only succeeded in hitting my heels against the parquet. After failing in this, she stood me in the corner, but although I stood there, I turned my head over my shoulder and shouted, "There is no Santa Claus, there is no Santa Claus," until finally she was forced to send me home. I went home shouting all the way, "There is no Santa Claus," but I never got over the feeling of the injustice with which I had been treated, deprived of candy and punished for telling the truth. When I recounted this to my mother, saying, "Wasn't I right? There is no Santa Claus, is there?" she replied, "There is no Santa Claus and there is no God, only your own spirit to help you." And that night, as I sat upon the rug at her feet, she read us the lectures of Bob Ingersoll.

It seems to me that the general education a child receives at school is absolutely useless. I remember that in the classroom I was either considered amazingly intelligent and at the head of my class, or quite hopelessly stupid and at the bottom of the class. It all depended on a trick of memory and whether I had taken the trouble to memorise the subject we were given to learn. And I really had not the slightest idea what it was about. Whether I was at the head or the foot of the class, it was all to me a weary time in which I watched the clock until the hand pointed to three, and we were free. My real education came during the evenings when my mother played to us Beethoven, Schumann, Schubert, Mozart, Chopin or read aloud to us from Shakespeare, Shelley, Keats or Burns. These hours were to us enchanted. My mother recited most of the poetry by heart and I, in imitation of her, one day at a school festival, at the age of six, electrified my audience by reciting William Lytle's "Antony to Cleopatra":

> *"I am dying, Egypt, dying!*
> *Ebbs the crimson life-tide fast."*

On another occasion when the teacher required of each pupil to write the history of their lives, my story ran somewhat in this wise:

"When I was five we had a cottage on 23rd Street. Failing to pay the rent, we could not remain there but moved to 17th Street, and in a short time, as funds were low, the landlord objected, so we moved to 22nd Street, where we were not allowed to live peacefully but were moved to 10th Street."

The history continued in this way, with an infinite number of removals. When I rose to read it to the school, the teacher became very angry. She thought I was playing a bad joke, and I was sent to the principal, who sent for my mother. When my poor mother read the paper she burst into tears and vowed that it was only too true. Such was our nomadic existence.

I hope that schools have changed since I was a little girl. My memory of the teaching of the public schools is that it showed a brutal incomprehension of children. I also remember the misery of trying to sit still on a hard bench with an empty stomach, or cold feet in wet shoes. The teacher appeared to me to be an inhuman monster who was there to torture us. And of these sufferings children will never speak.

I can never remember suffering from our poverty at home, where we took it as a matter of course; it was only at school that I suffered. To a proud and sensitive child the public school system, as I remember it, was as humiliating as a penitentiary. I was always in revolt against it.

When I was about six years old, my mother came home one day and found that I had collected half a dozen babies of the neighbourhood—all of them too young to walk—and had them sitting before me on the floor while I was teaching them to wave their arms. When she asked the explanation of this, I informed her that it was my school of the dance. She was amused, and placing herself at the piano, she began to play for me. This school continued and became very popular. Later on, little girls of the neighbourhood came and their parents paid me a small sum to teach them. This was the beginning of what afterwards proved a very lucrative occupation.

When I was ten years old the classes were so large that I informed my mother that it was useless for me to go to school any more, as it was only a waste of time when I could be making money, which I considered far more important. I put up my hair on the top of my head and said that I was sixteen. As I was very tall for my age every one believed me. My sister Elizabeth, who was brought up by our grandmother, afterwards came to live with us and joined in the teaching of these classes. We became in great demand and taught in many houses of the wealthiest people in San Francisco

CHAPTER TWO

AS my mother had divorced my father when I was a baby in arms, I had never seen him. Once, when I asked one of my aunts whether I had ever had a father, she replied, "Your father was a demon who ruined your mother's life." After that I always imagined him as a demon in a picture book, with horns and a tail, and when other children at school spoke of their fathers, I kept silent.

When I was seven years old, we were living in two very bare rooms on the third floor, and one day I heard the front door bell ring and, on going out into the hall to answer it, I saw a very good-looking gentleman in a top hat who said:

"Can you direct me to Mrs. Duncan's apartment?"

"I am Mrs. Duncan's little girl," I replied.

"Is this my Princess Pug?" said the strange gentleman. (That had been his name for me when I was a baby.)

And suddenly he took me in his arms and covered me with tears and kisses. I was very much astonished at this proceeding and ask him who he was. To which he replied with tears, "I am your father."

I was delighted at this piece of news and rushed in to tell the family.

"There is a man there who says he is my father."

My mother rose, very white and agitated, and, going into the next room, locked the door behind her. One of my brothers hid under the bed and the other retired to a cupboard, while my sister had a violent fit of hysterics.

"Tell him to go away, tell him to go away," they cried.

I was much amazed, but being a very polite little girl, I went into the hall and said:

15

"The family are rather indisposed, and cannot receive to-day," at which the stranger took me by the hand and asked me to come for a walk with him.

We descended the stairs into the street, I trotting by his side in a state of bewildered enchantment to think that this handsome gentleman was my father, and that he had not got horns and a tail, as I had always pictured him.

He took me to an ice-cream parlour and stuffed me with ice-cream and cakes. I returned to the family in a state of the wildest excitement and found them in a terribly depressed condition.

"He is a perfectly charming man and he is coming to-morrow to give me more ice-cream," I told them.

But the family refused to see him, and after a time he returned to his other family at Los Angeles.

After this I did not see my father for some years, when he suddenly appeared again. This time my mother relented sufficiently to see him, and he presented us with a beautiful house which had large dancing rooms, a tennis court, a barn and a windmill. This was due to the fact that he had made a fourth fortune. In his life he had made three fortunes and lost them all. This fourth fortune also collapsed in course of time and with it the house, etc., disappeared. But for a few years we lived in it and it was a harbour of refuge between two stormy voyages.

Before the collapse I saw my father from time to time, and learned to know that he was a poet, and to appreciate him. Among other poems of his was one which was in a way a prophecy of my entire career.

I am relating something of the history of my father because these early impressions had a tremendous effect on my after life. On the one hand I was feeding my mind with sentimental novels, while on the other I had a very practical example of marriage before my eyes. All my childhood seemed to be under the black shadow of this mysterious father of whom no one would speak, and the terrible word divorce was imprinted upon the sensitive plate of my mind. As I could not ask any one for the explanation of these things I tried to reason them out for myself. Most of the novels I read ended in marriage and a blissfully happy state of which there was no more reason to write. But in some of these books, notably George Eliot's "Adam Bede," there is a girl who does not marry, a child that comes unwanted, and the terrible disgrace which falls upon the poor mother. I was deeply impressed by the injustice of this state of things for women, and putting it together with the story of my father and mother, I decided, then and there, that I would live to fight against marriage and for the emancipation of women and for the right for every woman to have a child or children as it pleased her, and to uphold her right and her virtue. These may seem strange ideas for a little girl of twelve years old to reason out, but the circumstances of my life had made me very precocious. I enquired into the marriage laws and was indignant to learn of the slavish condition of women. I began to look enquiringly at the faces of the married women friends of my mother, and I felt that on each was the mark of the green-eyed monster and the stigmata of the slave. I made a vow then and there that I would never lower myself to this degrading state. This vow I always kept, even when it cost me the estrangement of my mother and the miscomprehension of the world. One of the fine things the Soviet Government has done is the abolishment of marriage. With them two people sign their names in a book and under the signature is printed: "This signature involves no responsibility whatever on the part of either party, and can be annulled at the pleasure of either party." Such a marriage is the only convention to which any free-minded woman could consent, and is the only form of marriage to which I have ever subscribed.

At the present time I believe my ideas are more or less those of every free-spirited woman, but twenty years ago my refusal to marry and my example in my own person of the right of the woman to bear children without marriage, created a considerable misunderstanding. Things have changed and there has been so great a revolution in our ideas that I think to-day every intelligent woman will agree with me that the ethics of the marriage code are an impossible proposition for a free-spirited woman to accede to. If in spite of this, intelligent women continue to marry, it is simply because they have not the courage to stand up for their convictions, and if you will read through a list of the divorces of the last ten years you will realise that what I say is true. Many women to whom I have preached the doctrine of freedom have weakly replied, "But who is to support the children"? It seems to me that if the marriage ceremony is needed as a protection to insure the enforced support of children, then you are marrying a man who, you suspect, would under certain conditions, refuse to support his children, and it is a pretty low-down proposition. For you are marrying a man whom you already suspect of being a villain. But I have not so poor an opinion of men that I believe the greater percentage of them to be such low specimens of humanity.

*   *   *

It was owing to my mother that, as children, our entire lives were permeated with music and poetry. In the evenings she would sit at the piano and play for hours, and there were no set times for rising or going to bed, nor any discipline in our lives. On the contrary, I think my mother quite forgot about us, lost in her music or declaiming poetry, oblivious of all around her. One of her sisters, too, our aunt Augusta, was remarkably talented. She often visited us and would have performances of private theatricals. She was very beautiful, with black eyes and coal black hair, and I remember her dressed in black velvet "shorts" as Hamlet. She had a beautiful voice and might have had a great career as a singer, had it not been that everything relating to the theatre was looked upon by her father and mother as pertaining to the Devil. I realise now how her whole life was ruined by what would be difficult to explain nowadays—the Puritan spirit of America. The early settlers in America brought with them a psychic sense which has never been lost entirely. And their strength of character imposed itself upon the wild country, taming the wild men, the Indians, and the wild animals in a remarkable manner. But they were always trying to tame themselves as well, with disastrous results artistically!

From her earliest childhood my aunt Augusta had been crushed by this Puritan spirit. Her beauty, her spontaneity, her glorious voice were all annihilated. What was it that made men at that time exclaim, "I would rather see my daughter dead than on the stage"? It is almost impossible to understand this feeling nowadays, when great actors and actresses are admitted to the most exclusive circles.

I suppose it was due to our Irish blood that we children were always in revolt against this Puritanical tyranny.

One of the first effects of our removal to the large house my father gave us, was the opening of my brother Augustin's theatre in the barn. I remember he cut a piece out of the fur rug in the parlour to use as a beard for Rip Van Winkle, whom he impersonated in so realistic a manner that I burst into tears, as I watched him from a cracker box in the audience. We were all very emotional and refused to be repressed.

The little theatre grew and became quite celebrated in the neighbourhood. Later on this gave us the idea of making a tournée on the coast. I danced, Augustin recited poems, and afterwards we acted a comedy in which Elizabeth and Raymond also took part. Although I was only twelve years old at the time and the others still in their teens, these tournées down the coast at Santa Clara, Santa Rosa, Santa Barbara, and so forth, were very successful.

The dominant note of my childhood was the constant spirit of revolt against the narrowness of the society in which we lived, against the limitations of life and a growing desire to fly eastward to something I imagined might be broader. How often I remember haranguing the family and my relations, and always ending with, "We *must* leave this place, we shall never be able to accomplish anything here."

* * *

Of all the family I was the most courageous, and when there was absolutely nothing to eat in the house, I was the volunteer who went to the butcher and through my wiles induced him to give me mutton chops without payment. I was the one sent to the baker, to entice him to continue credit. I took a real adventurous pleasure in these excursions, especially when I was successful, as I generally was. I used to dance all the way home with joy, bearing the spoils and feeling like a highwayman. This was a very good education, for from learning to wheedle ferocious butchers, I gained the technique which enabled me afterwards to face ferocious managers.

I remember once, when I was quite a baby, finding my mother weeping over some things which she had knitted for a shop and which had been refused. I took the basket from her, and putting one of the knitted caps on my head and a pair of knitted mittens on my hands, I went from door to door and peddled them. I sold everything and brought home twice the money mother would have received from the shop.

When I hear fathers of families saying they are working to leave a lot of money for their children, I wonder if they realise that by so doing they are taking all the spirit of adventure from the lives of those children. For every dollar they leave them makes them so much the weaker. The finest inheritance you can give to a child is to allow it to make its own way, completely on its own feet. Our teaching led my sister and me into the richest houses in San Francisco. I did not envy these rich children; on the contrary, I pitied them. I was amazed at the smallness and stupidity of their lives, and, in comparison to these children of millionaires, I seemed to be a thousand times richer in everything that made life worth while.

Our fame as teachers increased. We called it a new system of dancing, but in reality there was no system. I followed my fantasy and improvised, teaching any pretty thing that came into my head. One of my first dances was Longfellow's poem, "I shot an arrow into the air." I used to recite the poem and teach the children to follow its meaning in gesture and movement. In the evenings my mother played to us while I composed dances. A dear old lady friend who came to spend the evening with us very often, and who had lived in Vienna, said I reminded her of Fanny Elssler, and she would recount to us the triumphs of Fanny Elssler. "Isadora will be a second Fanny Elssler," she would say, and this incited me to ambitious dreams. She told my mother to take me to a famous ballet teacher in San Francisco, but his lessons did not please me. When the teacher told me to stand on my toes I asked him why, and when he replied "Because it is beautiful," I said that it was ugly and against nature and after the third lesson I left his class, never to return. This stiff and commonplace gym-

nastics which he called dancing only disturbed my dream. I
dreamed of a different dance. I did not know just what it
would be, but I was feeling out towards an invisible world
into which I divined I might enter if I found the key. My art
was already in me when I was a little girl, and it was owing
to the heroic and adventurous spirit of my mother that it
was not stifled. I believe that whatever the child is going
to do in life should be begun when it is very young. I wonder
how many parents realise that by the so-called education
they are giving their children, they are only driving them
into the commonplace, and depriving them of any chance of
doing anything beautiful or original. But I suppose this
must be so, or who would supply us with the thousands of
shop and bank clerks, etc., who seem to be necessary for
organised civilised life.

My mother had four children. Perhaps by a system
of coercion and education she might have turned us into
practical citizens, and sometimes she lamented, "Why must
all four be artists and not one practical?" But it was her
own beautiful and restless spirit that made us artists. My
mother cared nothing for material things and she taught us
a fine scorn and contempt for all such possessions as houses,
furniture, belongings of all kinds. It was owing to her example that I have never worn a jewel in my life. She taught
us that such things were trammels.

After I left school I became a great reader. There was a
public library in Oakland, where we then lived, but no matter
how many miles we were from it, I ran or danced or skipped
there and back. The librarian was a very wonderful and
beautiful woman, a poetess of California, Ina Coolbrith.
She encouraged my reading and I thought she always looked
pleased when I asked for fine books. She had very beautiful
eyes that glowed with burning fire and passion. Afterwards
I learnt that at one time my father had been very much in

love with her. She was evidently the great passion of his life and it was probably by the invisible thread of circumstance that I was drawn to her.

At that time I read all the works of Dickens, Thackeray, Shakespeare, and thousands of novels besides, good and bad, inspired books and trash—I devoured everything. I used to sit up at night, reading until dawn by the light of candles' ends which I had collected during the day. I also started to write a novel, and at this time I edited a newspaper, all of which I wrote myself, editorials, local news and short stories. In addition I kept a journal, for which I invented a secret language, for at this time I had a great secret. I was in love.

Besides the classes of children, my sister and I had taken some older pupils to whom she taught what was then called "Society dancing," the valse, mazurka, polka, and so forth, and among these pupils were two young men. One was a young doctor and the other a chemist. The chemist was amazingly beautiful and had a lovely name—Vernon. I was eleven years old at the time, but looked older as I had my hair up and my dresses long. Like the heroine of Rita, I wrote in my journal that I was madly, passionately in love, and I believe that I was. Whether Vernon was conscious of it or not, I do not know. At that age I was too shy to declare my passion. We went to balls and dances where he danced almost every dance with me and afterwards I sat up until the small hours recounting to my journal the terrifying thrills which I felt, "floating," as I put it, "in his arms." During the day he worked in a drug store in the main street and I walked miles just to pass the drug store once. Sometimes I mustered up enough courage to go in and say, "How do you do?" I also found out the house where he lodged, and I used to run away from home in the evening to watch the light in his window. This passion lasted two years and

I believed that I suffered quite intensely. At the end of the two years he announced his approaching marriage to a young girl in Oakland society. I confined my agonised despair to my journal and I remember the day of the wedding and what I felt as I saw him walking down the aisle with a plain girl in a white veil. After that I never saw him.

The last time I danced in San Francisco, there came into my dressing-room a man with snow-white hair, but looking quite young and extremely beautiful. I recognised him at once. It was Vernon. I thought that after all these years I might tell him of the passion of my youth. I thought he would be amused, but he was extremely frightened and talked about his wife, the plain girl, who it seems is still alive, and from whom his affections have never deviated. How simple some people's lives can be!

That was my first love. I was madly in love, and I believe that since then I have never ceased to be madly in love. At the present time I am convalescing from the last attack, which seems to have been violent and disastrous. I am, so to speak, in a convalescent entr'acte before the final act, or can it be that the show is over? I might publish my photograph and ask the readers what they think.

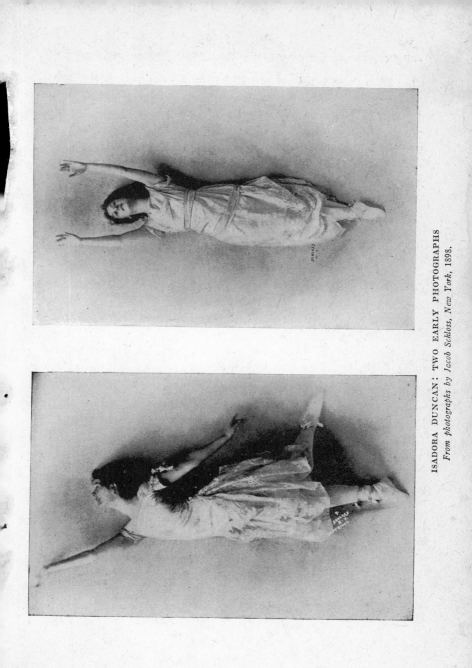

ISADORA DUNCAN: TWO EARLY PHOTOGRAPHS
From photographs by Jacob Schloss, New York, 1898.

CHAPTER THREE

UNDER the influence of the books I had read I planned
to leave San Francisco and go abroad. I had the
idea that I would leave with some great theatrical
company, and one day I went to see the manager of a
travelling company that was playing a week's engagement
in San Francisco and asked to dance before him. The trial
took place in the morning, on the big, black, bare stage.
My mother played for me. I danced in a little white tunic
to some of Mendelssohn's "Songs Without Words." When
the music was finished, the manager remained silent for a
while and then, turning to my mother, said:

"This sort of thing is no good for a theatre. It's more
for a church. I advise you to take your little girl home."

Disappointed, but not convinced, I made other plans for
leaving. I called the family to a council and in an hour's
harangue made clear to them all the reasons why life in San
Francisco was impossible. My mother was somewhat dazed,
but ready to follow me anywhere; and we two started out the
first—two tourist tickets to Chicago. My sister and two
brothers remained in San Francisco with the idea that when
I made the family's fortune they should follow us.

We had with us when we arrived at Chicago, on a hot
June day, a small trunk, some old-fashioned jewellery of my
grandmother's, and twenty-five dollars. I expected that I
would have an engagement at once, and that everything
would be very pleasant and simple. But this was not the
case. Carrying my little white Greek tunic about with me,
I visited and danced for one manager after another. But

their opinion was always the same as the first one's. "It's very lovely," they said, "but *not* for the theatre."

As the weeks went by our money was exhausted, and the pawning of my grandmother's jewellery did not bring in very much. The inevitable happened. We could not pay our room rent and all our baggage was kept, and one day we found ourselves on the street without a penny.

I still had a little real lace collar around the neck of my dress, and all that day I walked hours and hours in the broiling sun, endeavouring to sell that lace collar. Finally, in the late afternoon, I succeeded. (I think I sold it for ten dollars.) It was a very beautiful piece of Irish lace and brought me enough money to pay for a room. With the money which was left I had the idea of buying a box of tomatoes, and for a week we lived on those tomatoes—without bread or salt. My poor mother became so weak that she could not sit up any longer. I used to start out early every morning endeavouring to interview managers, but finally I decided to take any sort of work I could find and I applied to an employment bureau.

"What can you do?" said the woman at the counter.

"Anything," I answered.

"Well, you look as if you could do nothing!"

In desperation, I applied one day to the manager of the Masonic Temple Roof Garden. With a big cigar in his mouth and his hat over one eye, he watched my dance with a supercilious air, while I floated to and fro to the strains of Mendelssohn's "Spring Song."

"Well, you're very pretty," he said, "and graceful. And if you would change all that and do something with some pep in it, I'd engage you."

I thought of my poor mother fainting at home on the last of the tomatoes, and I asked him what he would consider something with pepper.

"Well," he said, "not the sort of thing you do. Something with skirts and frills and kicks. Now you might do the Greek thing first and then change to the frills and kicks and it might be an interesting turn."

But where was I to get the frills? I realised that asking for any loan or advance would be unprofitable and only said that I would return the next day with the frills and kicks and the pepper. I went out. It was a hot day—regular Chicago weather. I wandered along the street, tired and faint with hunger, when I saw before me one of Marshall Field's big shops. I went in and asked to see the manager, and I was shown into the office, where I found a young man sitting behind a desk. He had a kindly expression and I explained to him that I must have a skirt with frills by the next morning, and that if he would give me credit I could easily pay him from the engagement. I do not know what inspired this young man to comply with my request, but he did so. Years afterwards I met him in the person of the multi-millionaire, Mr. Gordon Selfridge. I bought stuff: white stuff and red stuff for petticoats, and lace frills. And with my bundle under my arm I went home, to find my mother at the last gasp. But she bravely sat up in bed and made my costume. She worked all night and by morning had the last frills sewn on. With this costume I returned to the Roof Garden manager. The orchestra was ready for the trial.

"What's your music?" he said.

I hadn't thought of this, but I said, "The Washington Post," which was then popular. The music started up and I did my best to give that manager a peppery dance, improvising as I went on. He was simply delighted, took the cigar out of his mouth and said:

"That's fine! You can come on to-morrow night, and I'll have a special announcement."

He paid me fifty dollars for the week and was kind enough to give it to me in advance.

I had a great success in this roof-garden under an assumed name, but the whole thing disgusted me, and when, at the end of the week, he offered me a prolonged engagement, or even a tour, I refused. We were saved from starvation, but I had enough of trying to amuse the public with something which was against my ideals. And that was the first and last time I ever did so.

I think this summer was one of the most painful episodes in my life, and each time since, that I have appeared in Chicago the sight of the streets has given me a sickening sensation of hunger.

But through all this terrible experience my most courageous mother never once suggested that we should go home.

One day some one gave me a card of introduction to a journalist, a woman called Amber, who was a sub-editor of one of the big Chicago newspapers. I went to see her. She was a tall, gaunt woman of about fifty-five, with red hair. I told her my ideas about dancing and she listened to me very kindly and invited me to come with my mother to "Bohemia" where, she said, we would meet artists and literary people. We went to the club that evening. It was on the top of a high building and consisted of some bare rooms with tables and chairs, crowded with the most extraordinary people I have ever met. In the midst of them was Amber, calling out in a voice like a man's:

"All good Bohemians rally round! All good Bohemians rally round!"

And each time she called the Bohemians to rally round, they lifted their beer mugs and responded with cheers and songs.

In the midst of this I came on with my religious dance. The Bohemians were nonplussed. They didn't know what to make of it. But in spite of it they thought I was a nice little girl, and invited me to come every evening and rally round with the good Bohemians.

The Bohemians were the most surprising group of people—poets, artists and actors of every nationality. They only seemed to have one thing in common: they were all without a cent. And I suspected many a Bohemian, like ourselves, would have had nothing to eat at all, if it had not been for the sandwiches and beer he found at the club, and which were mostly provided by the generosity of Amber.

Among the Bohemians there was a Pole called Miroski. He was a man of about forty-five, with a great shock of red, curling hair, a red beard, and piercing blue eyes. He generally sat in a corner and smoked a pipe and looked on at the "divertissements" of the Bohemians with a slightly ironical smile. But he alone, of all the crowd for whom I danced in those days, understood my ideals and my work. He, too, was very poor. Yet he often invited my mother and myself out to some little restaurant to dinner, or took us by a trolley car into the country, where we had lunch in the woods. He had a passion for goldenrod. Whenever he came to see me, he brought great armfuls of it, and the red-gold flowers of the goldenrod have always been associated in my mind with the red hair and beard of Miroski. . . .

He was a very queer man, poet and painter, and tried to earn his living by carrying on a business in Chicago. But he could never do it and half starved to death there.

At that time I was only a little girl, too young to understand his tragedy or his love. I suppose that in these sophisticated times nobody could realise how extraordinarily ignorant or innocent were the Americans of those days. My idea of life then was purely lyrical and romantic. I had not then experienced or come into contact with any of the physical reactions of love and it was a long time before

I even became aware of the insane passion with which I had inspired Miroski. This man of forty-five or so had fallen madly, insanely in love as only a Pole can love, with the naïve, innocent little girl that I then was. My mother evidently had no premonitions and allowed us to be alone a great deal. Tête-à-têtes together and long walks in the woods had the psychological effect. When, finally, he could no longer resist the temptation of kissing me and asked me to marry him, I believed that this would be the one great love of my life.

But the summer began to wane and we were absolutely without funds. I decided that there was nothing to be hoped for in Chicago and that we must leave for New York. But how? One day I read in the paper that the great Augustin Daly and his company, with Ada Rehan as star, were in town. I decided that I must see this great man who had the reputation of being the most art-loving and æsthetic theatre manager of America. I stood many afternoons and evenings at the stage door of the theatre, sending in my name over and over again with the petition to see Augustin Daly. I was told that he was much too busy and that I must see his under-manager. But this I refused, saying that I must see Augustin Daly himself on a very important matter. At last, one evening, at dusk, I was admitted into the presence of the potentate. Augustin Daly was a remarkably fine-looking man, but towards strangers he knew how to assume an absolutely ferocious expression. I was frightened, but mustered up courage and delivered a long and extraordinary speech.

"I have a great idea to put before you, Mr. Daly, and you are probably the only man in this country who can understand it. I have discovered the dance. I have discovered the art which has been lost for two thousand years. You are a supreme theatre artist, but there is one thing lacking in your theatre which made the old Greek theatre great, and this is the art of the dance—the tragic chorus. Without this it is a head and body without legs to carry it on. I bring you the dance. I bring you the idea that is going to revolutionise our entire epoch. Where have I discovered it? By the Pacific Ocean, by the waving pine-forests of Sierra Nevada. I have seen the ideal figure of youthful America dancing over the top of the Rockies. The supreme poet of our country is Walt Whitman. I have discovered the dance that is worthy of the poem of Walt Whitman. I am indeed the spiritual daughter of Walt Whitman. For the children of America I will create a new dance that will express America. I bring to your theatre the vital soul that it lacks, the soul of the dancer. For you know," I continued, trying not to heed the great manager's impatient interruption ("That's quite enough! That's *quite* enough!"), "for you know," I continued, raising my voice, "that the birth of the theatre was the dance, that the first actor was the dancer. He danced and sang. That was the birth of the tragedy, and until the dancer in all his spontaneous great art returns to the theatre, your theatre will not live in its true expression!"

Augustin Daly did not quite know what to make of this thin, strange child who had the audacity to harangue him in this manner. But all he replied was:

"Well, I have a little part in a pantomime that I am putting on in New York. You can report for rehearsals the first of October and if you suit you are engaged. What's your name?"

"My name is Isadora," I replied.

"Isadora. That's a pretty name," he said. "Well, Isadora, I'll see you in New York on the first of October."

Overcome with delight I rushed home to my mother.

"At last," I said, "some one appreciates me, Mamma. I

am engaged by the great Augustin Daly. We must be in New York by the first of October."

"Yes," said my mother, "but how are we going to get the railway tickets?"

Now that was the question. Then I had an idea. To a friend in San Francisco I sent the following telegram:

Triumphant engagement. Augustin Daly. Must reach New York first October. Wire a hundred dollars for fare.

And the miraculous happened. The money arrived. The money arrived and with it my sister Elizabeth and my brother Augustin who, inspired by the telegram, had decided that our fortunes were made. Still, we all managed to take the train for New York, wild with excitement and happy expectations. At last, I thought, the world will recognise me! If I had known the weary time ahead before this would come to pass, I might have lost courage.

Ivan Miroski was desperate with grief at the idea of parting from me. But we swore eternal love and I explained to him how easy it would be for us to marry when I had made a fortune in New York. Not that I believed in marriage, but at that time I thought it would be necessary to please my mother. I had not yet fully taken up the cudgels for free love for which I did battle later.

CHAPTER FOUR

MY first impression of New York was that it had far more beauty and art in it than Chicago. Again, I was glad to be by the sea once more. I have always felt stifled in inland cities.

We stopped at a boarding-house in one of the side streets off Sixth Avenue. There was a strange collection of people in this boarding-house. They, like the Bohemians, seemed to have but one thing in common: none were able to pay their bills, and they lived in a constant proximity to ejection.

One morning I reported at the stage door of Daly's theatre. Again I was admitted into the presence of the great man. I wanted to explain to him anew my ideas, but he seemed very busy and worried.

"We have brought over the great pantomime star, Jane May," he said, "from Paris. And there is a part for you if you can act in pantomime."

Now pantomime to me has never seemed an art. Movement is lyrical and emotional expression, which can have nothing to do with words and in pantomime, people substitute gestures for words, so that it is neither the art of the dancer nor that of the actor, but falls between the two in hopeless sterility. However, there was nothing to do but take the part. I took it home to study, but the whole thing seemed to me very stupid and quite unworthy of my ambitions and ideals.

The first rehearsal was a horrible disillusion. Jane May was a little lady with an extremely violent temper who took every occasion for bursting into a rage. When I was told that I must point to her to say YOU, press my heart to say LOVE, and then violently hit myself on the chest to say ME, it all seemed to be too ridiculous. And, having no heart in it, I did it so badly that Jane May was quite disgusted. She turned to Mr. Daly and explained that I had no talent whatever and could not possibly carry the part. When I heard this, I realised it would mean all of us being stranded in a terrible boarding-house at the mercy of a relentless landlady. I had in my mind's eye the vision of a little chorus girl who had been turned out into the streets the day before without her trunk, and I recalled all that my poor mother had gone through in Chicago. When I thought of all this, the tears came to my eyes and rolled down my cheeks. I suppose I looked very tragic and miserable, for Mr. Daly assumed a more kindly expression. He patted me on the shoulder and said to Jane May:

"You see, she is very expressive when she cries. She'll learn."

But these rehearsals were martyrdom to me. I was told to make movements which I considered very vulgar and silly and which had no real connection with the music to which they were made. However, youth is adaptable, and I finally managed to fall into the humour of the part.

Jane May acted the part of Pierrot and there was a scene where I was to make love to Pierrot. To three different bars in the music I must approach and kiss Pierrot three times on the cheek. At the dress rehearsal I did this with such energy that I left my red lips on Pierrot's white cheek. At which Pierrot turned into Jane May, perfectly furious, and boxed my ears. A charming entrance into theatrical life!

And yet, as the rehearsals advanced, I could not help but admire the extraordinary and vibrant expression of this pantomime actress. If she had not been imprisoned in the false and vapid form of pantomime, she might have been a great dancer. But the form was too limited. I always felt I wanted to say of pantomime:

"If you want to speak, why don't you speak? Why all this effort to make gestures as in a deaf and dumb asylum?"

The first night came. I wore a Directoire costume of blue silk, a blonde wig and a big straw hat. Alas for the revolution of art which I had come to give the world! I was completely disguised and not myself. My dear mother sat in the first row and she was rather bewildered. Even then she did not suggest that we should go back to San Francisco, but I could see that she was terribly disappointed. For so much striving to arrive at such a poor result!

During the rehearsals for that pantomime we had no money. We were put out of the boarding-house and took two bare rooms with nothing in them at all in 180th Street. There was no money for carfare and often I had to go on foot down to Augustin Daly's in 29th Street. I used to run on dirt, skip on pavement, and walk on wood to make the way seem shorter. I had all sorts of systems for that. I didn't eat lunch because I had no money, so I used to hide in the stage box during the lunch hour and sleep from exhaustion, then start rehearsing again in the afternoon without any food. I rehearsed for six weeks in this way before the pantomime opened, and then performed for a week before any payment was made.

After three weeks in New York the company went on the road on one night stands. I received fifteen dollars a week to pay all my expenses and sent half home to my mother that she might live. When we descended at a station, I did not go to a hotel, but carried my valise and went on foot looking for a boarding-house which would be cheap enough. My limit was fifty cents a day, everything included, and sometimes I had to trudge weary miles before I found this. And sometimes the quest landed me in very strange neighbourhoods. I remember one place where they gave me a room without a key and where the men of the house—mostly drunk —kept making continual attempts to get into my room. I was terrified and, dragging the heavy wardrobe across the room, barricaded the door with it. Even then I did not dare to go to sleep, but sat up on guard all night. I can't imagine any more God-forsaken existence than what they call "on the road" with a theatrical troupe.

Jane May was indefatigable. She called a rehearsal every day and nothing ever suited her.

I had a few books with me and I read incessantly. Every day I wrote a long letter to Ivan Miroski; I do not think I told him quite how miserable I was.

After two months of this touring, the pantomime returned to New York. The whole venture had been a distressing financial failure for Mr. Daly, and Jane May returned to Paris.

What was to become of me? Again I saw Mr. Daly and tried to interest him in my art. But he seemed quite deaf and indifferent to anything I could offer him.

"I am sending out a company with 'Midsummer Night's Dream,'" he said. "If you like, you might dance in the fairy scene."

My ideas on the dance were to express the feelings and emotions of humanity. I was not at all interested in fairies. But I consented and proposed that I should dance to the Scherzo of Mendelssohn in the wood scene before the entrance of Titania and Oberon.

When "Midsummer Night's Dream" opened, I was dressed in a long straight tunic of white and gold gauze with two tinsel wings. I objected very much to the wings. It seemed to me that they were ridiculous. I tried to tell Mr. Daly that I could express wings without putting on papier-mâché ones, but he was obdurate. The first night I came on the stage alone to dance. I was delighted. Here, at last, I was alone on a great stage with a great public before me, and I could dance. And I did dance—so well that the public broke into spontaneous applause. I had made what they call a hit. When I came out in the wings, I expected to find Mr. Daly delighted and receive his congratulations. Instead of this, he was in a towering rage. "This isn't a music-hall!" he thundered. Unheard of that the public should applaud this dance! Next night, when I came on to dance, I found all the lights were turned out. And each time I danced in "Midsummer Night's Dream" I danced in the dark. Nobody could see anything on the stage but a white fluttering thing.

After two weeks in New York, "Midsummer Night's Dream" also went on the road, and again I had the dreary journeys and the hunting for boarding-houses. Only, my salary was raised to twenty-five dollars a week.

A year passed by in this way.

I was extremely unhappy. My dreams, my ideals, my ambition: all seemed futile. I made very few friends in the company. They regarded me as queer. I used to go about behind the scenes with a book of Marcus Aurelius. I tried to adopt a Stoic philosophy to alleviate the constant misery which I felt. However, I made one friend on that trip—a young girl called Maud Winter who played Queen Titania. She was very sweet and sympathetic. But she had a strange mania of living on oranges and refusing other food. I suppose she was not made for this earth, for some years afterwards I read of her death from pernicious anæmia.

The star in Augustin Daly's company was Ada Rehan—a great actress, though a most unsympathetic person to her subordinates—and the only joy I had in the company was when I could watch her act. She was seldom with the road company with which I went, but when I returned to New York I often used to watch her performances of Rosalind,

Beatrice and Portia. She was one of the supremely great actresses of the world. But this great artist in ordinary life did not take any care to make herself loved by the people in the company. She was very proud and reserved and seemed to feel that it was an effort even to say good-day to us, for one day the following notice was posted in the wings:

The company are informed that they need not say good-day to Miss Rehan!

Indeed, in all the two years that I was with the Augustin Daly company, I never had the pleasure of speaking with Miss Rehan. She evidently considered all the minor people of the company as quite beneath her notice. I remember one day when she was kept waiting by some grouping of Daly's, she swept her hand over the heads of us all and exclaimed: "Oh, Guvnor, how can you keep me waiting for these nonentities!" (I, being one of the nonentities, did not appreciate the allusion!) I cannot understand how so great an artist and fascinating a woman as Ada Rehan could have made this mistake, and I can only account for it by the theory that at that time she was nearly fifty years old. She had long been the adoration of Augustin Daly and perhaps she resented his subsequently picking out of the company some pretty girl who would be for two or three weeks— or two or three months—suddenly lifted into leading parts for no apparent reason whatever, but possibly for some reason to which Miss Rehan objected. As an artist I had the greatest admiration for Ada Rehan and at that time it would have meant very much in my life to have had a little kindly encouragement from her. But in all those two years she never looked at me. Indeed, once I remember at the end of the "Tempest," where I danced for the pleasure of Miranda and Ferdinand at their nuptials, she distinctly turned away her head during the whole dance, which embarrassed me so much that I could hardly continue.

In the course of our tournée with "Midsummer Night's Dream" we finally arrived one day at Chicago. I was overjoyed to find my supposed fiancé. It was again summer, and every day that there was no rehearsal we went out into the woods and had long walks, and I learned more and more to appreciate the intelligence of Ivan Miroski. When, a few weeks later, I left for New York, it was with the understanding that he was to follow me there and that we would be married. My brother, hearing of this, fortunately made enquiries and found out that he had already a wife in London. My mother, aghast, insisted on our separation.

CHAPTER FIVE

THE whole family was now in New York. We had managed to take a studio with a bathroom, and as I wanted it to be free of all furniture in order to have space to dance in, we bought five spring mattresses. We hung curtains all round the walls of the studio, and in the daytime the mattresses were put up on end. We slept on the mattresses and had no beds, only a quilt over us. In this studio Elizabeth started school, as in San Francisco. Augustin had joined a theatrical company and was seldom at home. He was mostly on the road. Raymond ventured into journalism. In order to meet expenses, we rented the studio by the hour to teachers of elocution, music, singing, etc. But as there was only one room, this necessitated that the whole family went for a walk, and I remember trudging along Central Park in the snow, trying to keep warm. Then we would go back and listen at the door. There was one elocution teacher who always taught the same poem. It was "Mabel, little Mabel, with her face against the pane" and he used to repeat it with a pathos quite exaggerated. The pupil would repeat it in an expressionless voice and the teacher used to exclaim:

"But can't you *feel* the pathos of it? Can't you just *feel* it?"

At this time Augustin Daly had the idea of bringing over the "Geisha." He put me in, to sing in a quartette. And I had never been able to sing a note in my life! The other three said that I always put them out of tune, so I used to stand sweetly by with open mouth, but not uttering a sound. Mother used to say that it was extraordinary that the others should make such awful faces when they sang, whilst I never lost my sweet expression.

The stupidity of the "Geisha" was the last straw in my relations with Augustin Daly. I remember one day he came through the dark theatre and found me lying on the floor of a box, crying. He stooped down and asked me what was the matter, and I told him that I could no longer stand the imbecility of the things that went on in his theatre. He told me he did not like the "Geisha" any more than I did, but he had to think of the financial side of the affair. Then, to comfort me, Daly slipped his hand down the back of my dress, but the gesture simply made me angry.

"What's the good of having me here, with my genius," I said, "when you make no use of me?"

Daly only looked at me with a startled expression and said, "H'm!" then went away.

That was the last time I saw Augustin Daly: for a few days later, taking all my courage in my hands, I gave in my resignation. But I had learned to have a perfect nausea for the theatre: the continual repetition of the same words and the same gestures, night after night, and the caprices, the way of looking at life, and the entire rigmarole disgusted me.

I left Daly and returned to the studio in Carnegie Hall, and there was very little money, but again I wore my little white tunic and my mother played for me. As we had very little use of the studio during the day, my poor mother often played for me all night.

At this time I was much attracted by the music of Ethelbert Nevin. I composed dances to his "Narcissus," "Ophelia," "Water-Nymphs" and so forth. One day when I was practising in the studio, the door opened and there rushed in a young man with wild eyes, and hair standing on end. And although he was quite young, he seemed to be already attacked by that dreadful disease which afterwards caused his death. He rushed up to me, exclaiming:

"I hear you are dancing to my music! I forbid it, I forbid it! It isn't dance music, my music. Nobody shall dance it."

I took him by the hand and led him to a chair.

"Sit there," I said, "and I will dance to your music. If you don't like it, I swear I will never dance it again."

Then I danced his "Narcissus" for him. I had found in the melody the imagining of that youth Narcissus who stood by the brook until he fell in love with his own image, and in the end pined away and turned into a flower. This I danced for Nevin. The last note had hardly died away when he jumped up from the chair, rushed towards me and threw his arms around me. He looked at me and his eyes were filled with tears.

"You are an angel," he said. "You are a *devinatrice*. Those very movements I saw when I was composing the music."

Next I danced his "Ophelia" for him, and after that the "Water-Nymphs." He became more and more enthusiastically entranced. Finally he himself sat down at the piano and composed for me, on the instant, a beautiful dance which he called "Spring." It has always been a regret to me that this dance, although he played it for me many times, was never written down. Nevin was completely carried away and he proposed at once that we should give some concerts together in the small Music Room of Carnegie Hall. He would play for me himself.

Nevin himself arranged the concert, taking the hall, making the *réclame*, etc., and he came each evening to rehearse with me. I have always thought that Ethelbert Nevin had all the possibilities of a great composer. He might have been the Chopin of America, but the terrible struggle which he had to keep body and soul together in the cruel circumstances of his life was probably the cause of the terrible malady which caused his early death.

The first concert was a great success and was followed by others which caused quite a sensation in New York, and probably if we had been practical enough to find a good impresario at this moment, I would have begun a successful career then. But we were curiously innocent.

Many society women were in the audiences and my success led to engagements in different New York drawing-rooms. At this time I had composed a dance to the entire poem of Omar Khayyám as translated by FitzGerald. Sometimes Augustin read it aloud for me as I danced, sometimes my sister Elizabeth.

Summer was approaching. I was invited by Mrs. Astor to dance in her villa at Newport. My mother, Elizabeth and I went to Newport, which, at that time, was the most ultra-fashionable resort. Mrs. Astor represented to America what a Queen did to England. The people who came into her presence were more awed and frightened than if they had approached royalty. But to me she was very affable. She arranged the performances on her lawn, and the most exclusive society of Newport watched me dance on that lawn. I have a picture taken of this performance which shows the venerable Mrs. Astor sitting beside Harry Lehr, and rows of Vanderbilts, Belmonts, Fishes, etc., around her. Afterwards I danced in other villas in Newport, but these ladies were so economical of their *cachets* that we hardly made enough to pay the trip and our board. Also, although they looked upon my dancing and thought it very charming, they hadn't any of them the slightest understanding of what I was doing, and, on the whole, our visit to Newport left an impression of disappointment. These people seemed so enwrapped in snobbishness and the glory of being rich that they had no art sense whatever.

In those days they considered artists as inferior—a sort of upper servant. This feeling has changed very much since, especially since Paderewski became the Premier of a republic.

Just as the life in California did not satisfy me in any way, so I began to feel a strong wish to find some more congenial atmosphere than New York. And I dreamed of London, and the writers and painters one might meet there— George Meredith, Henry James, Watts, Swinburne, Burne-Jones, Whistler. . . . These were magic names, and, to speak the truth, in all my experience of New York I had found no intelligent sympathy or help for my ideas.

In the meantime Elizabeth's school had grown and we had removed from the Carnegie Hall studio to two great rooms on the ground floor of the Windsor Hotel. The price of these rooms was $90 a week, and we soon realised, with the prices people paid for dancing lessons, the impossibility of meeting this sum for rent, as well as other expenditures. In fact, though we were outwardly successful, our banking account at that time showed a deficit. The Windsor was a gloomy hotel and we found very little joy in living there and trying to meet these heavy expenses. One night my sister and I were sitting by the fire, wondering how we were going to find the necessary cash to foot the bill. Suddenly I exclaimed: "The only thing that can save us is for the hotel to burn down!" There was a very rich old lady who lived on the third floor in rooms filled with antique furniture and pictures, and she had a habit of coming down to the diningroom every morning at 8 o'clock sharp for her breakfast. We planned that I should meet her the next morning and ask her for a loan. Which I did. But the old lady was in a very bad temper and she refused the loan and complained of the coffee.

"I have stayed in this hotel for many years," she said,

"but if they don't give me better coffee, I am going to leave."

She did leave that afternoon, when the whole hotel went up in flames, and she was burned to a crisp! Elizabeth heroically saved her dancing school by her presence of mind, bringing them out of the building hand-in-hand, in Indian file. But we were unable to save anything, and we lost all of our belongings, including family portraits that were very precious to us. We went up to a room in the Buckingham Hotel on the same avenue as a refuge, and in a few days we found ourselves in the same state as when we came to New York, *i.e.*, without a penny. "This is fate," I said. "We must go to London."

CHAPTER SIX

ALL these misfortunes left us stranded in New York at the end of the season. It was then that I conceived the idea of going to London. After the Windsor Hotel fire we were without baggage, without even a necessary change of clothes. My engagement with Augustin Daly and my experiences when dancing before the smart set at Newport, and the New York Four Hundred, had left me in a state of bitter disillusion. I felt that if this was all the response America had to make, it was useless to knock any longer upon a door so closely shut; before so cold an audience. My great desire was to reach London.

The family was now reduced to four. Augustin, when on one of his journeys with a small road company, playing Romeo, had fallen in love with a sixteen-year-old child who played Juliet, and one day he came home and announced his marriage. This was taken as an act of treason. For some reason that I could never understand, my mother was furious. She acted in much the same way as she had done on the first visit from my father, which I have already described. She went into another room and slammed the door. Elizabeth took refuge in silence and Raymond became hysterical. I was the only one who felt any sympathy. I told Augustin, who was pale with anguish, that I would go with him to see his wife. He took me to a dreary lodging-house in a side street, where we climbed five flights of stairs to the room where we found Juliet. She was pretty and frail and looked ill. They confided to me that they were expecting a baby.

So, in our plans for London, Augustin was necessarily

left out. The family seemed to regard him as one who had fallen by the wayside and unworthy of the great future that we were seeking.

And now, once again, we found ourselves in a bare studio, with no funds, at the beginning of the summer. I had then a brilliant idea of soliciting the rich women, in whose salons I had danced, for a sum sufficient to take us to London. First of all I visited a lady who lived in a palatial mansion on 59th Street, overlooking Central Park. I told her of the Windsor Hotel fire, and how we had lost all our belongings, and of the lack of appreciation in New York, and of my certitude of finding recognition in London.

At last she moved towards her desk, and, taking up her pen, began to write out a cheque. She folded the cheque and gave it to me. I left her with tears in my eyes and skipped out of the house—but, alas! on reaching Fifth Avenue I found the cheque was for only fifty dollars, a sum quite insufficient to take the family to London.

I next tried the wife of another millionaire, who lived at the foot of Fifth Avenue, and I walked the fifty blocks between 59th Street and her palace. Here I was received even more coldly by an elderly woman who administered a rebuke on the impracticability of my request. She also explained to me that if I had ever studied ballet dancing she would have felt differently about it, and that she once knew a ballet dancer who had made a fortune! In the heat of pressing my suit I became quite faint and fell over sideways. It was four o'clock in the afternoon, and I had had no lunch. At this the lady seemed rather perturbed, and rang for a magnificent butler who brought me a cup of chocolate and some toast. My tears fell into the chocolate and on to the toast, but I still tried to persuade the lady of the absolute necessity of our trip to London.

"I shall be very famous some day," I told her, "and it

will redound to your credit that you recognised American talent."

At length this possessor of about sixty millions also presented me with a cheque—again for fifty dollars! But she added:

"When you make money, you will send this back to me."

I never sent it back, preferring rather to give it to the poor.

In this way I canvassed most of the millionaires' wives in New York, with the result that one day we had the magnificent sum of three hundred dollars for our trip to London. This sum was not even enough for second-class tickets on an ordinary steamer, if we were to arrive in London with any money whatever.

It was Raymond who had the bright idea of searching round the wharves until he found a small cattle boat going to Hull. The captain of this ship was so touched by Raymond's story that he consented to take us as passengers, although it was against the regulations of his ship, and one morning, with only a few handbags, for our trunks had all been burned in the Windsor Hotel fire, we embarked. I believe that it was this trip which was the great influence in making Raymond a vegetarian, for the sight of a couple of hundred poor struggling beasts in the hold, on their way to London from the plains of the Middle West, goring each other with their horns and moaning in the most piteous way, night and day, made a deep impression on us.

I have often thought of that voyage on the cattle boat when I have been in my luxurious cabin on one of the big liners, and of our irrepressible merriment and delight, and I have wondered if after all a continual atmosphere of luxury does not cause neurasthenia. Our nourishment was only salt beef and tea that tasted like straw, the berths were hard, the cabins small and the fare meagre, but we were very happy during the two weeks' journey to Hull. We were rather ashamed of going on this boat under our own name, so we signed under the name of my mother's mother—O'Gorman. I called myself Maggie O'Gorman.

The First Mate was an Irishman, with whom I spent the moonlit nights, up in the lookout, and he often said to me, "Sure, Maggie O'Gorman, I'd make a good husband to you if you would allow it." On some other nights the Captain, who was a fine man, would produce a bottle of whiskey and make us all hot toddies. Altogether it was a very happy time, in spite of the hardships, and only the bellowings and moanings of the poor cattle in the hold depressed us. I wonder if they still bring cattle over in that barbarous fashion.

The O'Gormans landed in Hull on a May morning, took the train, and a few hours later the Duncans arrived in London. I think it was through an advertisement in *The Times* that we found a lodging near the Marble Arch. The first days in London were spent entirely in driving about on penny 'busses, in a state of perfect ecstasy, and, in the amazement and delight of everything around us, we absolutely forgot how very limited were our resources. We went in for sightseeing, spending hours in Westminster Abbey, the British Museum, the South Kensington Museum, the Tower of London, visiting Kew Gardens, Richmond Park and Hampton Court, and coming home to our lodgings excited and weary, behaving, in fact, exactly like tourists with a father in America to send us funds. It was not until some weeks had passed that we were awakened from our tourist dream by an irate landlady asking for her bill to be paid.

And then one day we returned from the National Gallery where we had been hearing a most interesting lecture on the Venus and Adonis of Correggio to find the door slammed in our faces and the little baggage we had, inside, while we ourselves were on the doorstep. On examining our pockets we realised that we had about six shillings left between us. We turned towards the Marble Arch and Kensington Gardens, where we sat down on a seat to consider our next step.

CHAPTER SEVEN

IF we could see a psychical cinematograph of our own lives would we not be amazed, and exclaim, "Surely that did not happen to me?" Certainly the four people I remember walking about the streets of London might just as well have existed in the imagination of Charles Dickens, and at the present moment I can scarcely believe in their reality. That we youngsters could remain cheerful through such a series of disasters is not astonishing, but that my poor mother, who had already experienced so many hardships and troubles in her life, and who was no longer young, could take them as the ordinary run of things, seems incredible as I look back upon those days.

We walked along the streets of London with no money, no friends and no possible means of finding shelter for the night. We tried two or three hotels, but they were adamant upon the necessity of payment in advance, in default of luggage. We tried two or three lodging houses, but all the landladies acted in the same heartless manner. Finally we were reduced to a bench in the Green Park, but even then an enormous policeman appeared and told us to move on.

This continued for three days and three nights. We lived upon penny buns and yet, such was our amazing vitality, we spent our days in the British Museum. I remember I was reading the English translation of Winckelmann's "Journey to Athens" and, our strange situation quite forgotten, I wept, not for our own misfortunes, but over the tragic death of Winckelmann returning from his ardent voyage of discovery.

But with the dawn of the fourth day I decided that something must be done. Admonishing my mother, Raymond and Elizabeth to follow me and not to say a word, I walked straight into one of the finest hotels in London. I informed the night porter, who was half asleep, that we had just come on the night train, that our luggage would come on from Liverpool, to give us rooms in the meantime, and to order breakfast to be sent up to us, consisting of coffee, buckwheat cakes and other American delicacies.

All that day we slept in luxurious beds. Now and then I telephoned down to the porter to complain bitterly that our luggage had not arrived.

"It is quite impossible for us to go out without a change of clothes," I said, and that night we dined in our rooms.

At dawn of the next day, judging that the ruse had reached its limit, we walked out exactly as we had walked in, but this time without waking the night porter!

We found ourselves on the streets greatly refreshed and ready once again to face the world. That morning we strolled down to Chelsea and were sitting in the graveyard of the old church, when I noticed a newspaper lying on the path. Picking it up, my eyes fell upon a paragraph stating that a certain lady, in whose house I had danced in New York, had taken a house in Grosvenor Square and was entertaining largely. I had a sudden inspiration.

"Wait here," I said to the others.

I found my way alone to Grosvenor Square just before lunch, and found the lady at home. She received me very kindly, and I told her I had come to London and was dancing in drawing-rooms.

"That would be just the thing for my dinner-party on Friday night," she said. "Could you give some of your interpretations after dinner?"

I consented, and delicately hinted that a small advance

was necessary to hold the engagement. She was most gracious, and at once wrote out a cheque for £10, with which I raced back to the Chelsea graveyard, where I found Raymond holding a discourse on the Platonic idea of the soul.

"I am to dance Friday night at Mrs. X.'s house in Grosvenor Square; probably the Prince of Wales will be there; our fortunes are made!" and I showed them the cheque.

Then Raymond said, "We must take this money and find a studio and pay a month in advance, for we must never again subject ourselves to the insults of these low, common lodging-house women."

We searched for a studio and found a small one just off the King's Road, Chelsea, and that night we slept in the studio. There were no beds and we slept on the floor, but we felt that we were again living as artists and we agreed with Raymond that we could never again occupy so bourgeois a home as lodgings.

With what remained of the money, after paying the rent of the studio, we bought some canned food as provision for the future, and I bought a few yards of veiling at Liberty's, in which I appeared on Friday evening at Mrs. X.'s party. I danced the "Narcissus" of Nevin, in which I was a slight adolescent, for I was then very thin, enamoured of his own image in the water. I also danced the "Ophelia" of Nevin, and I heard people whisper, "Where did the child get that tragic expression?" At the close of the evening I danced Mendelssohn's "Spring Song."

My mother played for me; Elizabeth read some poems of Theocritus, translated by Andrew Lang, and Raymond gave a short conference upon the subject of dancing and its possible effect on the psychology of future humanity. This was slightly above the heads of the well-fed audience. but at the same time it was very successful and the hostess was delighted.

It was typical of an English well-bred assembly that no one remarked that I danced in sandals and bare feet, and transparent veils, although this simple apparition made the *klatch* of Germany some years later. But the English are such an extremely polite people that no one even thought of remarking upon the originality of my costume, and, alas! neither did they remark upon the originality of my dancing. Every one said, "How pretty," "Awfully jolly," "Thank you so much," or something of the sort—but that was all.

But from this evening I received many invitations to dance in many celebrated houses. One day I would find myself dancing before Royalty, or in the garden at Lady Lowther's, and the next with nothing to eat. For sometimes I was paid, more often I was not. Hostesses were apt to say: "You will dance before the Duchess of So-and-So, and the Countess of So-and-So, and so many distinguished people will see you that your name will be made in London."

I remember one day when I danced for four hours in aid of a charity performance, that, as a reward, a titled lady poured out my tea and gave me strawberries with her own hand, but I was so ill from not having had any solid food for some days that those strawberries and the rich cream made me very miserable indeed. At the same time another lady held up a huge bag filled with golden sovereigns and said: "Look at the mint of money you have made for our Blind Girls' Home!"

My mother and I were both too sensitive to tell these people of what unheard-of cruelty they were guilty. On the contrary we denied ourselves proper food in order to have the money to appear well-dressed and prosperous.

We bought some cot beds for the studio and hired a piano, but we spent most of our time in the British Museum, where

Raymond made sketches of all the Greek vases and bas-reliefs, and I tried to express them to whatever music seemed to me to be in harmony with the rhythms of the feet and Dionysiac set of the head, and the tossing of the thyrsis. We also spent hours every day in the British Museum Library, and we lunched in the Refreshment Room on a penny bun and café au lait.

We were crazy with enthusiasm at the beauty of London. All the things that were culture and architectural beauty I had missed in America, but now I was able to drink my fill of them.

Before we left New York a year had passed since I had last seen Ivan Miroski, and then, one day, I received a letter from a friend in Chicago telling me that he had volunteered for the Spanish War, had got as far as the camp in Florida, had there been stricken with typhoid fever, and had died. The letter was a terrible shock to me. I could not believe that the news was true. One afternoon I walked down to the Cooper Institute and looked through the files of old newspapers, and there I found, in very small print, among hundreds of others, his name among the dead.

The letter had also given me the name and address of his wife in London, so one day I took a hansom cab and started out to find Madame Miroski. The address was very far out, somewhere in Hammersmith. I was still more or less under the Puritanical influence of America and so I considered it dreadful that Ivan Miroski had left a wife in London of whom he had never spoken to me. So I told no one of my project. Giving the cabman the address, I drove for what appeared to be miles, almost to the outskirts of London. There were rows and rows of small grey houses, each one exactly like the other, with most melancholy and dingy front gates, each bearing a designation more imposing than its neighbour. There were Sherwood Cottage, Glen House,

Ellesmere, Ennismore and other totally inappropriate names, and finally Stella House, where I rang the bell and the door was opened by a more than usually gloomy London maid. I asked for Madame Miroski and was shown into a stuffy parlour. I was dressed in a white muslin Kate Greenaway dress, a blue sash under the arms, a big straw hat on my head, and my hair in curls on my shoulders.

I could hear feet trampling overhead, and a sharp, clear voice saying, "Now, girls, order, order." Stella House was a school for girls. I was labouring under an emotion that was a mixture of fright and, in spite of Ivan's tragic death, a gnawing jealousy, when there entered one of the strangest little figures I have ever seen in my life, not more than four feet high, thin to emaciation, with shining grey eyes, and sparse grey hair, a small white face with thin compressed pale lips.

Her welcome was not very cordial. I tried to explain who I was.

"I know," she said, "you are Isadora; Ivan wrote to me about you in many of his letters."

"I am so sorry," I faltered. "He never spoke to me about you."

"No," she said, "he would not, but I was to have gone out to him and now——he is dead."

She said this with such an expression of voice that I began to cry. Then she began to cry, too, and with that it was as though we had always been friends.

She took me up to her room, where the walls were covered with pictures of Ivan Miroski. There were pictures of him when he was young—a face of extraordinary beauty and force, and a picture which he had sent her in his uniform as a soldier, which she had encircled with crape. She told me the story of their life, how he had gone to seek his

ISADORA DUNCAN

as the First Fairy in "Midsummer Night's Dream"

fortune in America, only there was not enough money for both to go together.

"I was to have joined him," she said. "He always kept writing: 'In a very little while I shall have the money and you will come.'"

Years went by and she still kept her position as governess in a girls' school, and her hair had turned white and still Ivan had never sent her the money to go to America.

I contrasted the fate of this patient little old lady—for she seemed very old to me—with my own daring voyages, and I could not understand it. As she was Ivan Miroski's wife, why had she not gone to him, if she had wanted to? Even as a steerage passenger. For I was never able to understand, then or later on, why, if one wanted to do a thing, one should not do it. For I have never waited to do as I wished. This has frequently brought me to disaster and calamity, but at least I have had the satisfaction of getting my own way. How could this poor, patient little creature have waited, year after year, for a man who was her husband to send for her.

I sat in her room surrounded by the pictures of Ivan, she holding my hands in a tight grip and talking and talking about him, until I realised it was becoming dark.

She made me promise to come again, and I said she must come and see us, but she said she never had a moment, as she had to work from very early in the morning until late at night, teaching and correcting the girls' exercises.

As I had sent the cab away, I went home on the tops of 'busses. I remember I cried all the way home at the fate of Ivan Miroski and his poor little wife, but at the same time I had a strange exultant sense of power and a contempt for people who were failures, or who spent their lives waiting for things. Such is the cruelty of extreme youth.

Up to then I had been sleeping with Ivan Miroski's photograph and letters under my pillow, but from that day I consigned them to a closed packet in my trunk.

*   *   *

When the first month of our tenancy of the Chelsea studio was ended the weather was very hot, and we took a furnished studio which we found to let in Kensington. Here I had a piano and more room to work in. But suddenly, at the end of July, the London season closed, and there we were with August before us and very little money saved from the season. We spent the entire month of August between the Kensington Museum and the British Museum Library, and we often walked home, after the library closed, from the British Museum to our studio in Kensington.

One evening, to my astonishment, little Madame Miroski made her appearance and invited me to dinner. She was much excited. This visit meant a great adventure to her. She even ordered a bottle of Burgundy for our dinner. She asked me to tell her just how Ivan had looked in Chicago, and what he had said, and I told her how he loved to gather the goldenrod in the woods, how I had seen him one day with the sun shining on his red hair and his arms filled with goldenrod and how I always associated him with that flower. She wept and I also shed tears. We drank another bottle of Burgundy and indulged in a perfect orgy of reminiscences. Then she left me to find her way home by a labyrinth of omnibuses, back to Stella House.

September came, and Elizabeth, who had had some correspondence with the mothers of our former pupils in New York, one of whom sent her a cheque for her return passage, decided that she must go back to America and make some money.

"For," she said, "if I make money I can send some to you, and as you will soon be rich and famous, I can soon rejoin you."

I remember we went to a store in Kensington High Street and bought her a warm travelling coat, and finally we saw her off on the boat train, and we three who were left behind returned to the studio where we spent some days of absolute depression.

The cheery and gentle Elizabeth was gone. October loomed cold and dreary. We had our first taste of a London fog, and a régime of penny soups had perhaps rendered us anæmic. Even the British Museum had lost its charm. There were long days when we had not even the courage to go out, but sat in the studio wrapped in blankets, playing chequers on an improvised chequer-board with pieces of cardboard.

Just as I am astonished when I look back at our extraordinary buoyancy, so, when I look back on this period, I am astonished at the complete collapse of our spirits. There were days, in fact, when we no longer had the courage to get up in the morning, but slept all day.

At last there came a letter from Elizabeth enclosing a remittance. She had arrived in New York, had put up at the Buckingham Hotel in Fifth Avenue, opened her school and was doing well. This gave us heart. As the term of our studio had expired, we rented a small furnished house in Kensington Square. This gave us the privilege of a key to the Square gardens.

One night, in the Indian summer, Raymond and I were dancing in the gardens, when an extremely beautiful woman in a large black hat appeared and said, "Where on earth did you people come from?"

"Not from the earth at all," I replied, "but from the moon."

"Well," she said, "whether from the earth or the moon, you are very sweet; won't you come and see me?"

We followed her to her very lovely home in Kensington

Square where marvellous pictures by Burne-Jones and Rossetti and William Morris reflected her image.

She was Mrs. Patrick Campbell. She sat at the piano and played to us and sang old English songs, and then she recited poetry for us, and finally I danced for her. She was magnificently beautiful, with luxurious black hair, great black eyes, a creamy complexion and the throat of a goddess.

She made us all fall in love with her and that meeting with her definitely rescued us from the state of gloom and depression into which we had fallen. It also inaugurated the epoch of a change of fortune, for Mrs. Patrick Campbell expressed herself so delighted with my dancing, that she gave me a letter of introduction to Mrs. George Wyndham. She told us that as a young girl she had made her début at Mrs. Wyndham's house, reciting Juliet. Mrs. Wyndham received me most charmingly, and I had my first experience of an English afternoon tea before an open fire.

There is something about an open fire, bread and butter sandwiches, very strong tea, a yellow fog without and the cultural drawl of English voices which makes London very attractive and if I had been fascinated before, from that moment I loved it dearly. There was in this house a magic atmosphere of security and comfort, of culture and ease, and I must say I felt as much at home as a fish that has found the water to which it belongs. The beautiful library, too, attracted me very much.

It was in this house that I first noticed the extraordinary demeanour of good English servants, who move about with a sort of assured aristocratic manner of their own, and, far from objecting to being servants, or wishing to rise in the social scale as they do in America, they are proud of working "for the best families." Their fathers did it before them, and their children will do it after them. This is the kind of thing that makes for the calm and security of existence.

Mrs. Wyndham arranged for me to dance in her drawing-room one evening, and nearly all the artistic and literary people in London were present. Here I met a man who was to impress himself deeply on my life. He was a man of about fifty years of age at that time, with one of the most beautiful heads I have ever seen. Deep-set eyes under a prominent forehead, a classical nose and a delicate mouth, a tall, slender figure with a slight stoop, grey hair parted in the middle and waving over his ears, and a singularly sweet expression. This was Charles Hallé, the son of the famous pianist. It was strange that of all the young men I met at that time, who were quite ready to pay court to me, no one attracted me, in fact I did not even notice their existence, but I became at once passionately attached to this man of fifty.

He had been a great friend of Mary Anderson in her youth, and he invited me to tea at his studio where he showed me the tunic she had worn as Virgilia in "Coriolanus," and which he kept as a sacred memento. After this first visit our friendship became very deep and there was hardly an afternoon that I did not find my way to his studio. He told me many things about Burne-Jones, who had been his intimate friend, Rossetti, William Morris and all the school of Pre-Raphaelites; of Whistler and Tennyson, all of whom he had known very well. In his studio I spent enchanted hours, and it is to the friendship of this delightful artist that I partly owe the revelation of the art of the Old Masters.

At that time Charles Hallé was a Director of the New Gallery where all the modern painters exhibited. It was a very charming little gallery with a central court and a fountain, and Charles Hallé conceived the idea of my giving performances there. He introduced me to his friends Sir William Richmond, the painter, Mr. Andrew Lang, and Sir Hubert Parry, the composer, and each consented to give a

conference, Sir William Richmond upon dancing in its relation to painting, Andrew Lang on dancing in its relation to
the Greek myth, and Sir Hubert Parry on dancing in its
relation to music. I danced in the central court, round the
fountain, surrounded by rare plants and flowers and banks
of palms, and these functions were a great success. The
newspapers were enthusiastic and Charles Hallé was overjoyed at my success; every one of note in London invited
me to tea or dinner and we had a short period during which
fortune smiled upon us.

One afternoon at a crowded reception in Mrs. Ronald's
little house I was presented to the Prince of Wales, afterwards King Edward. He exclaimed that I was a Gainsborough beauty, and this appellation added to the general
enthusiasm of London Society.

Our fortunes having improved, we took a large studio in
Warwick Square, where I spent my days in working out the
new-found inspiration under the influence of what I had
seen of Italian art in the National Gallery, though I think
that at this period I was also strongly under the influence
of Burne-Jones and Rossetti.

At that moment there came into my life a young poet
with a soft voice and dreamy eyes, fresh from Oxford. He
was descended from a line of Stewarts and his name was
Douglas Ainslie. Every evening at dusk he appeared at
the studio with three or four volumes under his arm, and
read to me the poems of Swinburne, Keats, Browning, Rossetti and Oscar Wilde. He loved reading aloud and I adored
listening to him. My poor mother, who deemed that it was
absolutely necessary to act as chaperon on these occasions,
although she knew and loved this poetry, could not understand the Oxford manner of reciting poetry, and after an
hour or so, especially of William Morris, she used to fall

asleep, at which moment the young poet would lean forward and kiss me lightly on the cheek.

I was very happy in this friendship and between Ainslie and Charles Hallé I desired no other friends. Ordinary young men bored me exceedingly and though at the time there were many who, after seeing me dance in London drawing-rooms, would have been delighted to call upon me or take me out, my manner was so superior that they were completely frozen.

Charles Hallé lived in a little old house in Cadogan Street, with a very charming maiden sister. Miss Hallé was also most kind to me and would often invite me to little dinners where we three were alone, and it was with them that I first went to see Henry Irving and Ellen Terry. I saw Irving first in "The Bells," and his great art excited in me such enthusiasm and admiration that I lived under the impression of it and could not sleep for weeks. As for Ellen Terry, she became then, and ever after remained, the ideal of my life. And who that never saw Irving could ever comprehend the thrilling beauty and grandeur of his interpretations. It is impossible to describe the charm of his intellectual and dramatic power. He was an artist of such genius that his very defects became qualities to be admired. There was something of the genius and majesty of Dante in his presence.

One day in that summer Charles Hallé had taken me to see Watts, the great painter, and I danced for him in his garden. In his house I saw the marvellous face of Ellen Terry repeated many times in his pictures. We walked together in his garden, and he told me many beautiful things about his art and life.

Ellen Terry was then in the full maturity of her magnificent womanhood. She was no longer the tall, slender girl who had captured the imagination of Watts, but deep-bosomed, with swelling hips, and a majestic presence, very different from the present-day ideal! If audiences of to-day could have seen Ellen Terry in her prime, she would have been besieged with advice on how to become thin by dieting, etc., and I venture to say that the greatness of her expression would have suffered had she spent her time, as our actresses do now, trying to appear young and thin. She did not look slight or thin, but she was certainly a very beautiful example of womanhood.

Thus I came in contact, in London, with the highest intellectual and artistic personalities of the day. As the winter wore on there were fewer salons than in the season, and for a time I joined Benson's Company, but never got any further than playing the first fairy in the "Midsummer Night's Dream." It seemed that theatre managers were unable to understand my art, or to understand how my ideas might have been of benefit to their productions. This is strange when one considers how many bad copies of my schools have appeared since in the productions of Reinhardt, Gemier and others of the Advance-guard of the Theatre.

One day I had an introduction to Lady (then Mrs.) Tree. I went up to her dressing-room during a rehearsal, and found her most cordial. But when, following her instructions, I put on my dancing tunic and she took me on to the stage to dance for Beerbohm Tree and I danced Mendelssohn's "Spring Song" for him, he would hardly look at me and kept gazing in a distracted way up to the flies. I told him this story afterwards in Moscow when he had toasted me at a banquet as one of the world's greatest artists.

"What," he exclaimed, "I saw your dance, your beauty, your youth, and did not appreciate it? Ah! What a fool I was!" "And now," he added, "it is too late, too late!"

"It is never too late," I replied, and from that moment he gave me a tremendous amount of appreciation, about which I will speak later.

In fact, at that time, it was difficult for me to understand why, when I had awakened a frenzy of enthusiasm and admiration in such men as Andrew Lang, Watts, Sir Edwin Arnold, Austin Dobson, Charles Hallé—in all the painters and poets whom I had met in London, the theatre managers remained unmoved, as if the message of my art was too spiritual for their gross, materialistic comprehension of the art of the Theatre.

I worked in my studio all day and towards evening either the poet came to read to me or the painter took me out or watched me as I danced. They arranged never to come together as they had formed a violent antipathy to each other. The poet said he could not see how I could possibly spend so much time with that old fellow, and the painter said he could not understand how any intelligent girl could see anything in that jackanapes. But I was entirely happy in both friendships and really could not tell which I was most in love with. Only Sundays were always reserved for Hallé, when we lunched in his studio on a pâté de foies gras from Strasbourg, sherry and coffee, which he made himself.

One day he permitted me to don the famous tunic of Mary Anderson, in which I posed for him for many sketches.

And so the winter passed.

CHAPTER EIGHT

THERE was always a deficit between our expenditure and our earnings, but it was a period of peace. But this peaceful atmosphere had made Raymond restless. He left for Paris and in the spring he bombarded us with telegrams imploring us to come to Paris, so one day Mother and I packed up our belongings and took the Channel boat.

After the fogs of London we arrived on a spring morning at Cherbourg. France seemed to us like a garden and from Cherbourg to Paris we leaned out of our third-class window all the way. Raymond met us at the station. He had let his hair grow long over his ears, and wore a turned-down collar and a flowing tie. We were somewhat astonished at this metamorphosis but he explained to us that this was the fashion of the Latin Quarter where he lived. He took us to his lodging where we met a little midinette running down the stairs, and he regaled us on a bottle of red wine which, he said, cost thirty centimes. After the red wine we set out to look for a studio. Raymond knew two words of French and we walked along the streets saying *"Chercher atelier."* What we did not know was that *atelier* does not only mean a studio in France, but any kind of workshop. Finally, at dusk we found a studio in a courtyard, at the extraordinary price of fifty francs a month, furnished. We were overjoyed, and paid a month in advance. We could not imagine why it was so cheap, but that night we found out. Just as we had composed ourselves to rest, terrific earthquakes seemed to shake the studio and the whole thing seemed to jump into the air and then fall flat. This was repeated over and over again. Raymond went down to inspect and found that we were refuged over a night *imprimerie*. Hence the cheapness of the studio. It somewhat damped our spirits but, as fifty francs meant a great deal to us in those days, I proposed that it sounded like the sea and that we should pretend that we were at the seaside. The concierge provided the meals, twenty-five centimes for lunch and one franc a head for dinner, including wine. She used to bring up a bowl of salad and say with a polite smile, "Il faut tourner la salade, Monsieur et Mesdames, il faut tourner la salade."

Raymond gave up the midinette and devoted himself to me and we used to get up at five o'clock in the morning, such was our excitement at being in Paris, and begin the day by dancing in the gardens of the Luxembourg, walk for miles all over Paris and spend hours in the Louvre. Raymond had already got a portfolio of drawings of all the Greek vases, and we spent so much time in the Greek vase room that the guardian grew suspicious and when I explained in pantomime that I had only come there to dance, he decided that he had to do with harmless lunatics, so he let us alone. I remember we spent hours and hours sitting on the waxed floor, sliding about to see the lower shelves, or standing on tip-toe saying, "Look, here is Dionysus," or "Come here, here's Medea killing her children."

Day after day we returned to the Louvre, and could hardly be forced to leave at closing time. We had no money, we had no friends in Paris, but we wanted nothing. The Louvre was our Paradise, and I have since met people who saw us then—me in my white dress and Liberty hat, and Raymond in his large black hat, open collar and flowing tie—and say we were two bizarre figures, so young and so absolutely absorbed in the Greek vases. At the closing hour we walked back through the dusk, lingering before the statues in the Tuileries gardens, and when we had dined off white beans, salad and red wine, we were about as happy as any one could be.

Raymond was very clever with his pencil. In a few months he had copied all the Greek vases in the Louvre. But there exist certain silhouettes, which were afterwards published, which were not from Greek vases at all, but me, dancing in the nude, photographed by Raymond, which were passed off as Greek vases.

Besides the Louvre, we visited the Cluny Museum, the Carnavalet Museum, and Notre Dame, and all the other museums of Paris. I was especially entranced by the Carpeau group before the Opéra, and the Rude on the Arc de Triomphe. There was not a monument before which we did not stand in adoration, our young American souls uplifted before this culture which we had striven so hard to find.

Spring lengthened into summer and the great Exhibition of 1900 was opened, when, to my great joy, but to the discomfiture of Raymond, Charles Hallé appeared one morning at our studio in the Rue de la Gaieté. He had come over to see the Exhibition, and after that I was his constant companion. And I could not have had a more charming or intelligent guide. All day we roamed through the buildings and in the evening we dined at the Eiffel Tower. He was kindness itself, and when I was tired he would put me into a rolling chair, and I was often tired, for the art of the Exhibition did not seem to me at all equal to the art of the Louvre, but I was very happy, for I adored Paris and I adored Charles Hallé.

On Sundays we took a train and went into the country, to wander through the gardens of Versailles or the forest of Saint-Germain. I danced for him in the forest, and he made sketches of me. And so the summer passed. It was not so happy, of course, for my poor mother and Raymond.

One great impression remained with me of the Exhibition

of 1900—the dancing of Sadi Yacca, the great tragic dancer of Japan. Night after night Charles Hallé and I were thrilled by the wondrous art of this great tragedian.

Another, even greater impression, that has remained with me all my life, was the "Rodin Pavillon," where the complete works of the wonderful sculptor were shown for the first time to the public. When I first entered this Pavillon I stood in awe before the work of the great master. Without, at that time, knowing Rodin, I felt that I was in a new world, and each time I came I was indignant at the vulgar people who said "Where is his head?" or "Where is her arm?" I often turned and apostrophised the crowd, rating them soundly. "Don't you know," I used to say, "that this is not the thing itself, but a symbol—a conception of the ideal of life."

Autumn approached, and the last days of the Exhibition. Charles Hallé had to return to London, but before going he presented to me his nephew, Charles Noufflard. "I leave Isadora in your care," he said, when he was going. Noufflard was a young man of about twenty-five, more or less blasé, but he was completely captivated by the naïveté of this little American girl who had been confided to his care. He set out to complete my education in French art, telling me much about the Gothic, and making me appreciate for the first time the epochs of Louis XIII, XIV, XV and XVI.

We had left the studio in the Rue de la Gaieté and, with the remainder of our little savings, we took a large studio in the Avenue de Villiers. Raymond arranged this studio in a most original manner. Taking sheets of tin foil, he rolled them and placed them over the gas jets, allowing the gas to flare through them like old Roman torches, thereby considerably increasing our gas bills!

In this studio my mother revived her music and, as in our childhood's days, for hours and hours she would play Chopin, Schumann and Beethoven. We had no bedroom or a bathroom in our studio. Raymond painted Greek columns round the walls and we had a few carved chests in which we kept our mattresses. At night we took them from the chests and slept upon them. At this time Raymond invented his famous sandals, having discovered that all shoes were obnoxious. He was of an inventive disposition and he spent three-quarters of the night working out his inventions and hammering, while my poor mother and I had to sleep on the chests as best we could.

Charles Noufflard was a constant visitor and one day he brought to our studio two of his comrades, a pretty youth called Jacques Beaugnies, and a young literary man called André Beaunier. Charles Noufflard was very proud of me and delighted to show me to his friends as a phenomenal American product. Naturally I danced for them. I was then studying the music of Chopin's Preludes, Waltzes and Mazurkas. My mother played extremely well, with the firm, strong touch of a man, and with great feeling and insight, and she would accompany me for hours. It was then that Jacques Beaugnies had the idea of asking his mother, Madame de St. Marceau, the wife of the sculptor, to have me dance one evening for her friends.

Mme. de St. Marceau had one of the most artistic and chic salons in Paris and a rehearsal was arranged in the studio of her husband. At the piano sat a most remarkable man, with the fingers of a wizard. I was instantly attracted to him.

"Quel ravissement!" he exclaimed, "quel charme! Quelle jolie enfant!" And, taking me in his arms he kissed me on both cheeks, in French fashion. He was Messager, the great composer.

The evening of my début arrived. I danced before a group of people so kind, so enthusiastic, that I was quite overcome. They scarcely waited for the end of a dance to call out,

"Bravo, bravo, comme elle est exquise! Quel enfant!" and at the end of the first dance a tall figure, with piercing eyes, rose and embraced me.

"Quel est ton nom, petite fille?" he asked.

"Isadora," I replied.

"Mais ton petit nom?"

"When I was a little girl they called me Dorita."

"Oh, Dorita," he cried, kissing my eyes, my cheeks and my mouth, "tu es adorable," and then, Madame de St. Marceau took my hand and said,

"This is the great Sardou."

In fact that room held all who counted in Parisian life, and, when I left, covered with flowers and compliments, my three cavaliers, Noufflard, Jacques Beaugnies and André Beaunier escorted me home beaming with pride and satisfaction because their little phenomenon had been such a success.

Of these three young men the one who was to become my greatest friend was not the tall and pleasant Charles Noufflard, or the good-looking Jacques Beaugnies, but the rather under-sized pale-faced André Beaunier. He was pale and round-faced and wore glasses, but what a mind! I was always a "*cérèbrale*," and although people will not believe it, my love affairs of the head, of which I had many, were as interesting to me as those of the heart. André, who was at that time writing his first books, "Petrarch" and "Simonde," came every day to see me, and it was through him that I became acquainted with all the finest French literature.

By this time I had learned to read and converse fairly easily in French, and André Beaunier would read aloud to me in our studio for long afternoons and evenings. His voice had a cadence in it that was exquisitely sweet. He read to me the works of Molière, Flaubert, Théophile Gautier, Maupassant, and it was he who first read to me Maeterlinck's "Pélleas et Mélisande," and all the modern French books of the day.

Every afternoon there was a timid knock at the door of the studio. It was André Beaunier, always with a new book or magazine under his arm. My mother could not understand my enthusiasm for this man, who was not her *beau idéal* of what a lover should be, for, as I have said before, he was fat and small with small eyes and one had to be a "cerebrale" to understand that those eyes were sparkling with wit and intelligence. Often, when he had read to me for two or three hours, we went off on the top of a Seine 'bus and rode down to the Ile de la Cité to gaze at Notre Dame in the moonlight. He knew every figure of the façade and could tell me the history of every stone. Then we would walk home and now and then I would feel the timid pressure of André's fingers on my arm. On Sundays too, we would take a train and go out to Marly. There is a scene in one of Beaunier's books in which he describes these walks in the forest—how I used to dance before him down the paths, beckoning to him like a nymph or dryad bubbling with laughter.

He confided to me all his impressions and the sort of literature which he wished to write, which would certainly never have been of the "best seller" description, but I believe that the name of André Beaunier will go down the centuries as one of the most exquisite writers of his time. On two occasions André Beaunier showed great emotion. One was on the death of Oscar Wilde. He came to me white and trembling in a terrible state of depression. I had read and heard vaguely about Oscar Wilde but knew very little about him. I had read some of his poems and loved them and André told me something of his story, but when I questioned him as to the reason why Oscar Wilde was imprisoned, he blushed to the roots of his hair and refused to answer.

He held my hands and just trembled. He stayed with me

very late and kept on saying, "You are my only confidante," and he left me under the strange impression that some uncanny calamity had befallen the world. Again shortly after, he appeared one morning with a white tragic countenance. He would not confide to me what was the reason of his emotion, but remained silent with set face and eyes staring before him and on leaving kissed me on the forehead in such a significant manner that I had a premonition that he was going to his death and remained in painful anxiety until——three days later——he returned in brilliant spirits and confessed he had fought a duel and wounded his adversary. I never knew for what reason the duel took place. In fact I knew nothing of his personal life. He generally appeared at five or six each afternoon and then he read to me or took me for walks according to the weather or our mood. Once we sat at the opening where four roads cross in the Bois de Meudon. He named the right-hand, Fortune, the left Peace . . . and the road straight ahead Immortality and "Where we are sitting?" I asked. "Love," he replied in a low voice—— "Then I prefer to remain here," I exclaimed delighted——but he only said: "We can't remain here," and rose and walked very fast down the road straight ahead.

Very disappointed and puzzled I trotted after him calling out: "But why, but why, why do you leave me?" But he didn't speak again all the way home and left me abruptly at the door of my studio.

This quaint and passionate friendship had lasted over a year when in the innocence of my heart I had dreamt to give it another expression. One evening I plotted to send Mother and Raymond to the Opera and to be alone——that afternoon I clandestinely bought a bottle of champagne. That evening, I set a little table with flowers, champagne, two glasses ——and I donned a transparent tunic and wreathed my hair with roses and thus awaited André, feeling just like Thaïs.

He arrived, seemed very astonished and terribly embarrassed —he would hardly touch the champagne. I danced for him, but he seemed distrait and finally left abruptly saying he had a great deal of writing to finish that evening. I was left alone with the roses and the champagne and I wept bitterly.

When you recollect that at that time I was young and remarkably pretty, it's difficult to find an explanation of this episode and indeed I have never found one—but then I could only think in despair: *"He doesn't love me."* And as a result of hurt vanity and pique, I began a violent flirtation with one of the others of my trio of admirers who was tall and blond and handsome and as enterprising as André was backwards in embraces and kisses. But this experiment also ended badly, for one night after a real champagne dinner in a *Cabinet particulier* he took me to a hotel room booked as Mr. and Mrs. X. I was trembling but happy. At last I would know what love was. I found myself in his arms, submerged in a storm of caresses, my heart pounding, every nerve bathed in pleasure, my whole being flooded in ecstatic joy—I am at last awakening to life, I exulted—when suddenly he started up and falling on his knees beside the bed in undescribable emotion cried: "Oh—why didn't you tell me? What a crime I was about to commit— No, no you must remain pure. Dress, dress at once!"

And, deaf to my laments, he put my coat around me and hurried me to a cab—and all the way home swore at himself in such a savage manner that I was very frightened.

What crime, I asked myself, was he about to commit? I felt dizzy, ill and upset, again left at my studio door in a state of great discouragement. My young blond friend never returned; he left shortly after for the Colonies and when I met him years later, he asked: "Have you ever forgiven me?" "But, for what—?" I questioned. . . .

Such were my first youthful adventures at the borders of

the strange land of Love, which I longed to enter and which was denied to me for many years by this too religious and awe-inspiring effect which I produced upon my lovers—but this last shock had a decided effect upon my emotional nature, turning all its force toward my Art which gave me the joys which Love withheld.

* * *

I spent long days and nights in the studio seeking that dance which might be the divine expression of the human spirit through the medium of the body's movement. For hours I would stand quite still, my two hands folded between my breasts, covering the solar plexus. My mother often became alarmed to see me remain for such long intervals quite motionless as if in a trance—but I was seeking and finally discovered the central spring of all movement, the crater of motor power, the unity from which all diversities of movements are born, the mirror of vision for the creation of the dance—it was from this discovery that was born the theory on which I founded my school. The ballet school taught the pupils that this spring was found in the centre of the back at the base of the spine. From this axis, says the ballet master, arms, legs and trunk must move freely, giving the result of an articulated puppet. This method produces an artificial mechanical movement not worthy of the soul. I on the contrary sought the source of the spiritual expression to flow into the channels of the body filling it with vibrating light—the centrifugal force reflecting the spirit's vision. After many months, when I had learned to concentrate all my force to this one Centre I found that thereafter when I listened to music the rays and vibrations of the music streamed to this one fount of light within me—there they reflected themseves in Spiritual Vision not the brain's mirror, but the soul's, and from this vision I could express them in Dance—I have often tried to explain to artists this first basic theory of my Art. Stanislavski mentions my telling him of this in his book: "My Life in Art."

It would seem as if it were a very difficult thing to explain in words, but when I stood before my class of even the smallest and poorest children and said: "Listen to the music with your soul. Now, while listening, do you not feel an inner self awakening deep within you—that it is by its strength that your head is lifted, that your arms are raised, that you are walking slowly toward the light?" they understood. This awakening is the first step in the dance, as I conceive it.

Even the youngest child understands; from then on, even in walking, and in all their movements, they possess a spiritual power and grace which do not exist in any movement born from the physical frame, or created from the brain. This is the reason why quite small children in my school appearing in the Trocadero or the Metropolitan Opera House before vast audiences have been enabled to hold those audiences with a magnetism generally possessed only by very great artists. But when these children grew older the counteracting influences of our materialistic civilisation took this force from them—and they lost their inspiration.

The peculiar environment of my childhood and youth had developed this power in me to a very great degree, and in different epochs of my life I have been enabled to shut out all outside influences and to live in this force alone. So, after my rather pathetic efforts to gain earthly love, I had a sudden revulsion and return to this force.

Hereafter when André presented himself somewhat timidly and apologetically I deluged him for hours with my discourses on the Art of the Dance and a new school of human movement, and I must say that he never seemed bored or tired but would listen with the sweetest patience and sympathy while I explained to him each movement I had discovered. I also then dreamed of finding a first movement from which would be born a series of movements without my volition, but as the unconscious reaction of the primary movement. I had developed this movement in a series of different variations on several themes,—such as the first movement of fear followed by the natural reactions born of the primary emotion or Sorrow from which would flow a dance of lamentation or a love movement from the unfolding of which like the petals of a flower the dancer would stream as a perfume.

These dances were without actual music, but seemed to create themselves from the rhythm of some invisible music. From these studies I first attempted to express the preludes of Chopin. I was also initiated to the music of Gluck. My mother was never wearied of playing for me, and would repeat the entire score of "Orpheus" over and over until dawn appeared in the studio window.

That window was high, covering the entire ceiling and curtainless—so that always looking up she saw the sky, the stars, the moon—though sometimes the rain pelted down and little trickles of water fell to the floor, for top studio windows are seldom rainproof—also in winter the studio was dreadfully cold and full of drafts, and in summer we baked—and as there was only one room it was not always convenient for our different occupations. But the elasticity of youth defies discomfort, and my mother was an angel of self-effacement and abnegation, only desiring to be helpful to my work. At that time the Countess Greffuhle was the reigning Society Queen. I received an invitation to dance in her drawing-room, where a fashionable throng was gathered, including all the celebrities of Paris Society. The Countess hailed me as a renaissance of Greek Art, but she was rather under the influence of the "Aphrodite" of Pierre

Louys and his "Chanson de Bilitis," whereas I had the expression of a Doric column and the Parthenon pediments as seen in the cold light of the British Museum.

The Countess had erected in her drawing-room a small stage backed with a lattice, and in each opening of the lattice work was placed a red rose. This background of red roses did not at all suit the simplicity of my tunic or the religious expression of my dance, for, at this epoch, although I had read Pierre Louys and the "Chanson de Bilitis," the "Metamorphoses" of Ovid and the songs of Sappho, the sensual meaning of these readings had entirely escaped me, which proves that there is no necessity to censor the literature of the young. What one has not experienced, one will never understand in print.

I was still a product of American puritanism—whether due to the blood of my pioneer grandfather and grandmother, who crossed the Plains in a covered wagon in '49, cutting their road through virgin forests over the Rocky Mountains and across the burning plains, sternly keeping off or battling with the hordes of hostile Indians, or my Scottish blood on my father's side, or whatever it was—the land of America had fashioned me as it does most of its youth,—a Puritan, a mystic and a striver after the heroic expression rather than any sensual expression whatever, and I believe that most American artists are of the same mould. Walt Whitman, in spite of the fact that his writings were once prohibited and classed as undesirable literature, and in spite of his frequent proclaiming of the joys of the body, is at heart a Puritan and so are most of our writers, sculptors and painters.

Is it the great, rough land of America, or the broad open wind-swept spaces, or the shadow of Abraham Lincoln that looms over all, as compared to French sensual art? One might say that the American trend of education is to reduce the senses almost to nil. The real American is not a gold chaser or money lover, as the legend classes him, but an idealist and a mystic. Not that I mean for a moment to say that the American is without senses. On the contrary, the Anglo-Saxon in general, or the American with some Celtic blood is, when it comes to the crucial moment, more fiery than the Italian, more sensuous than the French, more capable of desperate excesses than are the Russians. But the habit of early training has enclosed his temperament in a wall of iron, frosted over, and these things only come to pass when some extraordinary incident of life breaks through his reserve. Then one might say that the Anglo-Saxon or Celt is of all the nations the most fiery lover. I have known such characters who go to bed with two suits of pyjamas: one silk, for softness near the skin and one woollen for warmth, with the *Times*, the *Lancet*, and a briar pipe, turn suddenly into satyrs such as would leave the Greeks behind, breaking into such a volcano of passion as would frighten an Italian for a week!

Therefore, that evening at the Countess Greffuhle's house, in an overcrowded salon full of marvellously dressed and bejewelled women, stifled by the perfume of the thousands of red roses, and stared at by a front row of *jeunesse dorée*, whose noses just reached the end of the stage and were almost brushed by my dancing toes, I was extremely unhappy and felt it was all a failure; but the next morning I received from the Countess a gracious little note, thanking me and telling me to call at the concierge's lodge for the *cachet*. I did not like having to call at the lodge, for I was over-sensitive about money, but the sum, after all, paid the rent of the studio.

Much pleasanter was an evening at the studio of the famous Madame Madeleine Lemaire, where I danced to the music of Orphée, and saw among the spectators, for the first time, the inspired face of the Sappho of France, the Comtesse de Noailles. Jean Lorrain was also present and described his impressions in the *Journal*.

In addition to the two greatest sources of our joy, the Louvre and the National Library, I now discovered a third: the charming library of the Opéra. The librarian took an affectionate interest in my researches and placed at my disposal every work ever written on dancing, and also all the books on Greek music and Theatre art. I applied myself to the task of reading everything that had ever been written on the Art of Dancing, from the earliest Egyptians to the present day, and I made special notes of all I read in a copy-book; but when I had finished this colossal experiment, I realised that the only dance masters I could have were Jean-Jacques Rousseau ("Emile"), Walt Whitman and Nietzsche.

One dark afternoon there was a knock at the studio door. A woman stood there. She was of such imposing stature and such powerful personality that her entrance seemed to be announced by one of those Wagnerian motifs, deep and strong, and bearing portents of coming events and, indeed, the motif then announced has run through my life ever since, bringing in its vibrations stormy, tragic happenings.

"I am the Princess de Polignac," she said, "a friend of the Countess Greffuhle. When I saw you dance your art interested me, and particularly my husband, who is a composer."

She had a handsome face, somewhat marred by a too heavy and protruding lower jaw and a masterful chin. It might have been the face of a Roman Emperor, except that an expression of cold aloofness protected the otherwise voluptuous promise of her eyes and features. When she spoke, her voice had also a hard, metallic twang which was mystifying as coming from her, whom one would have expected to have richer, deeper tones. I afterwards divined that these cold looks and the tone of her voice were really a mask to hide, in spite of her princely position, a condition of extreme and sensitive shyness. I spoke to her of my Art and my hopes, and the Princess at once offered to arrange a concert for me in her studio. She painted, and was also a fine musician, playing both the piano and the organ. The Princess seemed to sense the poverty of our bare, cold studio and our pinched looks, for, when abruptly leaving, she shyly placed an envelope on the table, in which we found two thousand francs.

I believe such acts as these are habitual with Madame de Polignac, in spite of her reputation of being rather cold and unsympathetic.

The next afternoon I went to her home, where I met the Prince de Polignac, a fine musician of considerable talent; an exquisite, slight gentleman, who always wore a little black velvet cap, which framed his delicate, beautiful face. I donned my tunic and danced for him in his music-room, and he was enraptured. He hailed me as a vision and a dream for which he had long waited. My theory of the relation of movement to sounds interested him deeply, as did all my hopes and ideals for the renaissance of the dance as an Art. He played for me delightfully on a charming old harpsichord, which he loved and caressed with his finely tapering fingers. I felt at once for him the warmth of appreciation, and when he finally exclaimed, "Quelle adorable enfant. Isadora, comme tu es adorable," I replied shyly, "Moi, aussi, je vous adore. Je voudrais bien danser toujours pour vous, et composer des danses réligieuses inspirées par votre belle musique."

And then we envisaged a collaboration. Alas, what a despairing waste there is on this earth. The hope of a collaboration, which would have been so precious to me, was soon afterwards cut short by his death.

The concert in the studio of the Princess was a great success and, as she had the generous idea of opening her studio to the public, and not limiting the audience to her personal friends, there followed a more general interest in my work. After this we also arranged a series of subscription concerts in our studio, which held an audience of twenty or thirty. The Prince and Princess de Polignac came to all these concerts, and I remember once, in his admiration, the Prince took off his little velvet cap and waved it in the air, crying "Vive Isadora."

Eugène Carrière and his family also came to those concerts and once Carrière did me the great honour of pronouncing a short discourse on the Dance. Among other things he said:

"Isadora, in her desire to express human sentiments, found in Greek art the finest models. Full of admiration for the beautiful bas-relief figures, she was inspired by them. Yet, endowed with an instinct for discovery, she returned to Nature, whence came all these gestures, and, believing in imitating and revivifying the Greek dance, she found her own expression. She thinks of the Greeks, and only obeys her own self. It is her own joy and her own grief which she offers us. Her forgetfulness of the moment and her search for happiness are her own desires. In recounting them to us so well, she invokes ours. Before the Greek works, revived for an instant for us, we are young with her, a new hope triumphs in us; and, when she expresses her submission to the inevitable, we, too, resign ourselves with her.

"The dance of Isadora Duncan is no longer a 'divertissement,' it is a personal manifestation, as a work of art more living, perhaps, and as fecund in inciting us to works for which we ourselves are destined."

CHAPTER NINE

ALTHOUGH my dancing was known and appreciated by many notable people, my financial situation was precarious, and we often worried terribly how to pay the rent of the studio, and as we often had no coal for the stove, we suffered from cold. Yet, in the midst of this poverty and deprivation, I can remember standing for hours, alone in our cold, bleak studio, waiting for the moment of inspiration to come to me to express myself in movement. At length my spirit would be uplifted, and I would follow the expression of my soul.

One day, as I was standing thus, there called on us a florid gentleman with an expensive fur collar on his coat, and a diamond ring. He said:

"I am from Berlin. We have heard of your barefoot act." (As you can imagine, this description of my Art shocked me dreadfully.) "I have come from the largest music hall to make an engagement with you at once."

He rubbed his hands and beamed as if he were bringing me a wonderful piece of luck, but I retired into my shell like a hurt snail and replied distantly, "Oh, thank you. I would never consent to take my art into a music hall."

"But you do not understand," he exclaimed. "The greatest artists appear in our hall, and there will be much money. I already offer you five hundred marks a night. There will be more later. You will be magnificently presented as the 'First Barefoot Dancer in the World.' (*Die erste Barfuss Tänzerin. Kolossal, kolossal. Das will so ein Erfolge.*) Of course you will accept?"

"Certainly not. Certainly not," I repeated, becoming angry. "Not on any terms."

"But this is impossible. Unmöglich. Unmöglich. I cannot take No for an answer. I have the contract ready."

"No," I said, "my Art is not for a music hall. I will come to Berlin some day, and I hope to dance to your Philharmonic Orchestra, but in a Temple of Music, not in a music hall with acrobats and trained animals. Quelle horreur! Mon Dieu! No, not on any terms. I bid you good day and adieu."

Looking at our surroundings and shabby clothes, this German impresario could hardly believe his ears. When he returned the next day, and the next, and finally offered me a thousand marks an evening for one month, he grew very angry and characterised me as a "Dummes Mädel," until finally I shouted at him that I had come to Europe to bring about a great renaissance of religion through the Dance, to bring the knowledge of the Beauty and Holiness of the human body through its expression of movements, and not to dance for the amusement of overfed Bourgeoisie after dinner.

"Please go away! Allez vous en!"

"You refuse one thousand marks a night?" he gasped.

"Certainly," I replied sternly, "and I would refuse ten thousand, one hundred thousand. I am seeking something which you don't understand." And, as he left, I added, "I will come to Berlin one day. I will dance for the countrymen of Goethe and Wagner, but in a theatre that will be worthy of them, and probably for more than a thousand marks."

My prophecy was fulfilled, for this same impresario had the grace to bring flowers to my loge three years afterwards in the Krol's Opera House with the Philharmonic Orchestra of Berlin playing for me, when the house was sold out for more than twenty-five thousand marks. He acknowledged his error with a friendly, "Sie hatten Recht, Gnädige Fraulein. Küss die Hand."

But for the time being we were very pressed for funds. Neither the appreciation of princes, nor my growing fame, brought us enough to eat. At that time there came frequently to our studio a diminutive lady who resembled an Egyptian princess, although she hailed from somewhere west of the Rockies and bore the name of her native State through a long and famous career. She sang like an enchantress. I noticed that little violet-scented notes were often poked under the door in the early morning hours, followed by the surreptitious disappearance of Raymond. As he was not in the habit of taking walks before breakfast, I put two and two together, and gathered my conclusions. And then one day Raymond announced to us that he was engaged in some capacity in a concert tour to America.

So Mother and I were left alone in Paris. As Mother was ailing, we moved to a little hotel on the Rue Marguerite where she could at last sleep in a bed without draughts from the cold floor, as in the studio, and where she could have regular meals, since we were *en pension*.

In the *pension* I noticed a couple who would have attracted attention anywhere. She, a remarkable looking woman of about thirty, with great eyes—the strangest I have ever seen—soft, deep, alluring, magnetic eyes, filled with fiery passion and, at the same time, with something of the submissive humility of a great Newfoundland dog. She had auburn hair, framing her face like flames, and every movement was vibrant with the appeal of love. I remember thinking that when one looked into her eyes it was like entering the crater of a volcano.

He, slight, with a fine brow and somewhat weary face for one so young. They generally had a third person with

them and were always absorbed in conversation so animated
and vital that it seemed as if this trio could never know
one minute of relaxation or boredom like ordinary people,
but were continually devoured by inward flames; his the
intellectual flame of pure beauty; hers, the passionate flame
of a woman ready to be devoured or destroyed by fire. Only
the third person had something more languorous, more of
the continual sensuous enjoyment of life.

One morning the young woman came to my table and said,
"This is mon ami, Henri Bataille. This, Jean Lorrain, who
has written of your Art, and I am Berthe Bady. We would
like to come one evening to your studio if you will dance
for us."

Of course I was thrilled and delighted. I had never heard
before, or, indeed, since, a voice of such magnetic warmth,
vibrant with life and love, as the voice of Berthe Bady. How
I admired her beauty! In those days, when women's fashions
were so unæsthetic, she always appeared clothed in some
marvellous, clinging gown of changing colours or glittering sequins. I saw her once in such a gown, her head
crowned with purple flowers, starting out for some assembly
where she was to read the poems of Bataille. I thought
surely no poet ever had a more beautiful Muse.

After that meeting they came often to our studio, and
Bataille once read his poems to us there. In this wise I,
a little, uneducated American girl, in some mysterious manner had found the key which opened to me the hearts and
minds of the intellectual and artistic élite of Paris; Paris,
which stands in our world, for our times, for what Athens
was in the epoch of the glory of Ancient Greece.

Raymond and I were in the habit of taking long walks
about Paris. In these rambles we often came across most
interesting places. For instance, one day we found, in the
Parc Monceau district, a Chinese Museum left by an eccen-

tric French millionaire.   Another day, it was the Musée
Guimet, with all its Oriental treasures, the Musée Carnavalet
where the mask of Napoleon thrilled us, or the Musée Cluny,
where Raymond spent hours before the Persian plates, and
where he fell madly in love with the Lady and the Unicorn
in a fifteenth century tapestry.

In our wanderings we came one day to the Trocadero.
Our eyes were arrested by a poster bearing the announcement of the appearance that afternoon of Mounet-Sully
in "Œdipus Rex," by Sophocles.   At that time the name
of Mounet-Sully was unknown to us, but we longed to see
the play.   We looked at the prices at the bottom of the
poster and consulted our pockets.   We had exactly three
francs and the lowest prices, in the upper tribunes, were
seventy-five centimes.   This meant going without dinner,
but we mounted up to the standing room at the back of
the tribunes.

On the stage of the Trocadero there was no curtain.   The
scene was set in a very poor imitation of what certain modern people consider to be Greek Art.   The Chorus entered,
badly dressed, in what certain books on costume describe
as Greek dresses.   Mediocre music, a sweet, insipid tune,
streamed up towards us from the orchestra.   Raymond
and I exchanged glances.   We felt that the loss of our
dinner had been a useless sacrifice, when there entered from
the portico on the left, which represented a palace, a figure.
Over the third-class operatic Chorus and the second-class
Comédie Française scene, he raised a hand:

"*Enfants du vieux Cadmus jeune postérité,*
　　Pourquoi vers ce palais vos cris ont-ils monté?
　　Et pourquoi ces rameaux suppliants, ces guirlandes?"

Ah, how shall I describe the emotion evoked by the first
accents of that voice?   I doubt whether in all the famous

days of antiquity, of the grandeur that was Greece, of the Dionysian Theatre, of the greatest days of Sophocles, whether in all Rome, or in any country, at any time, there was such a voice. And from that instant the figure of Mounet-Sully and the voice of Mounet-Sully, growing always greater, embracing all words, all arts, all dance, moved to such a stature and such a volume that the whole Trocadero, the height and the breadth of it was too small to contain this giant of art. Raymond and I from our place in the tribunes, caught our breath. We grew pale. We grew faint. Tears streamed from our eyes, and when finally the first act was over, we could only hug each other in our delirium of joy. There was an entr'acte in which we both decided that this was the apotheosis of our pilgrimage; the reason why we had come abroad.

The second act began, and the great tragedy unrolled itself before us. To the confidence of the triumphant young king came the first doubts, the first inquietudes. The passionate desire to know the truth at all costs, and then a supreme moment arrived. Mounet-Sully danced. Ah, here was what I had always envisaged—the great heroic figure dancing.

Again an entr'acte. I looked at Raymond. He was pale, his eyes burned, and we swayed. The third act. No one can describe it. Only those who have seen it, seen the great Mounet-Sully, can understand what we felt. When in the final moment of superb anguish, in his delirium and paroxysm of mixed horror, the horror of religious sin and of wounded pride, since it was he who had been the source of all evil, for which every one had been seeking, when, after having torn his own eyes from their sockets, when, at this moment, he knows he can no longer see and, calling his children to him, is left making his final exit, that vast audience of the Trocadero, six thousand people, were shaken with sobs.

Raymond and I descended the long staircase so slowly and reluctantly that finally the guards had to put us out. It was then that I realised that the great revelation of art had been given to me. Thenceforth I knew my way. We walked home like people tipsy with inspiration, and for weeks afterwards we lived upon this impression. How little did I ever dream then that one day I would stand on that same stage with the great Mounet-Sully!

*   *   *

Since viewing his work at the Exhibition, the sense of Rodin's genius had haunted me. One day I found my way to his studio in the Rue de l'Université. My pilgrimage to Rodin resembled that of Psyche seeking the God Pan in his grotto, only I was not asking the way to Eros, but to Apollo.

Rodin was short, square, powerful, with close-cropped head and plentiful beard. He showed his works with the simplicity of the very great. Sometimes he murmured the names for his statues, but one felt that names meant little to him. He ran his hands over them and caressed them. I remember thinking that beneath his hands the marble seemed to flow like molten lead. Finally he took a small quantity of clay and pressed it between his palms. He breathed hard as he did so. The heat streamed from him like a radiant furnace. In a few moments he had formed a woman's breast, that palpitated beneath his fingers.

He took me by the hand, took a cab and came to my studio. There I quickly changed into my tunic and danced for him an idyll of Theocritus which André Beaunier had translated for me thus:

> *"Pan aimait la nymphe Echo*
> *Echo aimait Satyr,* etc."

Then I stopped to explain to him my theories for a new dance, but soon I realised that he was not listening. He gazed at me with lowered lids, his eyes blazing, and then, with the same expression that he had before his works, he came toward me. He ran his hands over my neck, breast, stroked my arms and ran his hands over my hips, my bare legs and feet. He began to knead my whole body as if it were clay, while from him emanated heat that scorched and melted me. My whole desire was to yield to him my entire being and, indeed, I would have done so if it had not been that my absurd up-bringing caused me to become frightened and I withdrew, threw my dress over my tunic and sent him away bewildered. What a pity! How often I have regretted this childish miscomprehension which lost to me the divine chance of giving my virginity to the Great God Pan himself, to the Mighty Rodin. Surely Art and all Life would have been richer thereby!

I did not see Rodin again until two years later when I returned to Paris from Berlin. Afterwards, for years, he was my friend and master.

Quite different, but no less joyful, was the meeting with another great artist, Eugène Carrière. I was taken to his studio by the wife of the writer Keyzer, who had often taken pity on our loneliness and invited us to her family table, where her little daughter, who studied the violin, and her talented boy Louis, now well-known as a young composer, made such a perfect harmony around the evening lamp. I had noticed on the wall a strange, fascinating, sad picture. Madame Keyzer said, "It is my portrait by Carrière."

One day she took me to his house in the Rue Hégésippe Moreau. We climbed to the top floor studio where Carrière was surrounded by his books, his family and his friends. He had the strongest spiritual presence I have ever felt. Wisdom and Light. A great tenderness for all streamed from him. All the beauty, the force, the miracle of his pictures were simply the direct expression of his sublime soul. When

coming into his presence I felt as I imagine I would have
felt had I met the Christ. I was filled with such awe. I
wanted to fall on my knees, and would have done it, had not
the timidity and reserve of my nature held me back.

Madame Yorska, years after, describing this meeting,
writes:

"I remember better than I remember anything that happened when I was a young girl, except perhaps my first encounter with Eugène Carrière, in whose studio I met her, that
day her face and name gushed into my soul. I had knocked
at the door of Carrière's flat as usual with a beating heart.
I could never approach that Sanctuary of Poverty without
a desperate effort to choke down emotion. In that little
house in Montmartre, the magnificent artist worked in happy
silence amidst his adorable ones, wife and mother, all dressed
in black wool—children without toys, but faces so beaming
with affection for their great one. Ah! The sainted creatures.

"Isadora stood between the humble Master and his friend,
the quiet Metchnikoff of the Institut Pasteur. She was even
more still than either of these two; except for Lillian Gish,
I have never seen an American girl look so shy as she did
that day. Taking me by the hand, as one takes a child to
bring him nearer to something one wants him to admire,
Eugène Carrière said, as I stood gazing at her: 'C'est Isadora Duncan.' Then a silence to frame that name.

"Suddenly Carrière, who always spoke very low, proclaimed in a deep, loud voice: 'Cette jeune Américaine va
révolutionner le monde.'"

I can never pass Carrière's picture of his family in the
Luxembourg without tears, as I remember that studio where
I soon became a frequent guest. It is one of the fondest
memories of my youth that I was at once taken to their
hearts and admitted among them as a friend. Often since,
when I have doubted myself, I have thought of that ad-
mittance and regained confidence; for over my whole life has

been shed, like a benediction, the genius of Eugène Carrière, spurring me to keep to my highest ideal, beckoning me always toward a purer visitation in the holy vision of Art, and, strangely, when grief brought me almost to a madhouse, it was the work of Carrière near me that gave me faith to live.

No art has ever shown such force as his, no artist's life such divine compassion and help for the human beings around him. His pictures should not be in a museum, but be placed in a temple of Spiritual Force where all mankind could commune with his great spirit and be purified and blessed thereby.

CHAPTER TEN

THE Western nightingale had once said to me, "Sarah Bernhardt is such a great artist, what a pity, my dear, that she is not a good woman. Now there is Loie Fuller. She is not only a great artist but she is such a pure woman. Her name has never been connected with any scandal."

One night she brought Loie Fuller to my studio. Naturally I danced for her and explained to her all my theories, as I did for every one and, indeed, would have done for the plumber had he come in. Loie Fuller expressed herself filled with enthusiasm, and said she was leaving for Berlin the following day and proposed that I should join her in Berlin. She herself was not only a great artist but she was also managing Sada Yacco, whose art I admired so much. She suggested that I should give concerts through Germany with Sada Yacco. I was only too delighted to accept. And so it was arranged that I should join Loie Fuller in Berlin.

The last day André Beaunier came to bid me farewell. We took a last pilgrimage to Notre Dame, and he escorted me to the railway station. He kissed me farewell in his usual reserved manner, but it seemed to me that I caught a glint of anguish behind his spectacles.

I arrived in Berlin at the Hotel Bristol where, in a magnificent apartment, I found Loie Fuller surrounded by her entourage. A dozen or so beautiful girls were grouped about her, alternately stroking her hands and kissing her. In my rather simple up-bringing, although my mother certainly loved us all, she rarely caressed us, and so I was completely taken aback by coming upon this extreme atti-

tude of expressed affection, which was quite new to me.
Here was an atmosphere of such warmth as I had never met
before.

Loie Fuller's generosity was unbounded. She rang the
bell and ordered such a dinner that I could not help imagining what an extravagant price it would be. She was to
dance that night at the Winter Garden, but as I watched
her I wondered how she would be able to keep her engagement, for she seemed to be suffering from terrible pains in
the spine, for which her lovely entourage brought ice bags
from time to time and placed them between her back and the
back of the chair. "Just another ice bag, darling," she
would say, "it seems to make the pain go."

That night we all sat in the box to see Loie Fuller dance.
Had this luminous vision that we saw before us any relation
to the suffering patient of a few moments before? Before
our very eyes she turned to many coloured, shining orchids,
to a wavering, flowing sea flower, and at length to a spiral-
like lily, all the magic of Merlin, the sorcery of light, colour,
flowing form. What an extraordinary genius! No imitator
of Loie Fuller has ever been able even to hint at her genius!
I was entranced, but I realised that this was a sudden ebulli-
tion of nature which could never be repeated. She transformed herself into a thousand colourful images before the
eyes of her audience. Unbelievable. Not to be repeated or
described. Loie Fuller originated all the changing colours
and floating Liberty scarves. She was one of the first
original inspirations of light and changing colour. I returned to the hotel dazzled and carried away by this marvellous artist.

The next morning I went out to view Berlin for the first
time. At first I, who had already dreamed of Greece and
Greek Art, was momentarily impressed by the architecture
of Berlin.

"But this is Greece !" I exclaimed.

But after I examined it more closely I realised that Berlin did not resemble Greece. This was a Nordic impression of Greece. These columns are not the Doric columns which should soar into the skies of Olympian blue. These are the Germanic, pedantic, archælogical Professors' conception of Greece. And when I saw the Kaiserlich Royal Guard goose-step out of the Doric columns of the Potsdamer Platz, I went home to the Bristol and said, "Geben Sie mir ein Glas Bier. Ich bin müde."

We stayed some days in Berlin, and then left the Bristol Hotel to follow the Loie Fuller troupe to Leipsic. We left without our trunks, and even the modest trunk I brought from Paris was left behind with the rest. Why this should have happened with a successful music hall artist I could not at that time understand. After the luxurious life of champagne dinners and palatial hotel suites, I could not comprehend why we should be forced to leave without our trunks. Later I found out it was because of Sada Yacco, whom Loie Fuller was managing. She had made failures and Loie Fuller's receipts were drained to pay the deficits.

In the midst of these nereids, nymphs, iridescent apparitions, there was a strange figure in a black tailor-made. She was shy, reticent, with finely moulded yet strong face, black hair brushed straight back from her forehead, with sad, intelligent eyes. She invariably held her hands in the pockets of her suit. She was interested in art, and, especially, spoke eloquently of the art of Loie Fuller. She circulated around the bevy of brightly coloured butterflies like some scarab of ancient Egypt. I was at once attracted by this personality but felt that her enthusiasm for Loie Fuller possessed her entire emotional force, and she had nothing left for me.

In Leipsic, also, I went every night to see Loie Fuller,

from a box, and I was more and more enthusiastic about her marvellous ephemeral art. That wonderful creature—she became fluid; she became light; she became every colour and flame, and finally she resolved into miraculous spirals of flames wafted toward the Infinite.

In Leipsic I remembered once being awakened at two o'clock in the morning by hearing voices. The voices were confused, but I recognised that of a red-haired girl whom we called Nursey, because she was always ready to soothe and nurse any one who had a headache. From their excited whisperings I was able to glean that Nursey said she would go back to Berlin to consult with a certain person in order to procure sufficient funds to take us all to Munich. And then, in the middle of the night, this red-haired girl approached me and kissed me passionately, saying in fervid tones: "I am going away to Berlin." As it was only a couple of hours' journey, I could not imagine why she was so excited and upset about leaving us. She soon came back with the money to go to Munich.

From Munich we wished to go to Vienna. Again we were without sufficient funds and, as it seemed quite impossible, this time, to secure any, I volunteered to go to the American Consul for help. I told him that he must get us tickets for Vienna, and it was through my persuasion that we finally arrived there. At the Hotel Bristol we were accommodated in a most luxurious apartment, although we had appeared with practically no baggage. By this time, in spite of my admiration for the art of Loie Fuller, I began to ask myself why I had left my mother alone in Paris, and what I was doing in this troupe of beautiful but demented ladies. I had so far been but a helpless and sympathetic spectator of all these dramatic events *en route*.

In the Hotel Bristol at Vienna I was given as room-mate the red-haired girl called Nursey. About four o'clock one morning Nursey arose and, lighting a candle, advanced towards my bed proclaiming, "God has told me to choke you!"

Now I had heard that if a person suddenly goes mad, one should never cross them. In all my fear, I was able to control myself sufficiently to reply, "That's perfectly all right. But let me say my prayers first."

"All right," she consented, and put the candle on a little table near my bed.

I slipped out of bed and, as if the devil himself were after me, I flung open the door, flew down the long corridors, down the wide staircase, into the office of the hotel clerk, dressed as I was in my nightclothes, my curls streaming behind me, and cried, "Lady gone mad."

Nursey was hot upon my footsteps. Six hotel clerks leapt at her and held her prisoner until doctors arrived. The result of their consultation was so embarrassing to me that I decided to telegraph to my mother to come from Paris, which she did. When I told her all I felt about my present environment, my mother and I determined to leave Vienna.

It so happened that while I was in Vienna with Loie Fuller, I danced one night at the Künstler Haus for the artists. Each man came with a bouquet of red roses, and when I danced the Bacchanal I was completely covered with red roses. That evening there was present a Hungarian impresario, Alexander Gross. He came to me and said, "When you wish to find a future, seek me in Budapest."

And so, in this moment, when I was frightened to death by my surroundings, and desired to rush from Vienna with my mother, we naturally thought of Mr. Gross's offer and turned to Budapest in the hope of a brighter future. He offered me a contract to dance for thirty evenings by myself in the Urania Theatre.

This was the first time I ever had a contract to dance

before the public in a theatre, and I hesitated. I said, "My dancing is for the élite, for the artists, sculptors, painters, musicians, but not for the general public." But Alexander Gross protested that the artists were the most critical audience, and if they liked my dancing the public would like it a hundred times more.

I was persuaded to sign the contract, and the prophecy of Alexander Gross was fulfilled. The first night at the Urania Theatre was an indescribable triumph. For thirty nights I danced in Budapest to a sold-out house.

Ah, Budapest! It was the month of April. It was the spring-time of the year. One evening, shortly after the first performance, we were invited by Alexander Gross to have supper in a restaurant where the gypsy music was played. Ah, gypsy music! This was the first call to the awakening of my youthful senses. With such music what wonder that my budding emotions were beginning to flower. Is there any music like this—the gypsy music springing from the soil of Hungary? I remember, years after, talking to John Wanamaker. We were in the gramophone department of his store, and he was calling my attention to the wonderful music which his machines produced. I said to him, "Of all these finely constructed machines—products of skilled inventors—none could replace the gypsy music of a single Hungarian peasant playing on the dusty roads of Hungary. One Hungarian gypsy musician is worth all the gramophones in the world."

CHAPTER ELEVEN

THE beautiful city of Budapest was fairly bursting into blossom. Across the river, on the hills, lilacs were blooming in every garden. Every night the tempestuous Hungarian audience acclaimed me with frenzy, throwing their caps on the stage and crying: "Eljen."

One night, with the vision of the river flowing and rippling in the sunshine as I had seen it that morning, I sent word to the Director of the orchestra, and, at the end of the performance, improvised "The Blue Danube" of Strauss. The effect was an electric shock. The whole audience sprang to their feet in such a delirium of enthusiasm that I had to repeat the waltz many times before they would behave less like mad people.

That evening there was in the audience calling aloud with the rest, a young Hungarian of god-like features and stature, who was to transform the chaste nymph that I was, into a wild and careless Bacchante. Everything conspired for the change. The spring, the soft moonlight nights, and, when we left the theatre, the scent of the air, heavy with the perfume of the lilacs. The wild enthusiasm of the audience and the first suppers that I had ever eaten in company with absolutely care-free and sensual people, the music of the gypsies; the Hungarian goulasch, flavoured with paprika, and the heavy Hungarian wines—it was, indeed, the first time in my life that I was nourished, over-nourished and stimulated with an abundance of food—all brought about the first awareness of my body as something other than an instrument to express the sacred harmony of music.

100

My breasts, which until then had been hardly perceptible, began to swell softly and astonish me with charming but embarrassing sensations. My hips, which had been like a boy's, took on another undulation, and through my whole being I felt one great surging, longing, unmistakable urge, so that I could no longer sleep at night but tossed and turned in feverish, painful unrest.

One afternoon, at a friendly gathering, over a glass of golden Tokay, I met two large black eyes that burned and glowed into mine with such ardent adoration and Hungarian passion that in that one look was all the meaning of the spring in Budapest. He was tall, of magnificent proportions, a head covered with luxuriant curls, black, with purple lights in them. Indeed he might have posed for the David of Michael Angelo himself. When he smiled, between his red, sensual lips, gleamed strong, white teeth. From our first look every power of attraction we possessed rushed from us in mad embrace. From that first gaze we were already in each other's arms, and no power on earth could have prevented this.

"Your face is like a flower. You are my flower," he said, and over and over again he repeated "My flower—my flower," which in Hungarian means angel.

He gave me a small square of paper on which was written "Loge for the Royal National Theatre." That night Mother and I went to see him play Romeo. He was a fine actor and became the greatest in Hungary. His interpretation of Romeo's youthful flame achieved my conquest. I went to see him afterwards in his dressing-room. The whole company eyed me with curious smiles. Every one seemed to know already, and to be pleased. Only one, an actress, didn't seem pleased at all. He accompanied my mother and me to the hotel, where we had a little supper, as actors never dine before the play.

Afterwards, when my mother thought I was sleeping, I returned and met my Romeo in the salon of our apartment, which was separated from our bedroom by a long corridor. Then he told me that he had, that night, changed his interpretation of the part of Romeo, "I used to vault over the wall and begin at once to declaim in quite an ordinary voice:

'*He jests at scars that never felt a wound,*
  But, soft, what light through yonder window breaks?
It is the East, and Juliet is the Sun.'

But to-night, you remember, I whispered the words as if they choked me, for, since I met you, I know what love would do to Romeo's voice. Only now do I know. For, Isadora, you have made me for the first time know what Romeo's love was like. Now I will play the entire part differently," and he rose and repeated for me, scene for scene, the entire rôle, often stopping to say: "Yes, I see now that if Romeo really loved he would say it thus and thus—quite differently from what I imagined when first I played the part. Now I *know*. Ah, . . . adored, flower-faced girl, you have inspired me. By this love I will become indeed a great artist." So he declaimed the part of Romeo to me till the dawn crept in at the window.

I watched, and listened to him in raptures. Now and then I even ventured to give him the *réplique*, or suggest a gesture, and, in the scene before the Friar, we both knelt down and swore fidelity till death. Ah, youth and spring, and Budapest and Romeo! When I remember you, it does not seem so far away, but just as if it all happened last night.

One evening after his theatre and mine, we went into the salon quite unknown to my mother, who thought I was safe asleep. At first Romeo was happy just reciting his rôles, or speaking of his Art and the Theatre, and I was quite happy listening to him, but gradually I noticed that he seemed troubled and at times quite upset and speechless. He clenched his hands and appeared to feel quite ill, and at such times I noticed that his beautiful face became quite congested, his eyes inflamed, his lips swollen, and he bit them till the blood came.

I myself felt ill and dizzy, while an irresistible longing to press him closer and closer surged in me, until, losing all control and falling into a fury, he carried me into the room. Frightened but ecstatic, the realization was made clear to me. I confess my first impressions were a horrible fright, but a great pity for what he seemed to be suffering prevented me from running away from what was at first sheer torture.

That morning at dawn we left the hotel together, and taking a belated two-horse carriage, which we found in the street, we drove miles out, into the country. We stopped at a peasant's hut where the wife gave us a room with an old-fashioned four-poster bed. All that day we remained in the country, Romeo frequently hushing my cries and drying my tears.

I'm afraid I gave the public a very bad performance that evening, for I felt quite miserable. When, however, I met Romeo afterwards in the salon, he was in such a state of joy and elation that I felt repaid for all my suffering and only desired to recommence, especially as he assured me tenderly that I would finally know what Heaven was on earth. A prophecy which was soon fulfilled.

Romeo had a beautiful voice and he sang to me all the songs of his country and the songs of the gypsies, and taught me the words and meaning. One night Alexander Gross, having arranged for me a gala evening at the Budapest Opera House, I had the idea, after the programme

of Gluck's music, to bring on the stage a simple Hungarian
Gypsy Orchestra and dance the songs of the gypsies.   One
especially was a song of love.   It went thus:

>   *"Csak egy kis lány*
>   *van a világon*
>   *Az is az éi draga*
>   *galabom*
>   *A jó Isten de nagyon*
>   *zerethet*
>   *Hogy én nékem adott tégedet."*

which when translated means:

>   *"One little girl in the world exists.*
>   *She is my dear pigeon.*
>   *The good Lord must love me well*
>   *Because he gave me you."*

A sweet melody, full of passion, longing, tears, adoration.
I danced with such emotion as to bring the vast audience
to tears, and I ended with the Rakowsky March which, in my
red tunic, I danced as a Revolutionary Hymn to the Heroes
of Hungary.

The Gala ended the Budapest season and the next day
Romeo and I ran away for a few days in the country, staying in the peasant's hut.   We knew for the first time the
joy of sleeping all night in each other's arms, and
I had the unsurpassed joy of waking at dawn to find my
hair tangled in his black scented curls, and to feel his arms
around me.   We returned to Budapest, and the first cloud
in this Heaven was the anguish of my mother, and the
return from New York of Elizabeth, who seemed to think
I had committed some crime.   The anxiety of both of them

was so unbearable that at length I persuaded them to go
for a little trip to the Tyrol.

It was then, and always has been, the experience of my
temperament that no matter how violent the sensation or
passion, the brain worked at the same time with a lightning
and luxurious rapidity. I have, therefore, never, in the
slang sense, lost my head; on the contrary, the more acute
the pleasure of the senses, the more vivid the thought, and
when this reaches the state where the brain is the direct
critic of the senses, disappointing and even insulting the
pleasure for which the will to live clamours, the conflict is
such as to lead to a longing of the will for some soporific
to dull the incessant unwanted commentary of the intelligence. How I envy those natures which can give themselves entirely to the voluptuousness of the moment, without
fear of the critic who sits aloft and separates and insists
upon interjecting his view when least wanted, to the coupled
senses beneath.

And yet, there comes always the moment when, capitulat-
ing, the brain cries, "Yes. I admit all else in life, including
your Art, is as vapour and nonsense to the glory of this
moment, and, for this moment, willingly I abdicate to dissolu-
tion, destruction, death." So this defeat of the intelligence
is the final convulsion and sinking down into nothingness
that often leads to the gravest disasters—for the intelligence and the spirit.

So it was that, having learnt the desire, the gradual
approach of the ultimate madness of these hours, leading to the crucial and furious abandon of this final moment,
I no longer recked of the possible ruin of my Art, the
despair of my mother, or the ruin, and loss of the world in
general.

Let those judge me who can, but rather blame Nature or
God, that He has made this one moment to be worth more,

and more desirable, than all else in the Universe that we, who know, can experience. And naturally, just as the flight is high, so the crash of awakening is terrible.

Alexander Gross arranged for me a tour through Hungary. I gave performances in many towns, including Sieben Kirchen, where I was impressed by the story of the hanging of the seven Revolutionary Generals. In a great open field outside the town I composed a March in honour of those Generals, to the heroic and sombre music of Liszt.

Throughout this trip I received a wonderful ovation from the audiences in all these little Hungarian towns. In each of them Alexander Gross had a victoria waiting with white horses, and filled with white flowers, and I, dressed all in white, in the midst of cheers and shouts, was conducted through the town like some young visiting goddess from another world. But in spite of the ecstasy which my Art gave me, and the adulation of the public, I suffered continually with intolerable longing for my Romeo, especially at night when I was alone. I felt I would give all this success, and even my Art, for one moment in his arms again, and I ached for the day of my return to Budapest. The day came. Romeo certainly met me at the station with ardent joy, but I felt some strange change in him, and then he told me he was about to rehearse and make his début as Mark Antony. Was it that the artistic, intense temperament was so influenced by this change of rôle? I don't know, but I did know that the first naïve passion and love of my Romeo had changed. He spoke of our marriage as if it had already been definitely decided. He even took me to see some apartments, to choose one in which we should live. Inspecting bathroomless flats and kitchens up endless flights of stairs, I felt a strange chill and heaviness.

"What shall we do, living in Budapest?" I queried.

"Why," he replied, "you will have a box each night to see

me act, and then you will learn to give me all my *répliques* and help me in my studies."

He recited to me the part of Mark Antony, but now all the passionate interest centred in the Roman populace and I, his Juliet, was no longer the central interest.

One day, during a long stroll in the country, sitting by the side of a haystack, he finally asked me if I did not think I should do better to continue my career and leave him to his. These were not his exact words, but that was his meaning. I still remember the haystack and the field before us, and the cold chill that struck my breast. That afternoon I signed a contract with Alexander Gross for Vienna and Berlin, and all the cities of Germany.

I saw Romeo's début in Mark Antony. My last vision of him was the mad enthusiasm of the theatre audience, while I sat in a box swallowing my tears and feeling as if I had eaten bushels of broken glass. The next day I left for Vienna. Romeo had vanished. I said good-bye to Mark Antony, who seemed stern and so preoccupied that the journey from Budapest to Vienna was one of the bitterest and saddest I ever experienced. All joy seemed suddenly to have left the Universe. In Vienna I fell ill and was placed by Alexander Gross in a clinic.

I spent several weeks in utter prostration and horrible suffering. Romeo came from Budapest. He even made his cot in my room. He was tender and considerate, but awakening one morning at dawn, seeing the face of the nurse, a Catholic nun, banded in black, separating me from the form of my Romeo on the cot across the room, I heard the knell of Love's funeral.

I was a long time convalescing, and Alexander Gross took me to recover in Franzensbad. I was languid and sad, refusing to be interested either in the beautiful country or the kind friends about me. Gross's wife had come, and she tended me kindly through sleepless nights. Fortunately for me, probably, the expensive doctors and nurses had exhausted the bank account, and Gross arranged performances for me in Franzensbad, Marienbad and Carlsbad. So one day I opened my trunk again, and took out my dancing tunics. I remember bursting into tears, kissing my little red dress in which I danced all my Revolutionary dances, and swearing never to desert Art for love again. By this time my name had become magic in the country and I remember one night when I was dining with my manager and his wife, the crowd before the plate glass window of the restaurant became so dense that they broke the vast window, to the despair of the hotel manager.

The sorrow, the pains and disillusions of Love, I transformed in my Art. I composed the story of Iphigenia, her farewell to Life on the Altar of Death. Finally Alexander Gross arranged for my appearance in Munich, where I rejoined my mother and Elizabeth, who were delighted to see me again alone, although they found me changed and saddened.

Before I appeared in Munich, Elizabeth and I went to Abbazia and drove up and down the streets hunting for hotel accommodation. Unable to find any and having attracted considerable attention in this peaceful little town, we were seen by the Grand Duke Ferdinand, who was passing. He became interested and greeted us sympathetically. Finally he invited us to stay at his villa in the garden of the Hotel Stephanie. The whole episode was one of complete innocence, but it created a great scandal in Court circles. The grand ladies who soon began to call upon us, were not at all inspired by interest in my art, as I naïvely imagined at the time, but by the desire to discover our real status at the Duke's villa. These same ladies made deep curtseys every night before the Grand Duke's table in the hotel dining-room.

I followed the custom, curtseying more deeply than the others were able to do.

It was then that I inaugurated a bathing costume which has since become popular—a light blue tunic of finest crêpe de chine, low necked, with little shoulder straps, skirt just above the knees, with bare legs and feet. As the custom of the ladies of that epoch was to enter the water severely garbed in black, with skirt between the knees and ankle, black stockings and black swimming shoes, you can well imagine the sensation I created. The Grand Duke Ferdinand used to promenade the diving bridge with opera glasses which he riveted on me, murmuring in perfectly audible tones, "Ach, wie schön ist diese Duncan. Ach; wunder schön! Diese Frühlingzeit ist nicht so schön wie sie."

Some time afterward, when I danced at the Carl Theatre in Vienna, the Grand Duke, with his suite of handsome young aides-de-camps and lieutenants, came every night to the stage box and naturally people talked. But the Duke's interest in me was purely æsthetic and artistic. Indeed he seemed to shun the society of the fair sex, and was quite content with his entourage of beautiful young officers. I felt great sympathy for H. R. H. Ferdinand when I heard some years later that the Austrian Court had made a decree incarcerating him in a gloomy château in Salzburg. Perhaps he was a bit different from other people, but what really sympathetic person is not a little mad?

At that Villa in Abbazia there was a palm tree before our windows. It was the first time I had seen a palm tree growing in a temperate climate. I used to notice its leaves trembling in the early morning breeze, and from them I created in my dance that light fluttering of the arms, hands and fingers, which has been so much abused by my imitators; for they forget to go to the original source and contemplate the movements of the palm tree, to receive them inwardly before giving them outwardly. Often as I gazed at this palm tree all artistic thoughts left me, and I remembered only the moving lines of Heine:

"A lonely palm in the South . . ."

From Abbazia Elizabeth and I went to Munich. At that time all the life of Munich centred around the Künstler Haus, where the group of masters, Karlbach, Lembach, Stuck, etc., gathered each evening to imbibe the fine Münchener beer and discourse upon philosophy and art. Gross wished to arrange for my début in the Künstler Haus. Lembach and Karlbach were willing, only Stuck maintained that dancing was not appropriate to a Temple of Art like the Munich Künstler Haus. One morning I went to find Stuck at his house, in order to convince him of the worthiness of my Art. I took off my dress in his studio, donned my tunic, and danced for him, then talked to him for four hours without stopping, on the holiness of my mission and the possibility of the dance as an Art. He often told his friends afterwards that he was never so astonished in his life. He said he felt as if a Dryad from Mount Olympus had suddenly appeared from another world. Of course he gave his consent, and my début at the Munich Künstler Haus was the greatest artistic event and sensation that the town had experienced in many years.

Afterwards I danced at the Kaim Saal. The students went fairly crazy. Night after night they unharnessed the horses from my carriage and drew me through the streets, singing their student songs and leaping with lighted torches on either side of my victoria. Often, for hours, they would group themselves outside the hotel window and sing, until I threw them my flowers and handkerchiefs, which they would divide, each bearing a portion in their caps.

One night they bore me off to their student café, where they lifted me dancing from one table to another. All night they sang, and frequently came the refrain, "Isadora, Isadora, ach, wie schön das Leben ist." This night when recorded in *Simplissimus*, shocked some of the sober people of the town, but it was really a most innocent "rag," in spite of the fact that even my dress and shawl were torn to ribbons and worn in their caps when they carried me home at dawn.

Munich was, at that time, a veritable beehive of artistic and intellectual activities. The streets were crowded with students. Every young girl had a portfolio or music roll under her arm. Every shop window was a veritable treasury of rare books and old prints, and fascinating new editions. This, coupled with the marvellous collections of the museums, the crisp autumn air blowing from the sunny mountains, the visits to the studio of the silver-haired Meister, Lenbach, the frequenting of masters in philosophy, such as Carvelhorn and others, inspired me to return to my interrupted intellectual and spiritual conception of life. I began to study German, to read Schopenhauer and Kant in the original, and I could soon follow with intense pleasure the long discussion of the artists and philosophers and musicians who met each night in the Künstler Haus. I also learnt to drink the good Munich beer; and the recent shock to my senses was somewhat calmed.

One night at a special gala artistic performance at the Künstler Haus I was aware of a remarkable silhouette of a man sitting in the first row applauding. This silhouette recalled to mind that of the great master whose works were then being revealed to me for the first time. The same overhanging brow, prominent nose. Only the mouth was softer and possessed less strength. After the performance I learned that this was Siegfried Wagner, the son of Richard Wagner. He joined our circle and I had for the first time the pleasure of meeting and admiring one who was thereafter to count among my most treasured friends. His conversation was brilliant, with frequent recollections of his great father, which seemed to be always about his person as a sacred halo.

I was then, too, for the first time reading Schopenhauer, and I was carried away by the revelation of his philosophic enlightenment of the relation of music to the will.

This extraordinary spirit, or as the Germans called it *geist*, of the feeling of Holiness, *der Heiligthum des Gedankes* (the holiness of thought), that I met, made me often feel as if I had been introduced into a world of superior and God-like thinkers, the working of whose brains was far vaster, holier, than any I had encountered in the world of my travels. Here, indeed the philosophic conception seemed to be regarded as the highest point of man's satisfaction, only to be equalled by the still holier world of music. In the Munich museums the glorious works from Italy were also a revelation to me, and, realising how close we were to the borderline, following an irresistible impulse, Elizabeth, my mother and I took the train for Florence.

CHAPTER TWELVE

I SHALL never forget the marvellous experience of crossing the Tyrol, and then descending the sunny side of the mountain to the Umbrian plain.

We alighted from the train at Florence and spent several weeks in ecstatic wanderings through the galleries, gardens, olive orchards. At that time it was Botticelli who attracted my youthful imagination. I sat for days before the Primavera, the famous painting of Botticelli. Inspired by this picture, I created a dance in which I endeavoured to realise the soft and marvellous movements emanating from it; the soft undulation of the flower-covered earth, the circle of nymphs and the flight of the Zephyrs, all assembling about the central figure, half Aphrodite, half Madonna, who indicates the procreation of spring in one significant gesture.

I sat for hours before this picture. I was enamoured of it. A nice old guardian brought me a stool, and viewed my adoration with kindly interest. I sat there until I actually saw the flowers growing, the naked feet dancing, the bodies swaying; until the messenger of joy came to me and I thought: "I will dance this picture and give to others this message of love, spring, procreation of life which had been given to me with such anguish. I will give to them, through the dance, such ecstasy."

Closing time came, and I was still before the picture. I wanted to find the meaning of spring through the mystery of this beautiful moment. I felt that so far life had been a bungle, and blind seeking; I thought, if I can find the secret of this picture, I may show others the way to richness of life and development of joy. I remember that I already thought about life like a man who has been to the wars with good intentions and who has been terribly wounded, and who, on reflection, says: "Why should I not teach a gospel that will spare others from such mutilation?"

Such was my meditation before the Primavera of Botticelli in Florence, which I tried afterwards to transform into a dance. Oh, sweet, half-seen Pagan life, where Aphrodite gleamed through the form of the gracious but more tender Mother of Christ, where Apollo reached towards the first branches, with the likeness of St. Sebastian! I felt all this enter my bosom with a flood of peaceful joy, and I wished intensely to translate all this to my dance, which I named the Dance of the Future.

Here, in the rooms of an old palace, I danced for the artistic circle of Florence to the music of Monteverde and some melodies of earlier, anonymous masters. To one exquisite melody for the Viol d'Amour, I danced an angel playing on an imaginary violin.

With our usual careless disregard of the practical, our money had again come to an end, and we were obliged to telegraph to Alexander Gross to send us the necessary sum to join him in Berlin, where he was preparing for my début.

When we arrived in Berlin I was bewildered, in driving through the town, to find the entire city one flaming poster of my name, and the announcement of my début in Kroll's Opera House, with the Philharmonic Orchestra. Alexander Gross conducted us to a beautiful suite at the Hotel Bristol, in Unter den Linden, where the entire German Press appeared to be waiting for my first interview. From my studies in Munich and my experiences in Florence, I was in such a pensive and spiritual frame of mind that I greatly astonished these gentlemen of the Press by giving them, in my American German, a naïve and grandiose conception of the Art of the

Dance as a "grösste ernste Kunst," and one which would bring all the other arts to a new awakening.

How differently these German journalists listened than those to whom I explained my theories later on in America. They listened to me with the most reverent and interested contemplation, and next day there appeared long articles in the German newspapers treating my dance with grave and philosophic import.

Alexander Gross was a courageous pioneer. He had risked his entire capital on the launching of my performance in Berlin. He had spared no expense in advertising, having the first Opera House and the finest conductor, and if, when the curtain rose, revealing my simple blue curtains as scenery, and one small, slight figure on a huge stage, I had failed to arouse the applause at the first moment from the puzzled Berlin audience, it would have meant utter ruin for him. But he was a good prophet. I did what he had predicted. I took Berlin by storm. After I had danced for over two hours, the audience refused to leave the Opera House, but demanded encore after encore, until finally, in one enthusiastic rush, they came to the footlights. Hundreds of young students actually climbed upon the stage, until I was in danger of being crushed to death by too much adoration. For many nights following they repeated the charming ceremony which prevailed in Germany, of unhitching the horses from my carriage and drawing me through the streets in triumph, down Unter den Linden, to my hotel.

From that first night I was known to the German public by such names as "die göttliche, heilige Isadora." On one of these evenings Raymond suddenly returned from America. He had grown too homesick for us, and said he could remain separated from us no longer. We then revived a project which we had long cherished, of making a pilgrimage to the very holiest shrine of art, of going to our beloved Athens. I felt that I was only at the gateway of the study of my Art, and after a short season in Berlin I insisted, in spite of entreaties and lamentations from Alexander Gross, upon leaving Germany. We again took the train for Italy, with sparkling eyes and high-beating hearts, to make together our long-deferred trip to Athens, via Venice.

We stayed in Venice for some weeks, reverently observing the churches and galleries, but, naturally, Venice could not mean very much to us at that time. We admired a hundred-fold more the superior intellectual and spiritual beauty of Florence. Venice did not yield me its secret and its loveliness until years after, when I was there with a slight, olive-complexioned, dark-eyed lover. Then, for the first time I felt the sorcery of Venetian charms, but the first visit only left me impatient to take a boat and sail to higher spheres.

Raymond decided that our trip to Greece must be as primitive as possible, so, avoiding the big, comfortable passenger boats, we boarded a post steamer, a little boat that sailed between Brindisi and Santa Maura. At Santa Maura we alighted because the site of the ancient Ithaca was there, and there also was the rock from which Sappho had thrown herself in despair into the sea. Even now when I take this trip in my memory I recall those lines from Byron which came to me then:

> *"The Isles of Greece,*
> *The isles of Greece, the isles of Greece,*
> *Where burning Sappho loved and sung,*
> *Where grew the arts of war and peace,*
> *Where Delos rose and Phœbus sprung!*
> *Eternal summer gilds them yet,*
> *But all, except their sun, is set."*

From Santa Maura we took a little sailing boat at dawn,

with only two men, and on a burning July day, navigated through the blue Ionian Sea. We entered the Ambracian Gulf and landed at the little town of Karvasaras.

In hiring the smack, Raymond had explained with much pantomime, and some ancient Greek, that we wished our voyage as nearly as possible to resemble that of Ulysses. The fisherman didn't seem to understand much about Ulysses, but the sight of many drachmas encouraged him to set sail, although he was loath to go far, and pointed many times to the sky, saying, "Boom, Boom," and, with his arms indicating a storm at sea, to inform us that the sea was treacherous. And we thought of the lines in the Odyssey which described that sea:

> "So saying, he grasped his trident; gathered dense
> The clouds and troubled ocean; ev'ry storm,
> From every point he summoned, earth and sea
> Darkening, and the night fell black from Heav'n.
> The East, the South, the heavy blowing West,
> And the cold North Wind clear, assail'd at once
> His raft, and heaved on high the billowy flood.
> All hope, all courage, in that moment, lost."
>
> ODYSSEY V.

For there is no more changing sea than the Ionian Sea. We risked our precious lives in this voyage which might have turned out too much like that of Ulysses:

> "While thus he spoke, a billow on his head
> Bursting impetuous, whirl'd the raft around,
> And, dashing from his grasp the helm, himself
> Plunged far remote. Then came a sudden gust
> Of mingling winds, that in the middle snapp'd
> His mast, and, hurried o'er the waves afar,

> *Both sail and sail-yard fell into the flood.*
> *Long time submerged he lay, nor could with ease*
> *The violence of that dread shock surmount,*
> *Or rise to air again, so burthensome*
> *His drench'd apparel proved; but, at the last,*
> *He rose, and, rising, spitt'd from his lips*
> *The brine that trickled copious from his brows."*

And, further, when Ulysses was wrecked and meets Nausicaa:

> *"For I am one on whom much woe hath fall'n.*
> *Yesterday I escaped (the twentieth day*
> *Of my distress by sea) the dreary deep;*
> *For, all those days, the waves and rapid storms*
> *Bore me along, impetuous from the isle*
> *Ogyia; till at length the will of Heav'n*
> *Cast me, that I might also here sustain*
> *Affliction on your shores; for rest, I think,*
> *Is not for me. No. The immortal Gods*
> *Have much to accomplish ere that day arrive;*
> *But, oh, Queen, pity me! who after long*
> *Calamities endured, of all who live*
> *Thee first approach, nor mortal know beside*
> *Of the inhabitants of all the land."*
>
> ODYSSEY VI.

We stopped at the little Turkish town of Prevesa on the Epirus coast and bought provisions, a huge goat-cheese and quantities of ripe olives and dried fish. As there was no shelter on the sailing boat, I shall never forget, to my dying day, the smell of that cheese and fish, exposed all day to a blazing sun, especially as the little boat had a gentle but potent rolling gait of its own. Often the breeze ceased, and we were obliged to take to the oars. Finally, at dusk, we landed at Karvasaras.

The inhabitants all came down to the beach to greet us, and the first landing of Christopher Columbus in America could not have caused more astonishment among the natives —which grew to speechless curiosity when Raymond and I knelt down and kissed the soil, Raymond declaiming:

> *"Cold is the heart, fair Greece! that looks on thee,*
> *Nor feels as lovers o'er the dust they loved;*
> *Dull is the eye that will not weep to see*
> *Thy walls defaced, thy mouldering shrines removed."*

Indeed, we were half mad with joy. We wanted to embrace all the inhabitants of the village and cry, "At last we have arrived, after many wanderings, in the Sacred Land of Hellas! Salute, O Olympian Zeus! And Apollo! And Aphrodite! Prepare, O ye Muses, to dance again! Our singing may awaken Dionysus and his sleeping Bacchantes!"

> *"Up, O Bacchæ, wife and maiden,*
> *Come, O ye Bacchæ, come,*
> *Oh, bring the Joy-bestower,*
> *God-seed of God the Sower,*
> *Bring Bromios in his power*
> *From Phrygia's mountain dome;*
> *To street and town and tower,*
> *Oh, bring ye Bromios home!"*

> *"And don thy fawn-skin, fringed in purity*
> *With fleecy white, like ours."*

> *"I vowed with him, grey hair with snow-white hair,*
> *To deck the new God's thyrsus, and to wear*
> *His fawn-skin, and with ivy crown our brows."*

There was no hotel and no railroad in Karvasaras. That night we slept in one room, the only one the Inn could offer us. At least, we didn't sleep very much. First, because

Raymond discoursed all night on the Wisdom of Socrates,
and the Celestial Compensation of Platonic Love; and,
secondly, because the beds were made of single planks which
were very rough; and Hellas contained many thousands of
little inhabitants who wanted to feast on us.

At dawn we parted from the village, with Mother sitting
in a two-horse carriage containing our four valises, and we,
having cut staves from laurel trees, escorting her. The
whole village accompanied us a good part of the way. We
took the ancient road which Philip of Macedon had tramped
with his army over 2,000 years ago.

*   *   *

The road we took from Karvasaras to Agrinion winds
through mountains of savage, rugged grandeur. It was a
beautiful morning, the air clear as crystal. We sped along
on the light wings of youthful feet, often leaping and bound-
ing before the carriage, accompanying our steps with shouts
and songs of joy. When we crossed the River Aspropotamos
(the ancient Achelous) Raymond and I, in spite of the
tearful entreaties of Elizabeth, insisted upon going for a
dip, or baptism, in its limpid waters. We did not realise
how strong the current was, and were nearly carried away.

At one point in the journey, two savage sheep dogs raced
towards us across the entire valley from a distant farm.
They would have attacked us with the ferocity of wolves, had
not our valiant coachman frightened them off with his big
whip.

We had our lunch in a little wayside inn, where, for the
first time, we tasted wine preserved with resin in classic pig
skin. It tasted like furniture-polish, but, making wry faces,
we insisted that it was delicious.

At last we came to the ancient city of Stratos, which
was built upon three hills. This was our first adventure
among Greek ruins. The sight of Doric columns sent us

into ecstasies. We followed Raymond as he guided us to the site of the Theatre of the Temple of Zeus on the West Hill. In our vivid imaginations there arose a mirage in the setting sun—the city again covering the three hills, fair and beautiful.

By night we arrived at Agrinion, fairly exhausted, but in such a glow of happiness as rarely comes to the lot of mortals. The next morning we took the stagecoach down to Missolonghi, where we paid tribute to the flaming heart of Byron, enshrined in the remains of this heroic town, the ground of which is soaked with the blood of martyrs. Is it not strange to reflect that it was Byron who snatched the heart of Shelley from the red embers of the funeral pyre? Shelley's heart is now enshrined at Rome and it may be that the hearts of these two poets are still in mystic communion with each other from "The glory that was Greece, to the grandeur that was Rome."

All these memories subdued and saddened our effervescent pagan joy. The town still retains all the tragic atmosphere of Delacroix's famous picture, "La Sortie de Missolonghi," when almost all the inhabitants, men, women and children, were massacred in their desperate efforts to cut through the Turkish lines.

Byron died in Missolonghi in April, 1824. It was two years after, also in April, almost on the anniversary of Byron's death, that these martyrs joined him in the shadowy land; he, who was so ready to give all for their liberation. Is there anything more touching than Byron's death in that brave town of Missolonghi? His heart enshrined there among those martyrs who died that the world might again know the immortal beauty of Hellas. For, truly, all martyrdom is fruitful. With full hearts and tearful eyes we left Missolonghi in the dying light, watching it recede from the deck of the little steamer bound for Patras.

At Patras we had a hard struggle to decide between the attractions of Olympia and Athens, but a great, longing impatience for the Parthenon finally prevailed, and we took the train for Athens. The train sped through radiant Hellas. At one moment we glimpsed the snow-capped Olympus. At another we were surrounded by twisting, dancing nymphs and hamadryads of the olive groves. Our delight knew no bounds. Often our emotions were so violent that we could only find expression in tearful embraces. The stolid peasants at the little stations eyed us with wonder. They probably thought we were either drunk or crazy, whereas we were only exalted in our search for the highest and brightest of all wisdom—the blue eyes of Athena.

We arrived at violet-crowned Athens that evening, and the daybreak found us, with trembling limbs and hearts faint with adoration, ascending the steps of her Temple. As we mounted, it seemed to me that all the life I had known up to that time had fallen away from me as a motley garment; that I had never lived before; that I was born for the first time in that long breath and first gaze of pure beauty.

The sun was rising from behind Mount Pentelicus, revealing her marvellous clearness and the splendour of her marble sides sparkling in the sunlight. We mounted the last step of the Propylæa and gazed on the Temple shining in the morning light. With one accord we remained silent. We separated slightly from one another; for here was Beauty too sacred for words. It struck strange terror into our hearts. No cries or embraces now. We each found our vantage point of worship and remained for hours in an ecstasy of meditation which left us all weak and shaken.

We were now all together, my mother and her four children. We decided that the Clan Duncan was quite sufficient unto itself, that other people had only led us astray from

our ideals.   Also, upon viewing the Parthenon, it seemed
to us that we had reached the pinnacle of perfection.   We
asked ourselves why we should ever leave Greece, since we
found in Athens everything which satisfied our æsthetic
sense.   One might wonder why, at that time, after the public
success that I had had, and after my passionate interlude
in Budapest, I should have felt no longing to go back to
either.   The truth is that, when I had started on this pilgrimage, I had not had either the desire for fame nor for
making money.   It was purely a spiritual pilgrimage and it
seemed to me that the spirit which I sought was the invisible
Goddess Athena who still inhabited the ruined Parthenon.
Therefore we decided that the Clan Duncan should remain
in Athens eternally, and there build a temple that should
be characteristic of us.

From my Berlin performances there was in the bank a
sum which seemed to me inexhaustible, and, therefore, we
set out to find a suitable site for our Temple.   The only
one who was not perfectly happy was Augustin.   He brooded
for a long time, and finally confessed that he felt very lonesome for his wife and child.   We considered this a great
weakness on his part, but consented,—as he was already
married and had a child,—that there was nothing for us to
do but to send for them.

His wife arrived with the little girl.   She was fashionably
dressed and wore Louis XV heels.   We looked askance at
her heels, for we had already taken to sandals, so as not to
defile the white marble floor of the Parthenon.   But she
strongly objected to wearing sandals.   As for us, we had
decided that even the Directoire dresses which I wore, and
Raymond's knickerbockers, open collars and flowing ties
were degenerate garments, and we must return to the tunic
of the Ancient Greeks—which we did, much to the astonishment of the Modern Greeks themselves.

Having fitted ourselves out with tunic and chlamys and peplum, and having put fillets round our hair, we set out to find the site for our Temple. We explored Colonos, Phaleron and all the valleys of Attica, but could not find anything that was worthy of our Temple. Finally, one day in a walk toward Hymettus, where the beehives are from which the famous honey comes, we crossed a rise in the ground, and Raymond suddenly laid his staff upon the ground and shouted, "Look, we are on the same level as the Acropolis!" And sure enough, looking to the West, we saw the Temple of Athena, in startling propinquity, although we were in reality four kilometres distant from it.

But there were difficulties with this place. First, no one knew to whom the land belonged. It was so far from Athens, and frequented only by shepherds tending their flocks and goats. It took us a long time before we discovered that the land belonged to five families of peasants who had held it for over a hundred years. It was divided like a pie from the middle downwards in sections. After a long search we found the heads of these five families and asked them if they would sell. There was great astonishment among the peasants, as no one had ever evinced any interest in this land before. It was far from Athens, and was rocky soil, producing only thistles. Besides, there was no water anywhere near the hill. Nobody had considered this land of any value heretofore. But the moment that we let it be known that we wished to purchase it, the peasants who owned it gathered together and decided that the land was priceless. They asked a sum entirely out of proportion. Nevertheless the Clan Duncan was determined to buy this site, and we proceeded to deal with the peasants in this manner. We invited the five families to a banquet where we had lamb on the spit, and other kinds of tempting food. We also served much *raki*—the cognac of the country. At the feast, with the help of a little Athenian lawyer, we drew out a bill of sale to which the peasants, who were unable to write, put their marks. Although we paid somewhat dearly for the land, we esteemed that this banquet was a great success. The barren hillock, on the same level as the Acropolis, known since ancient times as Kopanos, now belonged to the Clan Duncan.

The next step was to secure paper and architectural instruments and make the plans for a house. Raymond found the exact model desired in the plan of the Palace of Agamemnon. He scorned the help of architects, and himself engaged the workmen and the stone carriers. We decided that the only stone worthy of our Temple was that from Mount Pentelicus, from whose sparkling sides were hewn the noble columns of the Parthenon. We, however, were modestly content with the red stone which is found at the base of the mountain. From then on, each day could be seen a long procession of carts, carrying these red stones; winding their tortuous way from Pentelicus to Kopanos. As each cartload of red stone was thrown down upon our ground, we became more and more delighted.

Finally arrived the momentous day when the corner-stone of our Temple was to be laid. We felt that this great event should be duly celebrated with a worthy ceremony. Goodness knows, not one of us was of a churchy turn of mind, each being completely emancipated through our ideas of modern science and free-thinking. Yet we thought it more beautiful and fitting to have this corner-stone laid in the Greek manner with a ceremony conducted by a Greek priest. We invited all the peasantry of the countryside for miles around to take part.

The old priest arrived, clothed in black robes and wearing a black hat with a black veil flowing from its ample crown. The priest asked us for a black cock to offer as a sacrifice.

This is the same rite, handed down through the Byzantine priests, from the time of the Temple of Apollo. With some difficulty the black cock was found and presented to the priest, with the sacrificial knife. In the meantime bands of peasants had arrived from all parts of the country. In addition, came some of the fashionable people from Athens. By sunset a great crowd was assembled on Kopanos.

With impressive solemnity the old priest commenced. He asked us to designate the exact line of the foundations of the house. We did this by dancing about it in a square which Raymond had already designed upon the ground. He then found the corner-stone nearest to the house and, just as the great red sun was setting, he cut the throat of the black cock and its crimson blood squirted upon the stone. Holding the knife in one hand and the slaughtered bird in the other, he solemnly promenaded three times around the square of the foundation. Then followed prayer and incantation. He blessed all the stones of the house and, asking us our names, he uttered a prayer in which we frequently heard the names *Isadora Duncan* (my mother), *Augustin, Raymond, Elizabeth* and *Little Isadora* (myself). Each time he pronounced our name Duncan, as though it were spelt Thuncan, with a hard th, instead of a D. Again and again he exhorted us to live piously and peaceably in this house. He prayed that our descendants also should live piously and peaceably in this house. When he had done with prayer, the musicians arrived with their primitive instruments of the country. Great barrels of wine and *raki* were opened. A roaring bonfire was set ablaze on the hill and we, together with our neighbours, the peasantry, danced and drank and made merry all through the night.

We decided to remain for ever in Greece. Not only that, but, as Hamlet says, we vowed, too, that there should be no more marriages. "Let those who are married remain married," etc.

We accepted Augustin's wife with ill-concealed reservation. But for our own part, we drew up a plan in a copy-book, which was to exclude all but the Clan Duncan, and therein we set down the rules for our lives to be spent on Kopanos. We did this somewhat on the same plan as Plato in his "Republic." It was decreed to arise at sunrise. We were to greet the rising sun with joyous songs and dances. Afterwards we were to refresh ourselves with a modest bowl of goat's milk. The mornings were to be devoted to teaching the inhabitants to dance and sing. They must be made to celebrate the Greek gods and to give up their terrible modern costumes. Then, after our light lunch of green vegetables, for we had decided to give up meat and become vegetarians, the afternoons were to be spent in meditation, and the evenings given over to pagan ceremonies with appropriate music.

Then began the building of Kopanos. As the walls of the palace of Agamemnon were about two feet thick, the walls of Kopanos must also be two feet thick. It wasn't until those walls were well under construction that I realised how much red stone from Pentelicus would be necessary, and also how much each cartload of stone cost. A few days later we decided to camp out on the spot for the night. And then it was suddenly and effectively brought to our consciousness that there was not a drop of water to be had for miles around! We looked at the heights of Hymettus where the honey was, and before our eyes were many springs and flowing rivulets. Then we gazed on Pentelicus, whose eternal snows were gushing cascades down the mountain side. Alas! We realised that Kopanos was completely dry and arid. The nearest spring was four kilometres away! But Raymond, nothing daunted, hired more workmen and

started them digging an artesian well. In the course of
the digging, he came upon different relics, and insisted there
had been an ancient village on these heights, but I have my
own reasons for thinking that it was only a cemetery, for
the deeper the artesian well was sunk the drier and drier
the ground became. At length, after several weeks of fruit-
less searching for water on Kopanos, we returned to Athens
to ask counsel of the prophetic spirits which we were sure
inhabited the Acropolis. We secured a special permit from
the city so that we could go there on moonlit evenings, and
we formed the habit of sitting in the amphitheatre of
Dionysus, where Augustin would give his recitations from
the Greek tragedies, and where we often danced.

We were completely self-sufficient in our Clan. We did
not mingle at all with the inhabitants of Athens. Even
when we heard one day from the peasants that the King of
Greece had ridden out to see our Temple, we remained
unimpressed. For we were living under the reign of other
kings, Agamemnon, Menelaus and Priam.

CHAPTER THIRTEEN

ONE moonlit night, when we were sitting in the Theatre of Dionysus, we heard a shrill boy's voice soaring into the night, with that pathetic, unearthly quality which only boys' voices have. Suddenly it was joined by another voice and another. They were singing some old Greek songs of the country. We sat enraptured. Raymond said, "This must be the tone of the boys' voices of the old Greek Chorus."

The next night this concert was repeated. As we distributed a great many drachmas, the third night the chorus was enlarged, and gradually all the boys of Athens gave themselves a rendezvous to sing to us by moonlight in the Theatre of Dionysus.

At this time we were very much interested in the subject of Byzantine music in the Greek Church. We visited the Greek Church and heard the wonderful plaintive chant of the Maître. We visited the seminary for young Greek priests just outside of Athens. They showed us their library of manuscripts, dating back through the Middle Ages. We were of the opinion, as are many distinguished Hellenists, that the hymns of Apollo, Aphrodite and all the pagan gods had found their way through transformations into the Greek Church.

Then was born in us the idea of forming once more the original Greek Chorus from these Greek boys. We held competitions each night in the Theatre of Dionysus and gave prizes to those who could present the most ancient Greek songs. We also enlisted the services of a Professor of Byzantine music. In this way we formed a chorus of ten boys who had the most beautiful voices in all Athens. The young Seminarist, who was also a student of Ancient Greek, helped us set this chorus to "The Suppliants" of Æschylus. These choruses are probably the most beautiful that have ever been written. One I especially recall portrays the fright of the maidens who gather around the altar of Zeus, seeking protection from their incestuous cousins coming across the sea.

And so, with our studies of the Acropolis, the building of Kopanos and the dancing of the choruses of Æschylus, we were completely immersed in our own work. Except for occasional excursions to the outlying villages, we desired nothing more.

We became greatly impressed upon reading of the Mysteries of Eleusis.

"Those mysteries of which no tongue can speak. Only blessed is he whose eyes have seen them; his lot after death is not as the lot of other men!"

We prepared to visit Eleusis, which is thirteen and a half miles from Athens. With bare legs, bare feet and sandals, we started to dance down the white and dusty road that skirts the ancient groves of Plato by the sea. We wished to propitiate the gods, and to that end substituted dancing for walking. We passed a little village of Daphnis and the Chapel of Hagia Trias. Through the opening in the hills we came in sight of the sea and the Island of Salamis, where we paused awhile to reconstruct the famous battle of Salamis, when the Greeks met and destroyed the Persian host, commanded by Xerxes.

Xerxes is said to have watched the battle, seated in his silver-footed chair on a hill in front of Mount Ægaleos. It was in the year 480 B.C. that the Greeks, with a fleet of three hundred ships, destroyed the Persians and won their independence. About six hundred picked Persian warriors

were stationed on an islet to cut off the Greeks, who were
to be wrecked and driven on shore. But Aristides, who had
been recalled from banishment and learned of the movements
of Xerxes to ruin the Greek fleet, outwitted the Persians.

> *"A Greek ship led on the attack*
> *And from the prow of a Phœnician struck*
> *The figure-head; and now the grapple closed*
> *Of each ship with his adverse desperate.*
> *At first the main line of the Persian fleet*
> *Stood the harsh shock; but soon their multitude*
> *Became their ruin; in the narrow firth*
> *They might not use their strength, and, jammed together,*
> *Their ships with brazen beaks did bite each other,*
> *And shattered their own oars. Meanwhile the Greeks*
> *Stroke after stroke dealt dexterous all around,*
> *Till our ships showed their keels, and the blue sea*
> *Was seen no more, with multitude of ships*
> *And corpses covered."*

We actually danced every step of the way. We only
stopped once at a little Christian Church, where the Greek
priest, who had been watching us with growing astonishment
coming up the road, insisted upon us visiting the Church
and having some of his wine. We spent two days in Eleusis,
visiting her mysteries. On the third day we returned to
Athens, but we did not return alone. We were accompanied
by a group of shadowy initiates, Æschylus, Euripides,
Sophocles and Aristophanes.

We had no desire to wander further. We had reached
our Mecca, which, for us, meant the splendour of perfection
—Hellas. I have since strayed from that first pure adoration of the wise Athena; and the last time I visited Athens,
I confess that it was no longer her cult that attracted me,

but rather the face of a suffering Christ in the little chapel of Daphnis. But at that time, in the morning of life, the Acropolis held for us all joy and inspiration. We were too strong, too defiant to understand pity.

Each dawn found us ascending the Propylon. We came to know the history of the sacred hill through all its successive periods. We brought our books and followed the history of each stone. We studied all the theories of distinguished archæologists as to the origin and meaning of certain marks and portents.

Raymond made some original discoveries of his own. He spent some time on the Acropolis with Elizabeth trying to find the old footprints of the goats who came up the stones to pasture upon the hill before it was built. They actually did trace some of the prints for the Acropolis was started at first merely by a group of goat-herds who sought shelter and protection for their flocks by night, and they succeeded in tracing definite criss-crossing of the paths taken by the goats. These date back at least a thousand years before the building of the Acropolis.

From the competition of a couple of hundred ragged urchins of Athens we, with the help of the young Seminarist, had selected ten with perfectly heavenly voices and, with his help, had begun to train them in singing the choruses. We found hidden in the ritual of the Greek Church strophe and antistrophe, so appropriate in harmony that they justified our conclusion that these were the very hymns to Zeus, Father, Thunderer and Protector; that they had been taken by the early Christians and transformed into hymns to Jehovah. In the library at Athens we found in different books on ancient Greek music just such gamuts and intervals. Upon making these discoveries, we lived in a state of feverish exaltation. At last, after two thousand years, we were able to bring to the world these lost treasures.

The Hotel d'Angleterre, where we stopped, generously put at my disposal a large salon where I could work each day. I spent hours fitting to the Chorus of the Suppliants the movements and gestures inspired by the rhythm of the music of the Greek Church. We were so intent and convinced of these theories that it never occurred to us to realise the comic mélange of religious expressions.

Athens was then, as it usually is, in a state of revolution. This time it was a revolution founded upon the difference of opinion between the Royal House and the students as to which version of the Greek language should be used upon the stage, the ancient or the modern. Crowds of students paraded the streets with banners in favour of the ancient Greek language. On the day of our return from Kopanos, they surrounded our carriage and acclaimed our Hellenic tunics and asked us to join their parade, which we did willingly, for Antique Hellas. From this meeting a representation was arranged at the Municipal Theatre by the students. The ten Greek boys and the Byzantine Seminarist, all attired in multi-coloured flowing tunics, sang the choruses of Æschylus in ancient Greek idiom, and I danced. This caused a delirium of joy among the students.

Then King George, hearing of this manifestation, expressed a wish to have the performance repeated at the Royal Theatre. But the performance given before the Royal Family and all the embassies of Athens in the Royal Theatre lacked all the fire and enthusiasm of that in the popular theatre for the students. The applause of the white-kid-gloved hands was not inspiring. When King George came behind the stage to my dressing-room and asked me to visit the Queen in the Royal box, although they seemed quite pleased, still I realised that there was no real spiritual love or understanding for my art. The Ballet will always be the dance *par excellence* for Royal personages.

These events took place at the same time that I discovered our bank account was depleted. I remember the evening after the Royal performance I could not sleep and, at dawn, I went all by myself, to the Acropolis. I entered the Theatre of Dionysus and danced. I felt it was for the last time. Then I ascended the Propylæa and stood before the Parthenon. Suddenly it seemed to me as if all our dreams burst like a glorious bubble, and we were not, nor ever could be, other than moderns. We could not have the feeling of the Ancient Greeks. This Temple of Athena before which I stood, had in other times known other colours. I was, after all, but a Scotch-Irish-American. Perhaps through some affinity nearer allied to the Red Indian than to the Greeks. The beautiful illusion of one year spent in Hellas seemed suddenly to break. The strains of Byzantine Greek music grew fainter and fainter, and through it all the great chords of the Death of Isolda floated upon my ears.

Three days later, amidst a great crowd of enthusiasts, and the weeping parents of the ten Greek boys, we took train from Athens for Vienna. At the station I wrapped myself in the Greek flag of white and blue, and the ten Greek boys and all the populace sang the beautiful Greek hymn:

> *"Op ta kokala vgalméni*
> *Ton Elinon to yera*
> *Chéré o chéré Elefteria*
> *Ké san prota andriomeni*
> *Chéré o chéré Elefteria."*

When I look back on this year spent in Greece I think it was really very beautiful, this effort to reach back over two thousand years to a beauty not perhaps understood by us, or understandable by others, a beauty of which Renan has written:

"Oh nobility! Oh simple and true beauty! Goddess whose worship signifies wisdom and reason. Thou whose temple is a lesson of eternal conscience and sincerity, too late I come to the threshold of thy mysteries; I bear to thy altar a load of remorse. It has cost me infinite seeking to find thee. The initiation that thou conferest on the Athenian at birth I have conquered by meditation, by much effort."

And so we left Hellas and arrived in the morning in Vienna, with our chorus of Greek boys and their Byzantine priest professor.

CHAPTER FOURTEEN

OUR desire to make the Greek Choruses and the ancient tragic dance live again was surely a very worthy effort, and one of utter impracticability. But after the financial successes of Budapest and Berlin, I had no desire to make a world tour, and only used the money that I had earned to build a Greek Temple and revivify the Greek Chorus. I look back now at our youthful aspirations as really curious phenomena.

And so we arrived one morning in Vienna and presented to a wondering Austrian public the Choruses of "The Suppliants" of Æschylus, intoned by our Greek boys on the stage, while I danced. As there were fifty "daughters of Danaus," I found it very difficult to express, in my slight figure, the emotions of fifty maidens all at once, but I had the feeling of multiple oneness, and did my best.

Vienna is only four hours from Budapest, but it is extraordinary, perhaps, that the year spent before the Parthenon, had so separated me from Budapest that I did not find it at all strange that Romeo never travelled those four hours to come to see me. Nor did I really think that he should have done so. I was so interested in the Greek Chorus that my devotion to it took all my energy and emotions. To tell the truth, I never thought of him. On the contrary, my being at that time was taken up with intellectual questions, and all this was admirably concentrated in a friendship I then had with a man who was, above all, a man of intelligence—Herman Bahr.

Herman Bahr had seen me dance a couple of years before in the Vienna Künstler Haus before the artists. On my return to Vienna with the Chorus of Greek boys, he was intensely interested. He wrote marvellous press criticisms in the Vienna *Neue Presse*.

Herman Bahr was at that time a man of perhaps thirty, with a magnificent head, covered with luxuriant brown hair and a brown beard. Although he often came to the Bristol after the performance and talked to me till dawn; although I often rose and danced strophe after strophe of the Greek Chorus to illustrate my meaning, nevertheless, between us was not the slightest hint of anything of a sentimental or emotional nature. Probably sceptics will find this hard to believe, but it is the very truth that from the experience of Budapest, for years after, my entire emotional reaction had such a revolution that I really believed I had finished with that phase, and in the future would only give myself to my Art. Now, considering that I was built rather on the lines of the Venus de Milo, this certainly was a bit astonishing, and so I regard it to-day. Strange as it may seem, after that brutal awakening, my senses slept; nor did I desire of them anything at all. All my life centred in my art.

My success in Vienna at the Karl Theatre was again achieved. The audience, who began by receiving the Chorus of the Suppliants with the ten Greek boys rather coldly, ended in a state of exalted enthusiasm when I danced the "Blue Danube" at the close of the performance. After the performance I made a speech explaining that it was not what I wanted; that I wished to give the spirit of Greek Tragedy. We must revive the beauty of the Chorus, I said. But still the audience shouted: "Nein. Mach nicht. Tanze. Tanze die Schöne Blaue Donau. Tanze noch einmal." And they applauded over and over again.

So, laden with new gold, we left Vienna and again arrived in Munich. The advent of my Greek Chorus in Munich caused a great stir in professorial and intellectual circles. The great Professor Furtwangler delivered a lecture, and discoursed on the Greek Hymns now set to music by the Byzantine professor of the Greek Church.

The students of the University were much "aufgeregt." In fact, our beautiful Greek boys made a profound hit. Only I, dancing as the fifty Danaïdes, felt very inadequate, and often, as the performance ended, I made a speech to explain that I should really be, not myself, but fifty maidens; that I was "furchtbahr traurig," that I was only one, but patience, "Geduld," I should soon form a school and transform myself into fifty "kleine Mädchen."

Berlin was less enthusiastic for our Greek Chorus and, although a distinguished Professor from Munich, Professor Cornelius, came to announce them, Berlin, like Vienna, cried, "Oh, dance the 'schöne blaue' Danube, and never mind the reconstruction of these Greek Choruses."

In the meantime the little Greek boys themselves were feeling the effects of their unaccustomed environment. I had received several complaints from our worthy Hotel proprietor of their bad manners and the violence of their tempers. It seems that they asked continually for black bread, black ripe olives and raw onions, and when these condiments were not in their daily menu, they became enraged with the waiters—going so far as to throw beefsteaks at their heads and attack them with knives. After they had been turned out of several first-class hotels, I was forced to fit up the front parlour rooms of my apartments in Berlin with ten cots, and install them with us.

As we considered them children, we used to solemnly take them all for a walk each morning in the Tiergarten, sandalled and accoutred as ancient Greeks. Elizabeth and I, walking at the head of this strange procession one morning, met the Kaiserin on horseback. She was so shocked and astonished that, at the next turning, she fell off her horse, for the good Prussian horse had also never seen anything like this, so he shied and acted badly.

These charming Greek children only remained with us for six months. Then we couldn't help noticing ourselves that their heavenly voices were becoming out of tune, and even the adoring Berlin public began to turn to one another in consternation. I bravely kept on trying to impersonate the fifty Danaïdes in supplication before the altar of Zeus, but it was a heavy task, especially when the Greek boys sang more than ordinarily false, and their Byzantine Professor seemed more and more distracted.

The Seminarist grew more and more vague about Byzantine music. He seemed to have left all his enthusiasm for it in Athens. Also his absences became more frequent and prolonged. The climax of all came when the police authorities informed us that our Greek boys were surreptitiously escaping from the window at night and, when we thought they were safely sleeping, they were frequenting cheap cafés and making the acquaintance of the lowest specimens of their compatriots which the city held.

Also, since they arrived in Berlin, they had completely lost that naïve and heavenly boyish expression which they had had on the evenings in the Dionysus Theatre, and each had grown half a foot. Every night at the theatre the Chorus of the Suppliants was becoming more and more off any key whatever. One could no longer excuse it on the ground that it was Byzantine. It was simply a fearful bad noise. So one day, after much worried consultation, we came to the decision to march all our Greek Chorus down to Wertheimer's big Department Store. We bought them all nice ready-made knickerbockers for the short boys and long trousers for the big boys, and then took them in taxis to the railroad station and, putting them all in second-class carriages, with a ticket for each to Athens, bade them a fond farewell. After their departure we put off the revival of Ancient Greek Music to a later date, and returned to the study of Christopher Gluck—Iphigenia and Orpheus.

From the beginning I conceived the dance as a chorus or community expression. Just as I had endeavoured to picture to the audience the sorrows of the daughters of Danaus, so I danced from "Iphigenia," the maidens of Chalcis playing with their golden ball on the suave sands, and later the sorrowful exiles at Tauris dancing with reluctant horror the blood sacrifices of their Hellenic countrymen and victims. I so ardently hoped to create an orchestra of dancers that, in my imagination, they already existed, and in the golden lights of the stage I saw the white supple forms of my companions; sinewy arms, tossing heads, vibrant bodies, swift limbs environed me. At the end of "Iphigenia" the maids of Tauris dance in Bacchanalian joy for the rescue of Orestes. As I danced these delirious rondos, I felt their willing hands in mine; the pull and swing of their little bodies as the rondos grew faster and madder. When I finally fell, in a paroxysm of joyous abandon, I saw them

"Drunken with wine, amid the sighing of flutes
Hunting desire thru woodland shades alone."

The weekly receptions at our house in Victoria Strasse now became the centre of artistic and literary enthusiasm. Here took place many learned discussions on the dance as a fine art; for the Germans take every art discussion most seriously and give the deepest consideration to it. My dance became a subject of violent and even fiery debates. Whole columns constantly appeared in all the papers, sometimes hailing me as the genius of a newly discovered Art, sometimes denouncing me as a destroyer of the real classic dance, *i.e.*, the Ballet. On my return from performances where the audience had been delirious with joy, I would sit far into the night in my white tunic, with a glass of white milk beside me, poring over the pages of Kant's "Critique of Pure Reason" from which, Heaven only knows how, I believed I was finding inspiration for those movements of pure beauty which I sought.

Among the artists and writers who frequented our house was a young man with a high forehead, piercing eyes behind glasses, who decided it was his mission to reveal to me the genius of Nietzsche. Only by Nietzsche, he said, will you come to the full revelation of dancing expression as you seek it. He came each afternoon and read me "Zarathustra" in German, explaining to me all the words and phrases that I could not understand. The seduction of Nietzsche's philosophy ravished my being, and those hours which Karl Federn devoted to me each day assumed a fascination so potent that it was with the greatest reluctance that my Impresario could persuade me to make even short tours to Hamburg, Hanover, Leipsic, etc., where excited, curious audiences and many thousand marks awaited my coming. I had no wish for the triumphal world tours of which he always talked to me. I wanted to study, continue my researches, create a dance and movements which then did not exist, and the dream of my School, which had haunted all my childhood, became stronger and stronger. This desire to remain in my studio and study drove my Impresario to absolute despair. He continually bombarded me with entreaties to travel, and continually came in, wailing with anguish, showing me newspapers which told how, in London and elsewhere, copies of my curtains, my costumes and my dances were being received, turned into certain success and hailed as original. But even this had no effect on me. His exasperation reached its climax when, as the summer approached, I declared my intention of spending the whole season in Bayreuth, to revel at last, from the real source, in the music of Richard Wagner. This decision was brought to a final determination when, one day, I received a visit from no less a person than the widow of Richard Wagner.

I have never met a woman who impressed me with such high intellectual fervour as Cosima Wagner, with her tall, stately carriage, her beautiful eyes, a nose perhaps too prominent for femininity and a forehead which radiated intelligence. She was versed in all the deepest philosophy and knew every phrase and note of the Master by heart. She spoke to me of my Art in the most encouraging and beautiful manner and then she spoke to me of Richard Wagner's distaste for the Ballet school of dancing, and costume; of his dream for the Bacchanal and the Flower Maidens; of the impossibility of fitting into Wagner's dream the execution of the Berlin Ballet actually engaged to perform at Bayreuth that season. She then asked me if I would consent to dance in the performances of "Tannhäuser": but there came the difficulty. With my ideals it was impossible for me to have anything to do with the Ballet, whose every movement shocked my sense of beauty, and whose expression seemed to me mechanical and vulgar.

"Oh, why have I not the school of which I dream," I exclaimed in response to her request; "then I could bring to you at Bayreuth a bevy of just those nymphs, fauns, satyrs and Graces, of which Wagner dreamed. But alone, what can I do? Nevertheless, I will come, and I will try to give at least an indication of the lovely, soft, voluptuous movements which I already see for the Three Graces."

CHAPTER FIFTEEN

I ARRIVED in Bayreuth on a lovely May day, and took rooms at the Hotel of the Black Eagle (Schwarz Adler). One of these was large enough to work in, and I installed a piano. Every day I received a little word from Frau Cosima, asking me to lunch or dinner, or to spend the evening at Villa Wahnfried, where hospitality was dispensed in a regal manner. Each day there were at least fifteen or more people to lunch. Frau Cosima, at the head of the table, presided with dignity, and with equal tact, for among her guests were included the greatest minds in Germany, artists and musicians, often Grand Dukes and Duchesses or Royal personages from all countries.

The tomb of Richard Wagner is in the garden of Villa Wahnfried and can be seen from the Library windows. After lunch Frau Wagner took my arm and we walked out into the garden, around the tomb. It was a promenade in which Frau Cosima conversed in tones of sweet melancholy and mystic hope.

In the evening there were often quartettes, in which each instrument was played by a celebrated virtuoso. The great figure of Hans Richter, the slight silhouette of Karl Muck, the charming Mottel, Humperdinck and Heinrich Thode, every artist of that time was received at Villa Wahnfried with equal kindness.

I was very proud that I should be admitted, in my little white tunic, to a galaxy of such distinguished and brilliant personages. I began to study the music of "Tannhäuser," that music which expresses all the frenzy of voluptuous longing of a "cerebrale"—for always this Bacchanal takes

143

place within the brain of Tannhäuser. The closed grotto of the satyrs and the nymphs and Venus was the closed grotto of Wagner's mind, exasperated by the continual longing for a sensual outlet which he could find only within his own imagination.

Of this Bacchanal I wrote:

"I am only able to give you a vague indication, only an indefinite sketch of what most dancers will be later on—masses rushing like whirlwinds in rhythms caught up by mad waves of this music, flowing with fantastic sensuality and ecstasy. If, with my force alone, I have the courage to dare a similar undertaking, it is because all that belongs to the domain of pure imagination. These are only the visions of Tannhäuser sleeping in the arms of Venus.

"In order to realise these dreams, a single gesture of appeal will be able to evoke a thousand extended arms, a single head tossed back will represent a bacchantic tumult which is the expression of burning passion in the blood of Tannhäuser.

"It seems to me that in this music is concentrated the unsatisfied senses, the mad longing, the passionate languor; in short, the whole cry of desire in the world.

"Can all this be expressed? Do not these visions exist only in the inflamed imagination of the composer, and can they be clothed in a manifested form?

"Why try this impossible effort? I repeat, I do not fulfill it, I only indicate it.

"And when these terrible desires arrive at paroxysm, when they attain the point where, breaking all the barriers, they rush forward like an irresistible torrent, I cover the scene with mists so that each one in his own way without seeing, can realise the dénouement in his imagination, which only outstrips any concrete vision.

"After this explosion and destruction, after this accomplishment which destroys in accomplishing, after all this comes peace.

"These are the Three Graces embodying the calm, the languor of satisfied amorous sensuality. In the dream of Tannhäuser they are interlaced and separated and, joining themselves together, become alternately unified and parted. They sing of the loves of Zeus.

"They tell of his adventures, of Europa carried over the waves. Their heads incline with love. They are inundated, they are drowned in the desire of Leda in love with the white swan. Thus they order Tannhäuser to repose in the whiteness of Venus's arms.

"Is it necessary to place before the eyes the gross representations of these visions? Do you not prefer, in peering into hazy space, to see Europa, one thin arm thrown round the neck of the large bull (she pressing the god to her) and waving to her companions, calling her from the river-bank, a final gesture of farewell?

"Would you not prefer to look into the shadows to see Leda, half covered by the wings of the swan, shivering before the approaching kiss?

"Perhaps you will reply, 'Yes; why are you there?' I will tell you simply—'I may indicate.' "

From morning to evening, in the red brick temple on the hill, I attended all the rehearsals, awaiting the first performance. "Tannhäuser," "The Ring," "Parsifal"—until I was in a constant state of intoxication from music. To understand them better, I learned all the text of the operas by heart, so that my mind was saturated with these legends, and my being was vibrating with the waves of Wagner's melody. I reached that state where all the outward world seemed cold, shadowy and unreal, and the only reality for me was what took place in the theatre. One day I was the blonde Segelinde, lying in the arms of her brother Sigmund, while the glorious spring song rose and throbbed.

> "*Frühling Zeit, Liebe Tanze . . .*
> *Tanze Liebe.*"

Next, I was Brünnhilde weeping her lost Godhead, and, again, Kundry uttering wild imprecation under the spell of Klingsor. But the supreme experience was when my soul arose, all trembling in the blood-lit goblet of the Grail. Such enchantment! Ah, I had indeed forgotten the Wise, Blue-eyed Athena and her Temple of Perfect Beauty on the hill of Athens. That other Temple on the hill of Bayreuth, with its waves and reverberations of magic, had entirely obliterated Athena's Temple.

The Hotel Black Eagle was crowded and uncomfortable. One day, in my wanderings about the gardens of the Hermitage, built by the mad Ludwig of Bavaria, I discovered an old stone house of exquisite architecture. It was the ancient hunting-lodge of the Margrave. It contained a very large and beautifully proportioned living-room, and old marble steps leading down to a romantic garden. It was in a state of terrible disrepair, inhabited by a large family of peasants, who had lived there for twenty years or so. I offered them a fabulous sum to leave, at least for the summer. Then I started painters and carpenters to work, had all the inside walls plastered and coloured a light, tender green; flew up to Berlin and ordered couches, cushions, deep wicker chairs and books. And, finally, I took possession of Phillip's Ruhe, as the hunting-lodge was called—Phillip's Rest. Afterwards I always thought of it as Heinrich's Himmel.

I was alone in Bayreuth. Mother and Elizabeth were summering in Switzerland. Raymond had returned to his beloved Athens to continue to build Kopanos. He sent me frequent telegrams reading "Artesian well progressing. Sure of water next week. Send funds." This went on until the accumulated expense of Kopanos took on such proportions as to fairly stagger me.

In the two years which had elapsed since Budapest, I had lived chastely, relapsing, in a curious manner, to the state in which I was as a virgin. Every atom of my being, brain and body had been absorbed in enthusiasm for Greece and, now, for Richard Wagner. I slept lightly and awoke singing the themes which I had studied the evening before. But Love was to awaken again within me, though in a very different form. Or was it the same Eros, only in another mask?

My friend Mary and I were alone in Phillip's Ruhe, for, as there was no servants' room, the valet and cook boarded in a small inn nearby. One night Mary called to me: "Isadora, I don't mean to frighten you, but come to the window. There, opposite, beneath a tree, every night after midnight that man looks up at your window. I'm afraid it's a burglar with evil intentions."

Sure enough, a small, slight man under a tree, stood looking at my window. I shivered with apprehension but, suddenly, the moon came out and lit up his face. Mary clutched me. We had both seen the exalted, uplifted visage of Heinrich Thode. We drew back from the window. I confess we were overcome with a fit of typical schoolgirl giggles—perhaps a reaction from the first fear.

"For a week he has been there like that every night," whispered Mary.

I told Mary to wait. I put on my coat over my nightdress and ran lightly out of the house, straight up to where Heinrich Thode stood.

"Lieber, treuer Freund," I said, "liebst du mich so?"

"Ja, ja—" he stammered. "Du bist mein Traum. Du meine Santa Clara."

I did not know then, but afterwards he told me he was writing his second great work, on the life of Saint Francis. His first had been the Life of Michael Angelo. Thode, like all great artists, lived in the moment's imagination of his work. At this moment he was Saint Francis, and he imagined me as Santa Clara.

I took his hand and drew him gently up the stairs, into the Villa, but he was like a man in a dream, and regarded me with eyes filled with prayer and light. As I returned his gaze, suddenly I was uplifted and, with him, traversed heavenly spheres or paths of shining light. Such exquisite ecstasy of love I had never felt before. It transformed my being, which became all luminous. After that gaze had lasted a while—I don't know how long in actual time—I felt weak and dizzy. All my senses swooned, and with an indescribable feeling of perfect bliss, I fainted in his arms. When I awoke, those wonderful eyes were still gazing into mine, and softly he quoted:

"Im Gluth mich Liebe senkte,
Im Gluth mich Liebe senkte!"

Again I experienced that transcendental, ethereal feeling of flight into the heavens. Thode leaned forward and kissed my eyes, my forehead; but these were not kisses of any earthly passion. Difficult as certain sceptics will find it to believe, it is nevertheless true that neither this night, until we parted at dawn, nor on each following night, when he came to the Villa, did Thode make one gesture of earthly force toward me. Always that luminous gaze, until, looking into his eyes, all faded around me and my spirit took wings on those astral flights with him. Nor did I wish for any earthly expression from him. My senses, which had slept for two years, were completely transformed into an ethereal ecstasy.

The rehearsal at Bayreuth began. With Thode I sat in the darkened theatre and listened to the first notes of the Prelude of "Parsifal." The feeling of delight through all my nerves became so poignant that the slightest touch of his arm sent such thrills of ecstasy through me that I turned sick and faint, with the sweet, gnawing, painful pleasure. It revolved in my head like a thousand whirls of myriad lights. It throbbed in my throat with such joy that I wanted to cry out. Often I felt his slight hand pressed over my lips to silence the sighs and little groans that I could not control. It was as if every nerve in my body arrived at that climax of love which is generally limited to the instant; and hummed with such insistence that I hardly knew whether it was utter joy or horrible suffering. My state partook of both, and I longed to cry out with Amfortas, to shriek with Kundry.

Each night Thode came to Phillip's Ruhe. He never caressed me as a lover, never sought even to undo my tunic or touch my breasts or my body in any way, although he knew that every pulse of it belonged only to him. Emotions I had not known to exist awoke under the gaze of his eyes. Sensations so ecstatic and terrible that I often felt the pleasure was killing me, and fainted away, to awaken again to the light of those wonderful eyes. He so completely possessed my soul that it seemed it was only possible to gaze into his eyes and long for death. For there was not, as in earthly love, any satisfaction or rest, but always this delirious thirst for a point that I required.

I completely lost my appetite for food, and even for sleep. Only the music of "Parsifal" brought me to the point where I dissolved into tears and wept, and that seemed to give some relief from this exquisite and terrible state of loving which I had then entered.

The spiritual will of Heinrich Thode was so strong that from these wild flights of ecstasy and fainting bliss, he could, when he pleased, awaken the attention of pure intelligence and, in the brilliance of these hours, when he discoursed to me on Art, I can only compare him to one other in the world—Gabriel D'Annunzio. Thode, in a way, resembled D'Annunzio. He was small of stature, with a wide mouth and strange green eyes.

Each day he brought me parts of his manuscript, Saint Francis. He read me each chapter as he wrote it. He also read me the entire Divine Comedy of Dante, from beginning to end. These readings occupied the hours far into the night, to the dawn. Often he left Phillip's Ruhe at sunrise. He staggered like a drunken man, although he had wet his lips with nothing but pure water during the reading. He was simply intoxicated with the divine essence of his supreme intelligence. On one of these mornings, as he was leaving Phillip's Ruhe, he grasped my arm in terror.

"I see Frau Cosima coming up the road!"

Sure enough, there, in the early morning light, Frau Cosima appeared. She was pale, and I would have thought wrathful. But this was not the case. We had had a dispute the day before about the meaning which I had put into my dance of the Three Graces of the Bacchanal of "Tannhäuser." That night, not being able to sleep, Frau Cosima had been turning over souvenirs and had found among the writings of Richard Wagner a small copy-book containing a description, more accurate than any yet published, of what he had meant by this Dance of the Bacchanal.

The dear woman had not been able to wait, but came to me at daybreak to acknowledge that I was right. Not only this, but, shaken and agitated, she said, "My dear child, you are surely inspired by the Master himself. See what he has written. It coincides exactly with your intuition. Hereafter, I will never interfere, but will give you free rein over the dance in Bayreuth."

I suppose it was at this time that there was the idea in Frau Cosima's mind that I should perhaps marry Siegfried and carry on with him the Master's tradition. But indeed, Siegfried, although he looked upon me with brotherly affection and was always my friend, had never the ghost of anything which hinted at being my lover. As for me, my whole being was absorbed with the superhuman love of Heinrich Thode, and I did not realise at that time what might have been of value for me in this combination.

My soul was like a battlefield where Apollo, Dionysus, Christ, Nietzsche and Richard Wagner disputed the ground. At Bayreuth I was buffeted between Venusberg and the Grail. I was taken up, swept along, carried away in the floods of Wagner's music and yet, one day during luncheon at Villa Wahnfried, I calmly announced,

"Der Meister hat einen fehler gemacht, eben so grosse wie seine Genie."

Frau Cosima fixed me with startled eyes. There was an icy silence.

"Yes," I continued with the extraordinary assurance which belongs to extreme youth, "der Grosse Meister hat einen grossen fehler gemacht. Die Musik-Drama, das ist doch ein unsinn."

The silence grew more and more troubled. I further explained that drama is the spoken word. The spoken word was born from the brain of man. Music is the lyric ecstasy. To expect a possible union between them is unthinkable.

I had uttered such blasphemy that nothing further was possible. I gazed innocently around me, to meet expressive visages of absolute consternation. I had said the untenable.

"Yes," I continued, "Man must speak, then sing, then dance. But the speaking is the brain, the thinking man. The singing is the emotion. The dancing is the Dionysian ecstasy which carries away all. It is impossible to mix in any way, one with the other. Musik-Drama kann nie sein."

I am glad that I was young in a day when people were not so self-conscious as they are now; when they were not such haters of Life and Pleasure. In the entr'acte of "Parsifal" people tranquilly drank beer, but this did not interfere with their intellectual and spiritual life. I often saw the great Hans Richter calmly drinking beer and eating sausages, which did not prevent him later from conducting like a demigod, nor did it hinder the people around him from carrying on a conversation of the highest intellectual and spiritual significance.

In those days, too, thinness was not equivalent to spirituality. People realised that the human spirit is something that works upward and is unfolded through tremendous energy and vitality. The brain, after all, is but the superfluous energy of the body. The body, like an octopus, will absorb everything it meets and only give to the brain what it finds unnecessary for itself.

Many of the singers of Bayreuth were of enormous stature, but when they opened their mouths their voices issued forth into the world of spirit and beauty where live the eternal gods. This was the reason why I maintained that these people were unconscious of their bodies, which were probably, for them, but masks of tremendous energy and power to express their god-like music.

CHAPTER SIXTEEN

WHEN I was in London, I had read the English translations of the works of Ernst Haeckel in the British Museum. I was greatly impressed by his lucid and clear expression of the different phenomena of the Universe. I wrote him a letter expressing my gratitude for the impression his books had made on me. There must have been something in this letter which arrested his attention, for afterwards, when I danced in Berlin, he replied to it.

At that time Ernst Haeckel was banished by the Kaiser, and could not come to Berlin, on account of his free speaking, but our correspondence had continued and when I was in Bayreuth I wrote and asked him to visit me and attend the Festspiel.

One rainy morning I took a two-horse, open carriage, as there were no autos in those days, and went to the train to meet Ernst Haeckel. The great man descended from the train. Although over sixty, he possessed a magnificent, athletic figure, with a white beard and white hair. He wore strange, baggy clothes, and carried a carpet bag. We had never met, but we recognised each other at once. I was immediately enfolded in his great arms and found my face buried in his beard. His whole being gave forth a fine perfume of health and strength and intelligence, if one can speak of the perfume of intelligence.

He came with me to Phillip's Ruhe, where we had his room decorated with flowers. Then I rushed down to Villa Wahnfried to tell the good news to Frau Cosima, that the great Ernst Haeckel had arrived and was my guest, and would come to hear "Parsifal." To my surprise this news was received most coldly. I had not realised that the crucifix over Frau Cosima's bed, and the rosary hanging on the night table were not merely ornaments. She really was a church-attending Catholic and a believer. The man who had written the "Riddle of the Universe," and who was the greatest iconoclast since Charles Darwin, whose theories he upheld, could not find a warm reception at Villa Wahnfried. In a naïve and direct manner, I expatiated on the greatness of Haeckel and my admiration for him. Frau Cosima reluctantly gave me the coveted place in the Wagner loge for him, for I was a very close friend of hers and she could not refuse me.

That afternoon, before the astonished audience, I promenaded during the entr'acte, in my Greek tunic, bare legs and bare feet, hand-in-hand with Ernst Haeckel, his white head towering above the multitude.

Haeckel was very quiet during the unfolding of Parsifal. Not until the third act did I understand that all this mystic passion did not appeal to him. His mind was too purely scientific to admit of the fascination of a legend.

As he received no invitation to dine or to be fêted at the Villa Wahnfried, I had the idea of giving an Ernst Haeckel Festival in his honour. I invited an amazing assembly of people, from King Ferdinand of Bulgaria, who was then visiting Bayreuth, and the Princess of Saxe-Meiningen, sister of the Kaiser, who was an extraordinarily broad-minded woman, to the Princess Henri of Reuss, Humperdinck, Heinrich Thode, etc.

I made a speech praising the greatness of Haeckel, then danced in his honour. Haeckel commented on my dance, likening it to all the universal truths of nature, and said that it was an expression of monism, in that it came from one source and had one direction of evolution. Afterwards, Von Barry, the famous tenor, sang. We had supper,

Haeckel acting as gaily as a boy. We feasted and drank and sang till morning.

Nevertheless, the next day, as every morning during his stay at Phillip's Ruhe, Haeckel rose with the sun. He used to come into my room and invite me to walk with him to the mountain top, which, I confess, I was not as keen to do as he was. But these walks were wonderful, because he commented upon every stone in the road, every tree and every geologic earth strata.

Finally, arriving at the mountain's height, he stood like some demi-god, observing the works of nature with a completely approving eye. He carried on his back his easel and paint-box, and made many sketches of the forest trees, and rock formations of the hills. Although he was a fairly good painter, his work naturally lacked the artist's imagination. It portrayed, rather, the skilled observation of the scientist. I do not mean that Ernst Haeckel could not appreciate art, but, to him, it was simply another manifestation of natural evolution. When I used to discourse to him of our enthusiasm for the Parthenon, he was much interested to know the quality of the marble, from which strata and which side of Mount Pentelicus it came, rather than to hear my praise of a gem of Phidias.

One night at Villa Wahnfried, King Ferdinand of Bulgaria had been announced. Every one rose and whispered to me to rise, but I was fiercely democratic and, instead, remained gracefully reclining on a couch à la Madame Récamier. Very soon Ferdinand asked who I was, and came towards me, to the scandal of all the other "hoheits" present. He simply seated himself beside me on the couch and began to talk at once most interestingly on his love for Greek antiquities. I told him of my dream of a school which would bring about a renaissance of the antique world and he said, in a voice that every one could hear, "It is a lovely idea. You must come and make your School in my Palace on the Black Sea."

The climax came when I asked him at dinner if he wouldn't come and have supper with me at Phillip's Ruhe some evening, after the performance, so that I could explain to him more about my ideals. He gracefully accepted the invitation. He kept his word and spent a charming evening with us at Phillip's Ruhe and I learned to appreciate this remarkable man, poet, artist, dreamer and truly royal intellect.

I had a butler with moustaches like the Kaiser. He was much impressed by Ferdinand's visit. When he brought in a tray with champagne and sandwiches, Ferdinand said, "No, I never touch champagne." But when he saw the label, "Oh, Möet et Chandon—yes—French champagne with pleasure. The truth is, I have been poisoned here with German champagne."

The visits of Ferdinand to Phillip's Ruhe, although we most innocently sat and discoursed on Art, also caused a hullabaloo in Bayreuth, because they took place at midnight. In fact, I could not do anything without seeming extravagantly different from other people, and therefore shocking.

Phillip's Ruhe contained many couches and cushions, rose-coloured lamps and no chairs. It was looked upon by some as a Temple of Iniquity. Especially since very often the great tenor Von Barry was inspired to sing all night and I danced, the village people considered it as a veritable witches' house and described our innocent revels as "terrible orgies."

Now there was at Bayreuth an Artists' cabaret called The Owl, and these people used to sing and drink all night, but that was considered all right because they acted in a manner which every one could understand, and because they wore ordinary clothes.

At Villa Wahnfried I met some young officers who invited me to ride with them in the mornings. I mounted in my Greek tunic and sandals, bareheaded, with my curls flying in the wind. I resembled Brünnhilde. As Phillip's Ruhe was some distance from the Festspiel Haus, I bought one of these horses from an officer, and I attended all the rehearsals à la Brünnhilde. As he was an officer's horse, the animal was used to spurs and was very difficult to manage. When he found himself alone with me, he indulged in all sorts of caprices. Among others, he used to stop at every public house on the road, where the officers had been accustomed to drink, and, planting his four feet on the ground, refuse to move until some laughing comrades of his former owner would come out and escort me further on my way. You can imagine the sensation my appearance created when I finally arrived before the entire audience assembled at the Festspiel Haus.

In the first performance of "Tannhäuser," my transparent tunic, showing every part of my dancing body, had created some stir amidst the pink-covered legs of the Ballet and at the last moment even poor Frau Cosima lost her courage. She sent one of her daughters to my loge, with a long white chemise, which she begged me to wear under the filmy scarf which served me for a costume. But I was adamant. I would dress and dance exactly my way, or not at all.

"You will see, before many years all your Bacchantes and flower maidens will dress as I do." This prophecy was fulfilled.

But at that time, there was much contention and hot discussion about my beautiful legs, whether my own satiny skin was quite moral or whether it should be covered with horrid salmon-coloured silk tights. Many times I declaimed myself hoarse on the subject of just how vulgar and inde-cent these salmon-coloured tights were and how beautiful and innocent the naked human body was when inspired by beautiful thoughts.

So here I was, a perfect pagan to all, fighting the Philistines. Yet here was a pagan about to be overcome by the ecstasy of a love born of the cult of St. Francis, and according to the rites of the silver trumpet, proclaiming the raising of the Grail.

In this strange world of legend the summer waned. The last days arrived. Thode left for a lecture tour. I also arranged for myself a tour of Germany. I left Bayreuth, but I carried a potent poison in my blood. I had heard the call of the Sirens. The yearning pain, the haunted remorse, the sorrowful sacrifice, the theme of Love calling Death—all were hereafter to obliterate for ever the clear vision of Doric Columns and the reasoning wisdom of Socrates.

The first stop on my tour was at Heidelberg. There I heard Heinrich lecture to his students. In alternate soft and thrilling tones, he discoursed to them of Art. Suddenly in the midst of his lecture he spoke my name and began telling these boys of a new æsthetic form brought to Europe by an American. His praise made me tremble with happiness and pride. That night I danced for the students and they made a great procession through the streets, and after it I found myself standing on the steps of the Hotel beside Thode, sharing this triumph with him. All the youth of Heidelberg adored him as I did. Every shop window held his picture, and every shop was filled with copies of my little book, "Der Tanz der Zukunft." Our names were linked together continually.

Frau Thode gave me a reception. She was a kindly woman, but seemed to me quite incapable of the high exaltation in which Heinrich lived. She was too thoroughly practical to be a soul-mate for him. As a matter of fact, towards the end of his life he left her, going away with a lady Pied Piper—a violinist—to live in a villa in the Garde See. Frau Thode had one brown eye and one grey, and that gave her a constantly uneasy expression. In a famous lawsuit later on, there was actually a family discussion as to whether she was the child of Richard Wagner or Von Bülow. Anyway, she was very kind to me, and if she felt any jealousy, she did not show it.

Any woman who could be jealous of Thode would have let herself in for a life of Chinese torture, for every one worshipped him—women and boys too. He was the magnetic centre of every gathering. It would be interesting to ask just what jealousy includes.

Though I had spent so many nights with Heinrich, there had been no sexual relations between us. Nevertheless, his treatment of me had so sensitised my entire being that it needed only a touch, sometimes a look, to give me all the keenest pleasure and intensity of love, the same relation to the actual pleasure, for instance, as one has in a dream. I suppose this state of things was too abnormal to last, for I finally could eat nothing at all, and was attacked by a queer faintness which gave to my dancing a more and more vaporous quality.

Alone on this tour, with a maid to care for me, I finally arrived at such a state that I continually heard Heinrich's voice calling to me in the night, and I was sure to receive a letter the next day. People began to worry about how thin I was, and commented upon my inexplicably emaciated looks. I could no longer eat or sleep, and often lay awake all night; my lithe, feverish hands, travelling over my body, which seemed to be possessed by thousands of demons, tried in vain to subdue or find some outlet for this suffering. Constantly I saw Heinrich's eyes and heard his voice. From such nights I often rose in agonised despair and took a train at two in the morning, travelling over half Germany only to be near him for an hour, and to return again alone on my tour to even greater torments. The spiritual ecstasy with which he had inspired me in Bayreuth gradually gave place to an exasperated state of uncontrollable desire.

This dangerous state was brought to an end by my manager bringing me a contract for Russia. St. Petersburg was only two days from Berlin, but from the moment of passing the frontier, it was as if one entered an entirely different world. From then on, the country became merged into great snowy plains and immense forests. The snow, so cold—glistening vast stretches—seemed to cool my heated brain.

Heinrich! Heinrich! He was back there in Heidelberg, telling beautiful boys about Michael Angelo's "Night" and the marvellous "Mother of God." Here was I, going further and further from him, into a land of vast, cold whiteness, only broken by poor villages (Isbas), from whose frost-covered windows gleamed a faint light. I could still hear his voice, but fainter. At last, the tantalising strains of Venusberg, the wails of Kundry and the agony cry of Amfortas were all frozen into one clear globe of ice.

That night in the sleeping car, I dreamt that I jumped out of the window, naked, into the snow, and was embraced and rolled and frozen in its icy arms. What would Dr. Freud have said of this dream?

CHAPTER SEVENTEEN

IT is impossible, is it not, to believe in a Providence or Guiding Destiny when one takes up the morning newspaper and reads of twenty people dead in a railway accident, who had not thought of death the day before; or of a whole town devastated with tidal wave or flood. Then why be so absurdly egotistical as to imagine a Providence guiding our small selves?

Yet there are things in my life so extraordinary as to make me believe at times in predestination. For instance, that train to St. Petersburg, instead of arriving at four in the afternoon, as scheduled, was stopped by snowdrifts and arrived at four the next morning, twelve hours late. There was no one at the station to meet me. When I descended from the train the temperature was ten degrees below zero. I had never felt such cold. The padded Russian coachmen were hitting their arms with their gloved fists to keep the blood flowing in their veins.

I left my maid with the baggage and, taking a one-horse cab, directed the driver to the Hotel Europa. Here I was, in the black dawn of Russia, quite alone, on the way to the Hotel when suddenly I beheld a sight equal in ghastliness to any in the imagination of Edgar Allan Poe.

It was a long procession that I saw from a distance. Black and mournful it came. There were men laden and bent under their loads—coffins—one after another. The coachman slowed his horse to a walk and bent and crossed himself. I looked on in the indistinct dawn, filled with horror. I asked him what this was. Although I knew no Russian, he managed to convey to me that these were the

161

workmen shot down before the Winter Palace the day before
—the fatal January 5, 1905, because, unarmed, they had
come to ask the Tsar for help in their distress—for bread
for their wives and children. I told the coachman to stop.
The tears ran down my face and were frozen on my cheeks
as this sad, endless procession passed me. But why buried
at dawn? Because later in the day it might have caused
more revolution. The sight of it was not for the city in the
daytime. The tears choked in my throat. With boundless
indignation I watched these poor grief-stricken workmen
carrying their martyred dead. If the train had not been
twelve hours late, I would never have seen this.

O dark and mournful night without one sign of Dawn,
O sad procession of poor stumbling forms,
Haunted, weeping eyes and poor hard worked rugged hands
Stifling with their poor black shawls
The sobs and moans beside their dead—
Guards walking stilted on either side.

If I had never seen it, all my life would have been different.
There, before this seemingly endless procession, this tragedy,
I vowed myself and my forces to the service of the people
and the down-trodden. Ah, how small and useless now
seemed all my personal love desires and sufferings! How
useless even my Art, unless it could help this. Finally the
last sad ones passed us. The coachman turned wonderingly
and watched my tears. Again he crossed himself with a
patient sigh, and spurred his horse toward the Hotel.

I mounted to my palatial rooms and slipped into the quiet
bed, where I cried myself to sleep. But the pity, the despairing rage of that dawn was to bear fruit in my life
thereafter.

The room of the Hotel Europa was immense and high-ceilinged. The windows were sealed and never opened. The air came through ventilators high in the wall. I awoke late. My manager called, bringing flowers. Soon my room was filled with flowers.

Two nights later I appeared before the élite of St. Petersburg society in the Saal des Nobles. How strange it must have been to those dilettantes of the gorgeous Ballet, with its lavish decorations and scenery, to watch a young girl, clothed in a tunic of cobweb, appear and dance before a simple blue curtain to the music of Chopin; dance her soul as she understood the soul of Chopin! Yet even for the first dance there was a storm of applause. My soul that yearned and suffered the tragic notes of the Preludes; my soul that aspired and revolted to the thunder of the Polonaises; my soul that wept with righteous anger, thinking of the martyrs of that funeral procession of the dawn; this soul awakened in that wealthy, spoilt and aristocratic audience a response of stirring applause. How curious!

The next day I received a visit from a most charming little lady, wrapped in sables, with diamonds hanging from her ears, and her neck encircled with pearls. To my astonishment she announced that she was the great dancer Kschinsky. She had come to greet me in the name of the Russian Ballet and invite me to a gala performance at the Opera that night. I had been used to receiving only coldness and enmity from the Ballet in Bayreuth. They had even gone so far as to strew tacks on my carpet so that my feet were torn. This change of sentiment was both gratifying and astounding to me.

That evening a magnificent carriage, warmed and filled with expensive furs, conducted me to the Opera, where I found a first tier box, containing flowers, bonbons and three beautiful specimens of the *jeunesse dorée* of St. Petersburg. I was still wearing my little white tunic and sandals, and must have looked very odd in the midst of this gathering of all the wealth and aristocracy of St. Petersburg.

I am an enemy to the Ballet, which I consider a false and preposterous art, in fact, outside the pale of all art. But it was impossible not to applaud the fairy-like figure of Kschinsky as she flitted across the stage, more like a lovely bird or butterfly than a human being.

In the entr'acte I looked about me, and saw the most beautiful women in the world, in marvellous décolleté gowns, covered with jewels, escorted by men in distinguished uniforms; all this display of luxurious riches so difficult to understand in contrast with the funeral procession of the previous dawn. All these smiling and fortunate people, what kinship had they with the others?

After the performance I was invited to supper in the palace of Kschinsky, and there met the Grand Duke Michael, who listened with some astonishment as I discoursed on the plan of a school of dancing for the children of the people. I must have seemed an utterly incomprehensible figure, but they all received me with the kindest cordiality and lavish hospitality.

Some days later I received a visit from the lovely Pavlowa; and again I was presented with a box to see her in the ravishing Ballet of Gisèle. Although the movement of these dances was against every artistic and human feeling, again I could not resist warmly applauding the exquisite apparition of Pavlowa as she floated over the stage that evening.

At supper in the house of Pavlowa, which was more modest than Kschinsky's palace, but equally beautiful, I sat between the painters Bakst and Benois, and met, for the first time, Serge Diaghileff, with whom I engaged in ardent discussion on the art of the dance as I conceived it, as against the Ballet.

That evening, at supper, the painter Bakst made a little

sketch of me which now appears in his book, showing my most serious countenance, with curls sentimentally hanging down on one side. It is curious that Bakst, who had some clairvoyant powers, read my hand that night. He found there two crosses. "You will have great glory," he said, "but you will lose the two creatures whom you love most on earth." At that time this prophecy was a riddle to me.

After supper the indefatigable Pavlowa danced again, to the delight of her friends. Although it was five o'clock in the morning before we left, she invited me to come at half-past eight the same morning, if I would like to see her work. I arrived three hours later (I confess I was considerably fatigued) to find her standing in her tulle dress practising at the bar, going through the most rigorous gymnastics, while an old gentleman with a violin marked the time, and admonished her to greater efforts. This was the famous master Petitpas.

For three hours I sat tense with bewilderment, watching the amazing feats of Pavlowa. She seemed to be made of steel and elastic. Her beautiful face took on the stern lines of a martyr. She never stopped for one moment. The whole tendency of this training seems to be to separate the gymnastic movements of the body completely from the mind. The mind, on the contrary, can only suffer in aloofness from this rigorous muscular discipline. This is just the opposite from all the theories on which I founded my school, by which the body becomes transparent and is a medium for the mind and spirit.

As twelve o'clock approached, there were preparations for luncheon, but, at the table, Pavlowa sat white and pale, and hardly touched food or wine. I admit I was hungry and ate many *podjarsky* cutlets. Pavlowa took me back to my hotel and then went to one of those interminable rehearsals at the Royal Theatre. I, very weary, fell upon my bed and slept soundly, praising my stars that no unkind fate had ever given me the career of a Ballet dancer!

The following day I also arose at the unheard-of hour of eight o'clock to visit the Imperial Ballet School, where I saw all the little pupils standing in rows, and going through those torturing exercises. They stood on the tips of their toes for hours, like so many victims of a cruel and unnecessary Inquisition. The great, bare dancing-rooms, devoid of any beauty or inspiration, with a large picture of the Tsar as the only relief on the walls, were like a torture chamber. I was more than ever convinced that the Imperial Ballet School is an enemy to nature and to Art.

After a week in St. Petersburg, I went to Moscow. The audience there was not, in the beginning, as enthusiastic as in St. Petersburg—but I will quote from the great Stanislavsky:

"At about this period, 1908 or 1909, I do not remember the date exactly, I came to know two great geniuses of the time who made a very strong impression on me,—Isadora Duncan and Gordon Craig. I appeared at Isadora Duncan's concert by accident, having heard nothing about her until that time, and having read none of the advertisements that heralded her coming to Moscow. Therefore I was very much surprised that in the rather small audience that came to see her there was a tremendous percentage of artists and sculptors with Mamontov at their head, many artists of the ballet, and many first-nighters and lovers of the unusual in the theatre. The first appearance of Duncan on the stage did not make a very big impression. Unaccustomed to see an almost naked body on the stage, I could hardly notice and understand the art of the dancer. The first number on the program was met with tepid applause and timid attempts at whistling. But after a few of the succeeding numbers, one of which was especially persuasive, I could no longer remain indifferent to the protests of the general public and began to applaud demonstratively.

"When the intermission came, I, a newly baptised disciple of the great artist, ran to the footlights to applaud. To my joy I found myself side by side with Mamontov, who was doing exactly what I was doing, and near Mamontov was a famous artist, a sculptor, and a writer. When the general run of the audience saw that among those who applauded were well-known Moscow artists and actors, there was a great deal of confusion. The hissing stopped, and when the public saw that it could applaud, the applause became general, and was followed by curtain calls, and at the end of the performance by an ovation.

"From that time on I never missed a single one of the Duncan concerts. The necessity to see her often was dictated from within me by an artistic feeling that was closely related to her art. Later, when I became acquainted with her methods as well as with the ideas of her great friend Craig, I came to know that in different corners of the world, due to conditions unknown to us, various people in various spheres sought in art for the same naturally born creative principles. Upon meeting they were amazed at the common character of their ideas. This is exactly what happened at the meeting I am describing. We understood each other almost before we had said a single word. I did not have the chance to become acquainted with Duncan on her first visit to Moscow. But during her second visit she came to our Theatre and I received her as a guest of honour. This reception became general, for our entire company joined me, as they had all come to know and love her as an artist.

"Duncan does not know how to speak of her art logically and systematically. Her ideas come to her by accident, as the result of the most unexpected everyday facts. For instance, when she was asked who taught her to dance, she answered:

" 'Terpsichore. I danced from the moment I learned to stand on my feet. I have danced all my life. Man, all humanity, the whole world, must dance. This was, and always will be. It is in vain that people interfere with this and do not want to understand a natural need given us by nature. *Et voilà tout*,' she finished in her inimitable Franco-American dialect. Another time, speaking of a performance of hers that was just over, during which visitors came to her dressing-room and interfered with her preparations she explained:

" 'I cannot dance that way. Before I go out on the stage, I must place a motor in my soul. When that begins to work my legs and arms and my whole body will move independently of my will. But if I do not get time to put that motor in my soul, I cannot dance.'

"At that time I was in search of that very creative motor, which the actor must learn to put in his soul before he comes out on the stage. Evidently I must have bored Duncan with my questions. I watched her during her performances and her rehearsals, when her developing emotion would first change the expression of her face, and with shining eyes she would pass to the display of what was born in her soul. In remembering all our accidental discussion of art, and comparing what she did to what I was doing, it became clear to me that we were looking for one and the same thing in different branches of art. During our talks about Art, Duncan continually mentioned the name of Gordon Craig, whom she considered a genius and one of the greatest men in the contemporary theatre.

" 'He belongs not only to his country, but to the whole world,' she said, 'and he must live where his genius will have the best chance to display itself, where working conditions and the general atmosphere will be best fitted to his needs. His place is in your Art Theatre.'

"I know that she wrote a great deal to him about me and our Theatre, persuading him to come to Russia. As for myself, I began to persuade the Direction of our Theatre to invite the great stage director to come so as to give our art a new impetus forward and to pour more yeast into the dough at the time when it seemed to us that our Theatre had broken through the blind wall before it at last. I must pay full justice to my comrades. They discussed the matter like true artists and they decided to spend a large sum of money in order to advance our art."

As much as the Ballet had filled me with horror, so the Stanislavsky Theatre thrilled me with enthusiasm. I went there every night that I was not dancing myself, and was received with the greatest affection by all the troupe. Stanislavsky came very often to see me and thought that by questioning me thoroughly, he would be able to transform all my dances into a new school of dancing in his theatre. But I told him that could only be done by beginning with children. Apropos of this, on my next visit to Moscow, I saw some young, beautiful girls of his troupe trying to dance, but the result was deplorable.

As Stanislavsky was exceedingly busy all day in his theatre with rehearsals, he was in the habit of coming to see me frequently after the performance. In his book he says of these talks: "I suppose I must have tired Duncan with my questions." No: he did not tire me. I was bursting with enthusiasm to transmit my ideas.

In fact the keen, snowy air, the Russian food, especially the caviar, had completely cured my wasting illness, caused by the spiritual love of Thode. And now my whole being longed for the contact of a strong personality. As Stanislavsky stood before me, I saw such an one in him.

One night I looked at him, with his fine handsome figure, broad shoulders, black hair just turning to grey on the temples, and something within me revolted at always playing this rôle of Egeria. As he was about to leave, I placed my hands on his shoulders and entwined them about his strong neck, then, pulling his head down to mine, I kissed him on the mouth. He returned my kiss with tenderness. But he wore a look of extreme astonishment, as if this were the last thing he expected. Then, when I attempted to draw him further, he started back and, looking at me with consternation, exclaimed, "But what should we do with the child?" "What child?" I asked. "Why, our child, of course. What should we do with it? You see," he continued in a ponderous manner, "I would never approve of any child of mine being raised outside my jurisdiction, and that would be difficult in my present household."

His extraordinary seriousness about this child was too much for my sense of humour, and I burst into laughter, at which he stared in distress, left me and hurried down the corridor of the hotel. I was still laughing at intervals all night. But, none the less, in spite of my laughter, I was exasperated, and angry too. I think I then thoroughly understood why some quite refined men might slam on their hats after certain meetings with the highly intellectual, and betake themselves to places of doubtful reputation. Well, being a woman, I couldn't do this; so I twisted and turned the rest of the night. In the morning I repaired to a Russian bath, where the alternate hot steam and cold water retoned my system.

And yet, in contradiction, the young men I had met in Kschinsky's loge, who would have given anything to be allowed to make love to me, bored me so by the first words they said to me, that they even froze my senses to the very centre of desire. I suppose this is what is called a "cerebrale." Certainly after the inspiring and cultured society of Charles Hallé and Heinrich Thode, I could not possibly stand the society of the *jeunesse dorée!*

Many years later, I told this story of Stanislavsky to his wife, who was overcome with merriment and exclaimed, "Oh, but that is just like him. He takes life so seriously."

Attack as I might, I received some sweet kisses, but otherwise I just met with a callous, solid resistance which there was no disputing. Stanislavsky didn't risk coming to my room again after the theatre, but one day he made me very happy by taking me out in an open sleigh to a restaurant in the country, where we had lunch in a private room. We drank vodka and champagne and we talked of Art, and I was finally convinced that it would take Circe herself to break down the stronghold of Stanislavsky's virtue.

I had often heard of the terrible dangers which young girls risked by going into theatrical life, but, as my readers can see from my career so far, it was just the opposite. I really suffered from too much awe and respect and admiration, which I inspired in my admirers.

* * *

In a brief visit to Kieff, after Moscow, hordes of students stood in the public square before the theatre and would not let me pass until I promised to give a recital where they could be present, as the prices of my performances were much too high for them. After I left the theatre they were

still there, manifesting resentment against the manager.   I
stood up in the sleigh and talked to them, saying how proud
and happy I would be if my art could inspire the intellectual
youth of Russia; for nowhere in the world do the students
care so much for ideals and art as in Russia.

This first visit to Russia was cut short by previous engagements which recalled me to Berlin.   Before I left I had
signed a contract to return in the spring.   In spite of the
shortness of my visit, I had left a considerable impression.
There were many quarrels for and against my ideals; and
one duel was actually fought between a fanatic *balletoman*
and a Duncan enthusiast.   It was from that epoch that the
Russian ballet began to annex the music of Chopin and
Schumann and wear Greek costumes; some ballet dancers
even going so far as to take off their shoes and stockings.

RAYMOND DUNCAN

CHAPTER EIGHTEEN

I RETURNED to Berlin with the determination to start my long dreamed-of School, no longer to delay it, but to start at once. I confided these plans to my mother and sister, Elizabeth, who were equally enthusiastic. We immediately set out to find a house for the future School, with such speediness as marked everything else we did. Within a week we found a villa, on Trauden Strasse in Grünewald, which was just passing from the workmen's hands, and we bought it.

We acted exactly as though we were people in Grimm's Fairy Tales. We went down to Wertheimer's and actually bought forty little beds, each covered with white muslin curtains, drawn back with blue ribbons. We set about to make of our Villa a real children's Paradise. In the central hall we placed a copy of the heroic figure of the Amazon twice the size of life. In the large dancing-room, the bas-reliefs of Luca della Robbia and the dancing children of Donatello. In the bedroom, the blue and white babies and the Madonna and Child, also in blue and white, encrusted with garlands of fruit—the work of Luca della Robbia.

I placed these different ideal representations of the child form in the School, the bas-reliefs and sculptures of dancing children in their youngest years, in books and paintings too, because they showed the child form as it was dreamed of by the painters and sculptors of all ages; paintings of children dancing on Greek vases, tiny figures from Tanagra and Bœotia, the group of Donatello's dancing children because it is a radiant child melody, and the dancing children of Gainsborough.

173

All these figures have a certain fraternity in the naïve grace of their form and their movements, as if the children of all ages met each other and joined their hands across the centuries, and the real children of my School, moving and dancing in the midst of these forms, would surely grow to resemble them, to reflect unconsciously, in their movements and their faces, a little of the joy and the same childlike grace. It would be the first step toward their becoming beautiful, the first step toward the new art of the dance.

I also placed in my School the figures of young girls dancing, running, jumping—those young girls of Sparta who, in the gymnasiums, were trained in severe exercises, so that they might become the mothers of heroic warriors; those fleet-footed runners who took the annual prizes, exquisite images in terra cotta, with flying veils and flowing garments; young girls dancing hand-in-hand, at the Panathenaeas. They represented the future ideal to attain, and the pupils of my school, learning to feel an intimate love for these forms, would grow each day to resemble them, and would become each day a little more imbued with the secret of this harmony, for I enthusiastically believed that it was only upon awakening the will for beauty that one could obtain beauty.

Also, in order to attain to that harmony I desired, they must each day go through certain exercises chosen with the aim in view. But these exercises were conceived in a way to coincide with their own intimate will, so that they accomplished them with good humour and eagerness. Each one was not only to be a means toward an end, but an end in itself, and that end was to render each day of life complete and happy.

Gymnastics must be the basis of all physical education; it is necessary to give the body plenty of air and light; it is essential to direct its development methodically. It is necessary to draw out all the vital forces of the body towards its fullest development. That is the duty of the professor of gymnastics. After that comes the dance. Into the body, harmoniously developed and carried to its highest degree of energy, enters the spirit of the dance. For the gymnast, the movement and the culture of the body are an end in themselves, but for the dance they are only the means. The body itself must then be forgotten; it is only an instrument, harmonised and well appropriated, and its movements do not express, as in gymnastics, only the movements of a body, but, through that body, they express also the sentiments and thoughts of the soul.

The nature of these daily exercises is to make of the body, in each state of its development, an instrument as perfect as possible, an instrument for the expression of that harmony which, evolving and changing through all things, is ready to flow into the being prepared for it.

The exercises commenced by a simple gymnastic preparation of the muscles, for their suppleness and their force; it is only after these gymnastic exercises that the first steps of the dance come. The first steps are to learn a simple, rhythmic walk or march, moving slowly to simple rhythm, then, to walk or march quickly to rhythms more complex; then to run, slowly at first, then jump slowly, at a certain moment in the rhythm. By such exercises one learns the notes of the scale of sounds, and thus my pupils learned the notes of the scale of movement. These notes, in consequence, are able to be agents in the most varied and most subtle harmonies of structure. These exercises, moreover, are only a part of their studies. The children were always clothed, too, in free and graceful draperies in their sports, in their playground, in their walks, in the woods; jumping, running naturally, until they should have learned to express themselves by movement as easily as others express themselves through speech or through song.

Their studies and their observations were not to be limited to the forms in art, but were, above all, to spring from the movements in Nature. The movements of the clouds in the wind, the swaying trees, the flight of a bird, and the leaves which turn, all were to have a special significance for them. They were to learn to observe the quality peculiar to each movement. They were to feel in their souls a secret attachment, unknowable to others, to initiate them into Nature's secrets; for all the parts of their supple bodies, trained as they would be, would respond to the melody of nature and sing with her.

To gather children for our School, we announced in the leading newspapers that the Isadora Duncan School was open for the adoption of talented children, with the purpose that they become disciples of that Art which I hoped to give to thousands of the children of the people. Certainly the sudden opening of this School, without the proper premeditation or capital or organisation, was the most rash undertaking imaginable; one that drove my manager to distraction. He was continually planning world tours for me and I was continually insisting upon, first, spending a year in Greece, which he called wasted time, and now, stopping my career altogether for the adoption and training of what he considered absolutely useless children. But this was quite in keeping with all our other undertakings, most unpractical and untimely and impulsive.

From Kopanos, Raymond sent us news more and more alarming. The well became increasingly expensive. Each week the possibility of finding water became fainter and fainter. The expenses of Agamemnon's Palace itself grew to such terrifying proportions that, in the end, I was obliged to desist. Kopanos has always remained a beautiful ruin on the hill, since used by each faction of Greek revolutionaries as a fortress. It is still standing there, perhaps as a hope for the future.

I decided that all my resources should be concentrated upon founding a school for the youth of the world, and I chose Germany as the centre of philosophy and culture, which I then believed it to be.

Flocks of children answered the announcement. I remember one day, returning from a matinée and finding the street blocked with parents and their offspring. The German coachman turned to me and said: "Eine verrückte dame die wohnt dort, die eine Ankundigung in die Zeitung gestellt hat dass sie Kinder sehr gern haben willt."

I was the "verrückte dame." I do not yet know exactly how we chose those children. I was so anxious to fill the Grünewald and the forty little beds, that I took the children without discrimination, or merely on account of a sweet smile or pretty eyes; and I did not ask myself whether or not they were capable of becoming future dancers.

One day in Hamburg, for instance, a man in a high hat and frock coat entered my hotel drawing-room, with a bundle in his arms, wrapped in a shawl. He placed this bundle on the table, and I opened it to find two great watchful eyes looking into mine, a child of about four, the most silent child I have ever seen. She did not utter a sound or say a word. The gentleman himself seemed to be very hurried. He asked me if I would take the child, and would hardly wait for a response. Looking from the baby face to his, I thought there was a significant resemblance which might account for his desire for secrecy and haste. With my usual lack of foresight, I consented to keep the child and he disappeared, nor did I ever see him again.

This was a mysterious way of leaving a child on my hands, as if she were a doll. In the train from Hamburg to Berlin, I discovered she had a high fever—a bad case of tonsillitis—and in Grünewald, for three weeks afterwards, we fought for her against death, with the aid of two nurses and the splendid doctor, Hoffa, the celebrated surgeon, who was so enthusiastic over the idea of my School that he gave his services for nothing.

Dr. Hoffa frequently said to me, "This is not a School. This is a hospital. All these children have hereditary taints, and you will find that it will be necessary to take the greatest care to keep them alive, much less teach them to dance." Dr. Hoffa was one of the greatest benefactors of humanity, a famous surgeon who was paid fabulous prices for his services, and then spent his entire fortune on a hospital for poor children, which he ran at his own expense, just outside Berlin. From the beginning of my School he constituted himself our doctor and surgeon in all matters concerning the health of the children and the sanitation of the School. In fact, without his untiring aid I could never have brought these children to the beautiful result of health and harmony which they afterwards attained. He was a great, robust, fine-looking man, with red cheeks, and possessed such a friendly smile that all the children loved him as much as I did.

The selection of the children, the organisation of the School, the commencing of the lessons and the routine of their lives took all our time. In spite of the warnings of my manager that successful copies of my work in the dance were collecting fortunes in London and elsewhere, nothing would make me stir from Berlin. Every day, from five o'clock until seven I taught these children to dance.

The children made phenomenal progress and I believe their good health was due to the very sane vegetarian diet advised by Dr. Hoffa. He was of the opinion that, at any

rate for the education of children, it is necessary to have a
diet of fresh vegetables, plenty of fruit, but no meat.

* * *

At that time my popularity in Berlin was almost unbelievable. They called me the Göttliche Isadora. It was even
bruited about that when sick people were brought into my
theatre they became well. And every matinée one could see
the strange sight of sick people being brought in on litters.
I had never worn any other dress than the little white tunic,
bare feet and sandals. And my audience came to my performances with an absolutely religious ecstasy.

One night, as I was returning from a representation, the
students took the horses out of my carriage and drew me
through the famous Sieges Allee. In the middle of the Allee,
they called for a speech. I stood up in the victoria—in
those days there were no automobiles—and I addressed the
students thus:

"There is no greater art," I said, "than the art of the
sculptor. But why do you, lovers of art, permit this horrible
outrage in the middle of your city? Look at these statues!
You are art students, but if you were really students of
art, you would take stones to-night and demolish them!
Art? They, art? No! They are the visions of the Kaiser."

The students were of my opinion and yelled their approba-
tion, and if it had not been for the police who came along,
we might have carried out my wish and destroyed those
horrible statues in the city of Berlin.

CHAPTER NINETEEN

ONE night in 1905 I was dancing in Berlin. Although as a rule I never notice the audience when I am dancing—they always seem to me like some great god representing Humanity—this evening I was aware of some personality sitting in the front row. Not that I looked, or saw, who it was, but I was psychically aware of its presence, and when the performance was over, there came into my loge a beautiful being. But he was very angry.

"You are marvellous!" he exclaimed. "You are wonderful! But why have you stolen my ideas? Where did you get my scenery?"

"What are you talking about? These are my own blue curtains. I invented them when I was five years old, and I have danced before them ever since!"

"No! They are my *décors* and my ideas! But you are the being I imagined in them. You are the living realisation of all my dreams."

"But who are you?"

Then came from his mouth these wonderful words:

"I am the son of Ellen Terry."

Ellen Terry, my most perfect ideal of woman! Ellen Terry . . . !

"Why, you must come home and have supper with us," said my unsuspecting mother. "Since you take such an interest in Isadora's art, you must come home to supper with us."

And Craig came home to supper.

He was in a wild state of excitement. He wanted to explain all his ideas about his art, his ambitions. . . .

ISADORA DUNCAN WITH HER PUPILS

And I was most interested.

But, one by one, my mother and the others became quite sleepy, and one by one, they went off to bed with various excuses, and we were left alone. Craig went on talking about the art of the theatre. He illustrated his art with gestures.

Suddenly, in the midst of all this, he said:

"But what are you doing here? You, the great artist, living in the midst of this family? Why, it's absurd! I was the one who saw and invented you. You belong to my scenery."

Craig was tall, willowy, with a face recalling that of his wonderful mother, but even more delicate in features. In spite of his height, there was something feminine about him, especially about the mouth, which was sensitive and thin-lipped. The golden curls of his boyhood pictures—Ellen Terry's golden-haired little boy, so familiar to London audiences—were somewhat darkened. His eyes, very near-sighted, flashed a steely fire behind his glasses. He gave one the impression of delicacy, a certain almost womanly weakness. Only his hands, with their broad-tipped fingers and simian square thumbs, bespoke strength. He always laughingly referred to them as murderous thumbs—"Good to choke you with, my dear!"

I, like one hypnotised, allowed him to put my cape over my little white tunic. He took my hand, we flew down the stairs to the street. Then he hailed a taxi and said, in his best German, "Meine Frau und mich, wir wollen nach Potsdam gehen."

Several taxis refused to take us, but finally we found one, and off we went to Potsdam. At dawn we arrived. We stopped at a little hotel that was just opening its doors, and we drank coffee. Then, as the sun was getting high in the heavens, we started back for Berlin.

We arrived in Berlin at about nine o'clock and then we

thought, "What are we to do?" We could not go back to my mother, so we went to see a friend called Elsie de Brugaire. Elsie de Brugaire was a Bohemian. She received us with most tender sympathy. She gave us some breakfast —scrambled eggs and coffee. She put me to sleep in her bedroom. I went to sleep and did not awake until evening.

Craig then took me up to his studio at the top of a high building in Berlin. There was a black, waxed floor with rose leaves, artificial rose leaves, strewn all over it.

Here stood before me brilliant youth, beauty, genius; and, all inflamed with sudden love, I flew into his arms with all the magnetic willingness of a temperament which had for two years lain dormant, but waiting to spring forth. Here I found an answering temperament, worthy of my metal. In him I had met the flesh of my flesh, the blood of my blood. Often he cried to me, "Ah, you are my sister." And I felt that in our love was some criminal incestuousness.

I do not know how other women remember their lovers. I suppose it is the correct thing to stop always at a man's head, shoulders, hands, etc., and then describe his clothes, but I always see him, as that first night in the studio, when his white, lithe, gleaming body emerged from the chrysalis of clothes and shone upon my dazzled eyes in all his splendour.

So must Endymion, when first discovered by the glistening eyes of Diana, in tall, slender whiteness, so must Hyacinthus, Narcissus and the bright, brave Perseus have looked. More like an angel of Blake than a mortal youth he appeared. Hardly were my eyes ravished by his beauty than I was drawn toward him, entwined, melted. As flame meets flame, we burned in one bright fire. Here, at last, was my mate; my love; my self—for we were not two, but one, that one amazing being of whom Plato tells in the Phædrus, two halves of the same soul.

This was not a young man making love to a girl. This was the meeting of twin souls. The light covering of flesh was so transmuted with ecstasy that earthly passion became a heavenly embrace of white, fiery flame.

There are joys so complete, so all perfect, that one should not survive them. Ah, why did not my burning soul find exit that night, and fly, like Blake's angel, through the clouds of our earth to another sphere?

His love was young, fresh and strong, and he had neither the nerves nor nature of a voluptuary, but preferred to turn from love-making before satiety set in, and to translate the fiery energy of his youth to the magic of his Art.

In his studio was no couch, no easy chair, and no dinner. We slept on the floor that night. He was penniless, and I didn't dare go home for money. I slept there for two weeks. When we wanted a dinner, he ordered one to be sent up, on credit, and I hid on the balcony until it came, then crept in and shared it.

My poor mother went around to all the police stations, and all the Embassies, saying that some vile seducer had run off with her daughter; while my impresario was wild with anxiety at my sudden disappearance. Vast audiences had been turned away, and no one knew what had happened. However, an announcement was wisely published in the papers to the effect that Miss Isadora Duncan had been taken seriously ill with tonsillitis.

When two weeks had passed, we returned to my mother's house; and, to tell the truth, in spite of my mad passion, I was a bit tired of sleeping on a hard floor, and having nothing to eat except what he could get from the delicatessen, or when we sallied out after dark.

When my mother saw Gordon Craig, she cried, "Vile seducer, leave the house!"

She was furiously jealous of him.

Gordon Craig is one of the most extraordinary geniuses of our epoch—a creature like Shelley, made of fire and lightning. He was the inspirer of the whole trend of the modern theatre. True, he has never taken an active part in the practical life of the stage. He has stayed apart and dreamed, and his dreams have inspired all that is beautiful in the modern theatre to-day. Without him, we should never have had Reinhardt, Jacques Copeau, Stanislavsky. Without him, we would still be back in the old realistic scenery, every leaf shimmering on the trees, all the houses with their doors opening and shutting.

Craig was a brilliant companion. He was one of the few people I have ever met who was in a state of exaltation from morning till night. Even with the first cup of coffee, his imagination caught fire and was sparkling. An ordinary walk through the streets with him was like a promenade in Thebes of Ancient Egypt with a superior High Priest.

Whether due to his extraordinary near-sightedness or not, he would suddenly stop, take out his pencil and paper-block and, looking at a fearful specimen of modern German architecture, a *neuer kunst praktisch* apartment house, explain how beautiful it was. He would then commence a feverish sketch of it which, when completed, resembled the Temple of Denderah of Egypt.

He always entered in a state of wild excitement over a tree or a bird or a child he had seen on his way. One never spent a dull moment with him. No, he was always either in the throes of highest delight, or the other extreme, in those moods which suddenly followed after, when the whole sky seemed to turn black, and a sudden apprehension filled all the air. One's breath was slowly pumped from the body, and nothing was left anywhere but the blackness of anguish.

Unfortunately, as time progressed, these dark moods became more and more frequent. Why? Well, principally because whenever he said, "My work. My work!" as he often did, I replied gently, "Oh, yes, your work. How wonderful. You are a genius—but, you know, there is my School"; and his fist would come down on the table, "Yes, but my work." And I would answer, "Certainly, very important. Your work is the setting, but the first is the living being, for, from the soul radiates everything. First, my School, the radiant human being moving in perfect beauty; then your work, the perfect setting for this being."

These discussions often ended in thunderous and gloomy silences. Then the woman in me, alarmed, would awaken, "Oh, darling, have I offended you?" And he, "Offended? Oh, no! All women are damned nuisances, and you are a damned nuisance, interfering with my work. My work! My work!!"

He would go out, slamming the door. Only the noise of the slammed door would awaken me to the terrible catastrophe. I would await his return and, when he didn't return, spend the night in stormy and tragic weeping. Such was the tragedy. These scenes oft repeated, ended by making life quite inharmonious and impossible.

It was my fate to inspire the great love of this genius; and it was my fate to endeavour to reconcile the continuing of my own career with his love. Impossible combination! After the first few weeks of wild, impassioned love-making, there began the waging of the fiercest battle that was ever known, between the genius of Gordon Craig and the inspirations of my Art.

"Why don't you stop this?" he used to say. "Why do you want to go on the stage and wave your arms about? Why don't you stay at home and sharpen my lead pencils?"

And yet Gordon Craig appreciates my Art as no one else has ever appreciated it. But his *amour propre*, his jealousy as an artist, would not allow him to admit that any woman could really be an artist.

* * *

My sister Elizabeth had formed for the Grünewald School a committee of very prominent and aristocratic women of Berlin. When they learned of Craig, they sent me a long letter, couched in majestic terms of reproach and said that they, members of the good bourgeois society, could no longer be patronesses of a school where the leader had such loose ideas of morals.

Frau Mendelssohn, wife of the great banker, was chosen by these ladies to present to me this letter. When she came with this tremendous parchment, she looked at me a bit unsteadily and suddenly bursting into tears, threw the letter on the floor, and taking me in her arms, cried: "Don't think I ever signed that wretched letter. As for the other ladies, there is nothing to be done with them. They will no longer be patrons of this School. Only they still believe in your sister, Elizabeth."

Now Elizabeth had her own ideas, but she did not make them public, so I saw the creed of these ladies was that anything is right if you don't talk about it! These women so roused my indignation that I took the Philharmonic Saal and gave a special lecture on the dance as an art of liberation, and ended with a talk on the right of woman to love and bear children as she pleased.

Of course, people will respond, "But what about the children?" Well, I could give the names of many prominent people who were born out of wedlock. It has not prevented them from obtaining fame and fortune. But leaving that, I said to myself, How can a woman go into this marriage contract with a man who she thinks is so mean that, in case of a quarrel, he wouldn't even support his own children? If she thinks he is such a man, why should she marry him? I suppose truth and mutual faith are the first principles of love. At any rate, I believe as a wage-earning woman, that if I make the great sacrifice of strength and health and even risk my life, to have a child, I should certainly not do so if, on some future occasion, the man can say that the child belongs to him by law, and he will take it from me and I shall see it only three times a year!

A very witty American writer once replied to his mistress, when she said: "What would the child think of us if we were not married?" by saying: "If your child and my child were that sort of child, we would not care what it thought of us."

Any intelligent woman who reads the marriage contract, and then goes into it, deserves all the consequences.

This lecture caused considerable scandal. Half of the audience sympathised with me, and the other half hissed and threw anything that came to their hands on to the stage. In the end, the unconsenting half left the hall, and I was left with the others, and we had an interesting debate on the rights and wrongs of women, which was considerably in advance of the Woman's Movement of the present day.

I continued to live in our apartment in Victoria Strasse, whereas Elizabeth went out to live at the School. My mother vacillated between the two places. From now on, my mother, who had, during all the times of privation and disaster, borne her troubles with such extraordinary courage, began to find life very dull. Perhaps this was on account of her Irish character, which could not stand prosperity as well as adversity. Her temper became most uneven. Indeed, she was often in such moods that nothing pleased her. For the first time since our voyage abroad, she began to express a longing for America, and said how much better everything was there—the food, and so forth.

When we took her to the best restaurant in Berlin, thinking to please her, and asked her, "Mother, what will you have to eat?" she would reply "Give me shrimps." If they were not in season, she would expatiate against the country, the misery of a land where shrimps did not exist and she would refuse to eat anything at all. If there happened to be shrimps, she would again complain, saying how much better the shrimps were in San Francisco.

I think that this turning of her character was probably due to the habitual state of virtue in which my mother had lived, for so many years devoting herself only to her children. Now that we found interests so absorbing that they continually took us away from her, she realised that she had actually wasted the best years of her life on us, leaving nothing for herself; as I think so many mothers do, especially in America. These uncertain humours on her part increased more and more and she continually expressed the desire to return to her native town, until at last she did so, shortly afterwards.

*   *   *

My mind dwelt always upon that villa in Grünewald, with its forty little beds. How inexplicable is fate, for certainly, had I met Craig a few months sooner, there would have been no villa, no School. In him I found such completion that I would have felt no need for founding a School. But now that this dream of my childhood was actually commenced, it became an *idée fixe*.

Shortly after, I discovered—and there could not be the slightest doubt about it—that I was pregnant. I dreamt that Ellen Terry appeared to me in a shimmering gown, such as she wore in "Imogene," leading by the hand a little blonde child, a little girl who resembled her exactly, and, in her marvellous voice, she called to me—"Isadora, love. Love. . . . Love. . . ."

From that moment I knew what was coming to me out of the shadowy world of Nothingness before Birth. Such a

EDWARD GORDON CRAIG
Original photograph by Edward Steichen

child would come, to bring me joy and sorrow. Joy and Sorrow! Birth and Death! Rhythm of the Dance of Life!

The divine message sang in all my being. I continued to dance before the public; to teach my School, to love my Endymion.

Poor Craig was restless, impatient, unhappy, bit his nails to the quick, exclaiming often: "My work. My work. My work."

Always the savage Nature interfering with Art. But I was comforted by my lovely dream of Ellen, and this dream was repeated again twice.

* * *

Spring arrived. I had a contract for Denmark, Sweden and Germany. In Copenhagen what surprised me most was the extraordinarily intelligent and happy look on the faces of the young women, striding along the streets alone and free, like boys, with their student caps placed on their black curls. I was astonished. I had never seen such fine girls. And it was explained to me that this was the first country to win the vote for women.

I had to take this tour because of the depleting expenses of the School. I had drawn upon my entire reserve funds and had no money left.

At Stockholm I had a very enthusiastic audience and, after the performance, the girls from the Gymnastic School escorted me to my hotel, leaping and galloping beside my carriage to express their delight at seeing me. I visited their Gymnastic Institution, but my visit did not leave me an ardent devotee. It seems to me that Swedish gymnastics are meant for the static, immobile body, but take no account of the living, flowing, human body. Also it regards the muscles as an end in themselves, instead of recognising them merely as the mechanical frame, a never-ending source of growth. The Swedish Gymnasium is a false system of body culture, because it takes no account of the imagination, and thinks of the body as an object, instead of vital, kinetic energy.

I visited the schools and explained this as best I might to the pupils. But, as I expected, they did not understand much.

While I was in Stockholm I sent an invitation to Strindberg, whom I greatly admired, to come and see me dance. He replied that he never went anywhere, that he hated human beings. I offered him a seat on the stage, but even then he did not come.

After a successful season in Stockholm, we returned to Germany by water. On the boat I became quite ill, and I realised that it would be better for me to cease making any more tours for the time being. Anyway, I had a great longing to be alone, and to retire far from the gaze of human beings.

In the month of June, after a short visit to my School, I had an intense desire to be near the sea. I went first to The Hague, and from there to a little village called Nordwyck, on the shores of the North Sea. Here I rented a little white villa in the dunes, called Villa Maria.

I was so inexperienced as to think that having a baby was a perfectly natural process. I went to live in this villa, which was a hundred miles from any town, and I engaged a village doctor. In my ignorance I was quite content to have this village doctor who, I think, was only used to peasant women.

From Nordwyck to the nearest village, Kadwyck, was about three kilometres. Here I lived, all by myself. Each day I walked from Nordwyck to Kadwyck and back. Always I had this longing for the sea; to be alone in Nordwyck, in the little white villa, quite isolated among the sand dunes which stretched for miles on either side of the lovely country. I lived in the Villa Maria for June, July and August.

In the meantime I kept up an active correspondence with my sister Elizabeth, who was in charge of the Grünewald School in my absence. During that month of July, I wrote in my diary precepts for the teaching of the School, and I worked out a series of five hundred exercises which would take the pupils from the simplest movements to the most complex, a regular compendium of the dance.

My little niece Temple, who was being educated at the Grünewald School, came to spend three weeks with me. She used to dance by the sea.

Craig was restless. He came and went. But I was no longer alone. The child asserted itself now, more and more. It was strange to see my beautiful marble body softened and broken and stretched and deformed. It is an uncanny revenge of Nature, that the more refined the nerves, the more sensitive the brain, the more all this tends to suffering. Sleepless nights, painful hours. But joy too. Boundless, unlimited joy, when I strode every day over the sands between Nordwyck and Kadwyck, with the sea, the great waves, looming on one side, and the swelling dunes on the other, along the deserted beach. Almost always, on that coast, the wind blows, sometimes a gentle, billowing zephyr, sometimes a breeze so strong that I had to struggle against it. Occasionally the storms grew terrific, and the Villa Maria was rocked and buffeted all night like a ship at sea.

I grew to dread any society. People said such banalities. How little is appreciated the sanctity of the pregnant mother. I once saw a woman walking alone along the street, carrying a child within her. The passers-by did not regard her with reverence, but smiled at one another derisively, as though this woman, carrying the burden of coming life, was an excellent joke.

I closed my doors to every visitor except a good and faithful friend who came over from The Hague on his bicycle, bringing me books and magazines, and cheering me with his discourses on recent art, music and literature. At that time he was married to a great poetess of whom he spoke often with worshipful tenderness. He was a methodical man. He came on certain days, and even a big storm did not deter him from his schedule. Except for him, I was mostly alone with the sea and the dunes and the child, who seemed already to have a great, strong impatience to enter the world.

As I walked beside the sea, I sometimes felt an excess of strength and prowess, and I thought this creature would be mine, mine alone, but on other days, when the sky was grey and the cold North Sea waves were angry, I had sudden, sinking moods, when I felt myself some poor animal in a mighty trap, and I struggled with an overwhelming desire to escape, escape. Where? Perhaps even into the midst of the sullen waves. I struggled against such moods and bravely overcame them, nor did I ever let any one suspect what I felt, but nevertheless, such moods were waiting for me at odd hours, and were difficult to avoid. Also I thought that most people were receding from me. My mother seemed thousands of miles away. Craig was also strangely remote, and always immersed in his art, whereas I could think less and less of my art, and was only absorbed in this fearful, monstrous task which had fallen to me; this maddening, joy-giving, pain-giving mystery.

How long and torturous lagged the hours. The days, weeks, months, how slowly they passed! With alternate hope and despair, I often thought of the pilgrimage of my childhood, my youth, my wanderings in distant countries, my discoveries in Art, and they were as a misty, far-away Prologue, leading up to this—the before-birth of a child. What any peasant woman could have! This was the culminating point of all my ambitions!

Why wasn't my dear mother with me? It was because she had some absurd prejudice that I should be married. But she had been married, had found it impossible, and had divorced her husband. Why should she want me to enter the trap where she had been cruelly bitten? I was against marriage with every intelligent force of my being. I believed it then and still believe it to be an absurd and enslaving institution, leading—especially with artists—inevitably to the divorce courts, and preposterous and vulgar lawsuits. If any one doubts what I say, just let them make up a little tally of all the artists divorced, and all the scandals in the American papers in the last ten years. Yet the dear public loves its artists and could not live without them, I suppose.

In August there came to stay with me, as a nurse, a woman who afterwards became my very dear friend, Marie Kist. I have never met a more patient, sweeter or kinder one. She was a great comfort. From now on, I confess, I began to be assailed with all sorts of fears. In vain I told myself that every woman had children. My grandmother had eight. My mother had four. It was all in the course of life, etc. I was, nevertheless, conscious of fear. Of what? Certainly not of death, nor even of pain—some unknown fear, of what I did not know.

August waned. September came. My burden had become very heavy. Villa Maria was perched on the dunes. One mounted by a flight of almost one hundred steps. Often I thought of my dancing, and sometimes a fierce regret for my Art assailed me. But then I would feel three energetic kicks, and a form turning within me. I would smile and think,

after all, what is Art but a faint mirror for the Joy and
Miracle of Life?

More and more my lovely body bulged under my astonished gaze. My hard little breasts grew large and soft and
fell. My nimble feet grew slower, my ankles swelled, my
hips were painful. Where was my lovely, youthful Naiad
form? Where my ambition? My fame? Often, in spite of
myself, I felt very miserable and defeated. This game with
the giant Life was too much. But then I thought of the
child to come, and all such painful thoughts ceased.

Helpless, cruel hours of waiting in the night; lying on
the left side the heart is smothered; turning on the right
side, still no comfort; finally lying on the back; always a
prey to the energy of the child, trying with one's hands
pressed on the swelling body to give a message to the child.
Cruel hours of tender waiting in the night. What seems
countless nights passing like this. With what a price we
pay for the glory of motherhood.

One day I had an intensely happy surprise. A sweet
friend I had known in Paris—her name was Kathleen—came
from Paris and said she had the intention of staying with
me. She was a magnetic person, filled with life and health
and courage. She afterwards married the explorer—
Captain Scott.

We were all sitting at tea one afternoon, when I felt a
thud as if some one had pounded me in the middle of the
back, and then a fearful pain, as if some one had put a
gimlet into my spine and was trying to break it open.
From that moment the torture began, as if I, poor victim,
were in the hands of some mighty and pitiless executioner.
No sooner had I recovered from one assault than another
began. Talk about the Spanish Inquisition! No woman
who has borne a child would have to fear it. It must have
been a mild sport in comparison. Relentless, cruel, knowing

no release, no pity, this terrible, unseen genie had me in his grip, and was, in continued spasms, tearing my bones and my sinews apart. They say such suffering is soon forgotten. All I have to reply is that I have only to shut my eyes and I hear again my shrieks and groans as they were then, like something encircling me apart from my self.

It is unheard-of, uncivilised barbarism, that any woman should still be forced to bear such monstrous torture. It should be remedied. It should be stopped. It is simply absurd that with our modern science painless childbirth does not exist as *a matter of course.* It is as unpardonable as if doctors should operate for appendicitis without an anæsthetic! What unholy patience, or lack of intelligence, have women in general that they should for one moment endure this outrageous massacre of themselves?

For two days and two nights this unspeakable horror continued. And, on the third morning, this absurd doctor brought out an immense pair of forceps and, without an anæsthetic of any sort, achieved the butchery. I suppose that, perhaps with the exception of being pinned underneath a railway train, nothing could possibly resemble what I suffered. Don't let me hear of any Woman's Movement or Suffragette Movement until women have put an end to this, I believe, wholly useless agony, and insist that the operation of childbirth, like other operations, shall be made painless and endurable.

What insane superstition stands in the way of such a measure? What lackadaisical, criminal inattention? Of course one can reply that all women don't suffer to this degree. No, neither do the Red Indians, the peasants or the African Negroes. But the more civilised the woman, the more fearful the agony, the useless agony. For the sake of the civilised woman, a civilised remedy to this horror should be found.

Well, I did not die because of it. No, I didn't die—nor does the poor victim taken timely from the rack. And then, you may say, when I saw the baby I was repaid. Yes, certainly I had a consummate joy, but nevertheless I tremble with indignation even to-day when I think of what I endured, and of what many women victims endure through the unspeakable egotism and blindness of men of science who permit such atrocities when they can be remedied.

Ah, but the baby! The baby was astonishing; formed like a Cupid, with blue eyes and long, brown hair, that afterwards fell out and gave place to golden curls. And, miracle of miracles, that mouth sought my breast and bit with toothless gums, and pulled and drank the milk that gushed forth. What mother has ever told the feeling when the babe's mouth bites at her nipple, and the milk gushes from her breast? This cruel, biting mouth, like the mouth of a lover, and our lover's mouth, in turn, reminding us of the babe.

Oh, women, what is the good of us learning to become lawyers, painters or sculptors, when this miracle exists? Now I knew this tremendous love, surpassing the love of man. I was stretched and bleeding, torn and helpless, while the little being sucked and howled. Life, life, life! Give me life! Oh, where was my Art? My Art or any Art? What did I care for Art! I felt I was a God, superior to any artist.

During the first weeks, I used to lie long hours with the baby in my arms, watching her asleep; sometimes catching a gaze from her eyes; feeling very near the edge, the mystery, perhaps the knowledge of Life. This soul in the newly created body which answered my gaze with such apparently old eyes—the eyes of Eternity—gazing into mine with love. Love, perhaps, was the answer of all. What words could describe this joy? What wonder that I, who am not a writer, cannot find any words at all!

We returned to Grünewald with the baby and my sweet friend Marie Kist. All the children were delighted to see the baby. I said to Elizabeth, "She is our youngest pupil." Every one asked, "What shall we name her?" Craig thought of a wonderful Irish name, Deirdre. Deirdre—beloved of Ireland. So we called her Deirdre.

Little by little my strength came back. Often I stood before the wonderful Amazon, our votive statue, with sympathetic understanding, for she, too, was never to be so gloriously fit for the battle again.

CHAPTER TWENTY

JULIETTE MENDELSSOHN, living in her palatial villa with her rich banker husband, was our near neighbour. She took a lively interest in my School, in spite of her renegade bourgeois friends. One day she invited all of us to dance before my adored Idol—Eleanora Duse.

I presented Gordon Craig to Duse. She was at once charmed and interested in his views of the theatre. After a few meetings of mutual enthusiasm, she invited us to come to Florence, and wished Craig to arrange a representation. So it was decided that Gordon Craig was to create the scenes for Ibsen's "Rosmersholm," for Eleanora Duse, in Florence. We all took the train de luxe for Florence—Eleanora Duse, Craig, Marie Kist, the baby and I.

I nursed the baby on the way and my milk became somewhat churned, so I had to supplement it with some prepared food in bottles. Nevertheless, I was supremely happy. The two most adored beings in the world for me had met; Craig would have his work, Duse a setting worthy of her genius.

Arriving in Florence, we put up at a small hotel near the Grand, where Eleanora was installed in the Royal suite.

The first discussions began—discussions in which I played the interpreter for Craig, who could understand neither French nor Italian, and Duse, who knew not a word of English. I found myself between these two great geniuses, forces which, oddly enough, from the very beginning seemed in opposition to each other. I only hoped to make each happy and to please both. This I accomplished by a certain amount of misrepresentation. I hope some of the lies which

I told in interpreting may be forgiven me, for they were in a holy cause. I wanted this great production to come off, and it would never have done so if I had really told Eleanora Duse what Craig said to her; and if I had repeated Duse's orders to Craig exactly as she expressed them.

In the first scene in "Rosmersholm," I believe Ibsen describes the sitting-room as "comfortably furnished in old-fashioned style." But Craig had been pleased to see the interior of a great Egyptian Temple with enormously high ceiling, extending upward to the skies, with walls receding into the distance. Only, unlike an Egyptian Temple, at the far end there was a great, square window. In Ibsen's description, the window looks out into an avenue of old trees leading to a courtyard. Craig had been pleased to see this in dimensions of ten metres by twelve. It looked out upon a flaming landscape of yellows, reds and greens, which might have been some scene in Morocco. It could not possibly have been an old-fashioned courtyard.

Eleanora, looking rather disconcerted, said, "I see this as a small window. It cannot possibly be a large one."

To which Craig thundered in English, "Tell her I won't have any damned woman interfering with my work!"

Which I discreetly translated to Eleanora, "He says he admires your opinions and will do everything to please you."

Then, turning to Craig, I again diplomatically translated Duse's objections as, "Eleanora Duse says, as you are a great genius, she will not make any suggestions on your sketches, but will pass them as they are."

These conversations sometimes went on for hours. Many times they occurred during the feeding time for the baby, nevertheless I was always on hand to play the important rôle of pacifying interpreter. I often suffered agonies when it was past milking time, while I explained to those artists what they did *not* say to each other! I was at the time in a certain tired state. My health was run down. These wearing interviews turned my period of convalescence into a very painful one. But in view of the great artistic event which was to take place, the production of "Rosmersholm," with Craig creating the scene for Eleanora Duse, I felt that no sacrifice on my part was too much.

Then Craig immured himself in the theatre, where he began, with dozens of huge pots of paint before him, and a big brush, to paint the scene actually himself. For he could find no Italian workmen who understood just what he meant. He could not find the proper canvas, so he took sacking and had it sewed together. For days, a chorus of old Italian women sat upon the stage and stitched sacking. Young Italian painters rushed about the stage, trying to carry out orders given by Craig, while Craig, with his long hair tossed about, shouted to them, dipped the brushes into the paint boxes, mounted ladders in perilous positions; stayed in the theatre all day and almost all night. He did not come out, even to eat. If I had not brought him a little luncheon basket at lunch time, he would not have had anything to eat at all.

One command he gave, "Keep Duse out of the theatre. Do not let her come here. If she does, I will take the train and go away."

Whereas Duse was filled with desire to see what was going on. It was my task, without offending her, to keep her from going to the theatre. I used to take her for long walks in the Gardens, where the lovely statues and exquisite flowers calmed her nerves.

I shall never forget the picture of Duse, walking through those gardens. She did not look like a woman of this world, but rather like some divine image of Petrarch or Dante, who found herself upon the terrestrial sphere by some mischance. All the populace made way for her and stared at us with respectful but curious eyes. Duse did not like to be stared at by the public. She took all the little by-paths and small alleys, to avoid the popular gaze. Nor had she any love for poor humanity as I had. She considered most of these people as "canaille," and used to speak of them as such.

This was due mostly to her over-sensitive nature, rather than anything else. She thought they were critical of her. When Duse came into personal contact with people, no one could be more sympathetic and kindly.

I will always remember those walks in the Gardens; the poplar trees, the magnificent head of Eleanora Duse, for, as soon as we found ourselves alone, she would pull off her hat and let her raven locks, just turning grey, free to the breeze. Her wonderfully intellectual forehead and her marvellous eyes —I shall never forget them. Sorrowful eyes, yet, when this face lit up in enthusiasm, I have never seen a more beatific expression of joy in any human face or in any work of art!

The *décors* for "Rosmersholm" were progressing. Each time I went to the theatre to take Craig his luncheon or his dinner, I found him in a state bordering between anger and frantic joy. One hour he believed it would be the greatest vision the artistic world would see. The next, he would cry that he could get nothing in this country—no paints, no good workmen; that he must do everything himself.

The hour approached when Eleanora should see the completed scene—I had especially kept her away by such manœuvres as I could invent. When the day arrived, I called for her at the appointed hour and took her to the theatre. She was in a state of intense nervous excitement which, I feared, might at any moment break out, like a stormy day, into a violent tempest. She met me in the lobby of her hotel. She was enveloped in a big brown fur coat, with a brown fur cap which resembled that of a Russian Cossack. It was placed at an angle over her eyes. For although Duse

at times in her life, by the advice of her kind friends patron-
ised the fashionable dressmakers, she could never wear a
modish dress or look in any way chic. Her dress was always
up on one side and down on the other. Her hat was always
crooked. No matter how costly her garments, she never
seemed to wear them, but appeared to condescend to carry
them on her.

On our way to the theatre, I was so wrought up that I
could hardly speak. Again, with great diplomacy, I kept
her from rushing to the stage door, but I had the front door
of the theatre especially opened and led her into a box.
There was a long wait, in which I suffered untold agonies, as
she kept saying, "Will my window be just as I see it? Where
is this scene?"

I held her hand tightly, kept patting it and saying: "In
a little while— You will soon see. Have patience." But I
was overcome with fear at the thought of that little window,
which had now taken on the most gigantic dimensions
imaginable.

From time to time one heard Craig's voice, in exasperated
tones, now trying to speak in Italian, now just saying,
"Damn! Damn! Why didn't you put this here? Why don't
you do what I tell you?" Then silence again.

Finally, after what seemed hours of waiting, when I felt
Eleanora's rising temper was ready to break out at any
moment, the curtain slowly rose.

Oh, how can I describe what appeared before our astonished, enraptured eyes? Did I speak of an Egyptian
Temple? No Egyptian Temple has ever revealed such
beauty. No Gothic Cathedral, no Athenian Palace. Never
have I seen such a vision of loveliness. Through vast blue
spaces, celestial harmonies, mounting lines, colossal heights,
one's soul was drawn toward the light of this great window
which showed beyond, no little avenue but the infinite uni-

verse. Within these blue spaces was all the thought, the meditation, the earthly sorrow of man. Beyond the window was all the ecstasy, the joy, the miracle of his imagination. Was this the living-room of Rosmersholm? I do not know what Ibsen would have thought. Probably he would have been as we were—speechless, carried away.

Eleanora's hand grasped mine. I felt her arms around me. She had me in a strong embrace. I saw the tears were running down her beautiful face. For some time we sat, clutched in one another's arms, silent—Eleanora from her admiration and joy of art, and I from the great relief I found when she was pleased, after all my previous misgivings. So we remained. Then she took me by the hand and dragged me from the box, striding with her long steps through the dark corridor up to the stage. She stood upon the stage, and in that voice which was Duse, called: "Gordon Craig! Come here!"

Craig came from the side wing, looking as shy as a boy. Duse enveloped him in her arms and then, from her lips, came such a string of Italian words of adulation that I could not translate them fast enough for Craig. They flowed from her lips like water streaming from a fountain.

Craig did not weep from emotion as we did, but he remained for a long time silent, which, on his part, was a sign of great feeling.

Duse then called all the company to her. They had been waiting unconcernedly behind the stage. She made them an impassioned speech in this wise:

"It is my destiny to have found this great genius, Gordon Craig. I now intend to spend the rest of my career (*sempre, sempre*) devoting myself only to showing the world his great work."

She then went on with renewed eloquence to denounce the

whole modern trend of the theatre, all modern scenery, the modern conception of an actor's life and vocation.

Holding the hand of Craig all the time she spoke, and turning again and again to him, she told of his genius and of the new great resurrection of the theatre. "Only through Gordon Craig," she said over and over again, "will we poor actors find release from this monstrosity, this charnel house, which is the theatre of to-day!"

Imagine my joy at all this. I was then young and inexperienced. I believed, alas, that, in moments of great enthusiasm, people actually meant all they said. I pictured Eleanora Duse placing her splendid genius at the service of my great Craig's Art. I pictured the future as one untold triumph for Craig, and splendour for the Art of the theatre. I did not count, alas, upon the frailty of human enthusiasm, more especially the frailty of a woman's enthusiasm. And Eleanora was only a woman, with all her genius—as was proved later.

The first evening of "Rosmersholm" an immense, expectant public filled the theatre in Florence. When the curtain rose, there was one gasp of admiration. The result could not have been otherwise. That single performance of "Rosmersholm" is remembered in Florence to this day by connoisseurs of Art.

Duse, with her marvellous instinct, had donned a gown of white with great wide sleeves that fell at her sides. When she appeared, she looked less like Rebecca West than a Delphic Sybil. With her unerring genius, she adapted herself to every great line and to each shaft of light which enveloped her. She changed all her gestures and movements. She moved in the scene like some prophetess announcing great tidings.

But when the other actors came on—Rosmer, for instance, who put his hands in his pockets—they seemed to be like stage hands who had walked on by mistake. It was positively painful. Only the man who played Brendel fitted perfectly with the marvellous surroundings when he declaimed the words: "When I have been wrapped in a haze of golden dreams that have descended on me; when new, intoxicating, momentous thoughts have had their birth in my mind, and I have been fanned by the beat of their wings as they bore me aloft—at such moments I have transformed them into poetry, into visions, into pictures."

We returned from this performance in high spirits. Craig was radiant with joy. He saw his future before him, a series of great works all devoted to Eleanora Duse, of whom he now spoke with praise as great as was his indignation before. Alas, for human frailty. This was to be the one and only night of Duse's genius displayed in Craig's setting. She was playing a repertory programme. Each night a different play appeared.

After all this excitement was over I called at my bank one morning to find my account completely depleted. The coming of the baby, the needs of the Grünewald School, our journey to Florence, all this had exhausted my reserve funds. It was absolutely necessary to think of some way of replenishing the coffers, and there arrived a timely invitation from an impresario in St. Petersburg, asking if I were ready to dance again, and offering me a contract for a tour in Russia.

So I left Florence, giving the baby to Marie Kist to take care of, and leaving Craig in the care of Eleanora, while I took the express train via Switzerland and Berlin to St. Petersburg. As you can imagine, it was a very sad journey for me. The first separation from my baby, and also the separation from Craig and Duse were very painful. Also my health was in a precarious condition, and as the baby was only half-weaned, it was necessary to have the milk drawn from my breasts with a little machine. This was a ghastly experience for me and caused me many tears.

Further and further north the train sped, until I arrived again in those plains of snow and forest, which now seemed more desolate than ever. Also, as I had been too intent upon Duse and Craig to think of my own art, I was not in the least prepared for the ordeal of a tour. However, the good Russian audience received me with its usual enthusiasm and overlooked any shortcomings there may have been in the performance. Only I remember that often when I danced, the milk overflowed, running down my tunic, and causing me much embarrassment. How difficult it is for a woman to have a career!

Of this tour in Russia, I do not remember very much. Needless to say, my heart was pulling me back to Florence by all its strings. Therefore I cut the tour as short as possible and accepted an engagement to tour Holland, as it would bring me a little nearer to my school and to those I so longed to see.

The first night I appeared on the stage in Amsterdam, a strange illness overcame me. I think it had something to do with the milk, what they call milk fever, and after the performance I fell prone upon the stage and had to be carried back to the hotel. There for days and weeks I lay in a darkened room packed in ice bags. They called it neuritis, a disease for which no doctor has been able to find a cure. For weeks I could eat nothing and was fed on a little milk with opium, and went from one delirium into another, and finally into unconscious sleep.

Craig came flying up from Florence and was devotion itself. He stayed with me for three or four weeks and helped to nurse me, until one day he received a telegram from Eleanora, "I am giving Rosmersholm in Nice. Scene unsatisfactory. Come at once."

I was partly convalescent at the time so he left for Nice, but directly I saw this telegram I had a terrible premonition of what would happen to those two when I was not there to interpret, and to smooth over their differences.

Craig appeared one morning in the old Nice Casino, which was horrible, to find that, without the knowledge of Eleanora, they had cut his scenery in two. Naturally when he saw his work of art, his masterpiece, his child that he had laboured to bring forth with such energy in Florence, thus amputated, massacred before his eyes, Craig flew into one of those terrible rages of which he was at times the victim, and, what was worse, thus addressed the form of Eleanora, who was at that time standing on the stage:

"What have you done?" he stormed at her. "You have ruined my work. You have destroyed my art! You, from whom I expected so much."

He went on and on mercilessly, until Eleanora, who certainly was not used to being spoken to in this manner, became furious. As she told me later: "I have never seen such a man. I have never been talked to like this. He towered more than six feet, arms folded in Britannic furor, saying fearful things. No one has ever treated me so. Naturally I could not stand it. I pointed to the door and said, 'Go. I never want to see you again.'"

And that was the end of her intention to devote her entire career to the genius of Gordon Craig.

* * *

I arrived in Nice so weak that I had to be carried from the train. It was the first night of the Carnival, and on the way to the hotel my open carriage was assailed by a band of Pierrot masks of all descriptions, whose grimaces seemed to me like the Dance Macabre before ultimate death.

In a hotel near to mine Eleanora Duse also lay ill. She sent me many tender messages. She also referred her doctor,

Emil Bosson, to me, and he not only tended me with great devotion but, from that time, became one of my greatest friends for life. My convalescence was long, and I was entwined in a network of pain.

My mother joined me and also my faithful friend, Marie Kist, with the baby. The baby was fine and strong and each day grew more beautiful. We moved to Mont Boron, where we looked over the sea on one side and, on the other, to the top of the mountain where Zarathustra had meditated with his serpent and his eagle. On the sunny terrace where we lived, I gradually came back to life. But it was a life more heavily burdened with financial difficulties than ever, and to meet them I returned, as soon as I was able, to my Holland tour, but I still felt very weak and despondent.

I adored Craig—I loved him with all the ardour of my artist soul, but I realised that our separation was inevitable. Yet I had arrived at that frenzied state when I could no longer live with him or without him. To live with him was to renounce my art, my personality, nay, perhaps, my life, my reason itself. To live without him was to be in a continual state of depression, and tortured by jealousy, for which, alas! it now seemed that I had good cause. Visions of Craig in all his beauty in the arms of other women haunted me at night, until I could no longer sleep. Visions of Craig explaining his art to women who gazed at him with adoring eyes—visions of Craig being pleased with other women—looking at them with that winning smile of his— the smile of Ellen Terry—taking an interest in them, caressing them—saying to himself, "This woman pleases me. After all Isadora is impossible."

All this drove me to fits of alternate fury and despair. I could not work, I could not dance. I did not care at all whether the public liked it or not.

I realised that this state of things must cease. Either Craig's Art or mine—and to give up my Art I knew to be impossible: I should pine away—I should die from chagrin. I must find a remedy and I thought of the wisdom of the Homeopaths. And as everything that we wish for very much comes, the remedy came.

He entered one afternoon: fair, debonair, young, blond, perfectly dressed. He said: "My friends call me Pim."

I said, "Pim, what a charming name. Are you an artist?"

"Oh, no!" he disclaimed, as if I had accused him of some crime.

"Then what have you? A Great Idea?"

"Oh, dear no. I have no ideas at all," he said.

"But a purpose in life?"

"Not any."

"But what do you do?"

"Nothing."

"But you must do something."

"Well," he replied reflectively, "I have a lovely collection of eighteenth century snuff boxes."

Here was my remedy. I had signed a contract to tour Russia—a long, arduous tournée, not only through North Russia, but South Russia and the Caucasus as well, and I dreaded the long journeys alone.

"'Will you come with me to Russia, Pim?"

"Oh, I should just love to," he replied quickly, "only there is my mother. I might persuade her, but there is also some one"—and Pim blushed—"some one who loves me very much—who would, perhaps, not consent to let me go."

"But we might go clandestinely," and so it was planned that after my last performance in Amsterdam an auto should meet us at the stage door, and carry us away into the country. We had arranged for my maid to take the luggage by the express, which we were to pick up at the next station outside Amsterdam.

It was a very foggy, cold night and over the fields hung a thick mist. The chauffeur did not wish to go fast, as the road ran by a canal.

"It is very dangerous," he cautioned, and crept along.

But this danger was nothing to that of being followed, and suddenly Pim looked behind and exclaimed:

"My God, she is pursuing us!"

I needed no explanation.

"She probably has a pistol," said Pim.

"Schnell, schneller!" I said to the chauffeur, but he only pointed to where a gleam through the fog showed the waters of the canal. It was very romantic, but finally he out-witted the pursuers' car and we arrived at the station and stopped at the hotel.

It was two o'clock in the morning. The old night porter thrust his lantern into our faces.

"Ein zimmer," we said in chorus.

"Ein zimmer—Nein, nein. Sind sie verheirathet?"

"Ja, ja," we replied.

"Oh, nein, nein," he grunted. "Sie sind nicht verheirathet. Ich weiss. Sie sehen aus viele zu glücklich"; and in spite of our protests he separated us in two rooms at either end of a long corridor, and took a malign delight in sitting up all night between the two, with his lantern on his knees, and each time that Pim or I put out a head, he raised the lantern and said:

"Nein, nein: nicht verheirathet—nicht möglich—nein, nein."

In the morning, a trifle tired after this game of hide and seek, we took the Rapide to Petersburg, and I have never made a pleasanter journey.

When we arrived at Petersburg I was perplexed when the

baggage porter demanded eighteen trunks from the train, all marked with Pim's initials.

"But what is this?" I gasped.

"Oh, that is only my luggage," said Pim. "This for my neckties; these two for my lingerie; these for my *complets* and these for my boots. Then this one contains my extra fur-trimmed waistcoats—so appropriate for Russia."

In the Hotel de l'Europe was a broad staircase and down this staircase Pim would come flying every hour dressed in a different coloured *complet*, wearing a different cravat —to the admiration of all beholders. For he was always exquisitely dressed and was, in fact, the criterion of fashion of The Hague. The great Dutch painter Van Vley was painting his portrait, with a background of tulips—golden tulips—purple tulips—rose-coloured tulips—and indeed his whole appearance had the fresh and attractive look of a bed of spring tulips. His golden hair like a bed of golden tulips; his lips like rose tulips, and when he embraced me I felt as though I were floating away on a bed of thousands of tulips in the spring of Holland.

Pim was pretty—blond, blue-eyed—with no intellectual complex. His love exemplified to me Oscar Wilde's saying, "Better the pleasure that lasteth for the moment, than the sorrow which endureth for ever." Pim gave the pleasure which lasteth for a moment. Heretofore love had brought me Romance, Ideal and Suffering. Pim brought me pleasure—just pure delightful pleasure—and at a moment when I most needed it, for without his ministrations I might have sunk into a hopeless neurasthenic. The presence of Pim gave me new life, new vitality. Perhaps for the first time I knew the joy of being simply, frivolously young. He laughed at everything, skipped and danced about. I forgot my chagrin and lived in the moment and was careless and

happy.   As a consequence my performances bubbled over
with renewed vitality and joy.

It was at this time that I composed the "Moment Musicale" which had such a success with the Russians that I
had to repeat it five or six times each evening. The "Moment Musicale" was Pim's dance—the "pleasure of the
moment"—the Musical Moment.

ISADORA DUNCAN

Photograph by Arnold Genthe

CHAPTER TWENTY-ONE

IF I had only visioned the dance as a Solo, my way would have been quite simple. Already famous, sought after in every country, I had only to pursue a triumphal career. But, alas! I was possessed by the idea of a school—a vast ensemble—dancing the Ninth Symphony of Beethoven. At night, I had only to shut my eyes and these figures danced through my brain in mighty array, calling on me to bring them to life. "We are here. You are the one at whose touch we might live!" (The Ninth Symphony: "Millionen Umschlingen.")

I was possessed by the dream of Promethean creation that, at my call, might spring from the Earth, descend from the Heavens, such dancing figures as the world had never seen. Ah, proud, enticing dream that has led my life from one catastrophe to another! Why did you possess me? Leading, like the light of Tantalus, only to darkness and despair. But no! Still flickering, that light in the darkness must eventually lead me to the Glorious Vision, at last realised. Small fluttering light, just ahead of my stumbling footsteps, I still believe, I still follow you—to find those superhuman creatures that in Harmonious Love will dance the Great Vision of Beauty the world awaits.

With these dreams I returned to Grünewald to teach the little group who were already learning to dance with such beauty as to strengthen my faith in the ultimate perfection of an orchestra of dancers—an orchestra which would be to sight what the great symphonies were to sound.

Now resembling the Loves of a Pompeian frieze, now the youthful Graces of Donatello, or, again, the airy flights of

213

Titania's following, I taught them to weave and entwine, to part and unite, in endless rounds and processions.

Each day they grew stronger, more lithe, and the light of inspiration and divine music shone in their youthful forms and faces. The sight of these dancing children was so beautiful that it awakened the admiration of all artists and poets.

Nevertheless it became more and more difficult to meet the expenses of the School, so I conceived the idea of taking them with me to different countries, in order to seek if there were a single Government which would recognise the beauty of this education for children and give me the chance I needed to experiment with my project on a larger scale.

At the end of each performance, I made an appeal to the public for help to find some way of giving to others, from my own life, the discovery I had made, and which might liberate and illumine the lives of thousands.

It became clearer and clearer to me that in Germany I would not find the support I needed for my School. The Kaiserin's views were so Puritanical that when she visited a sculptor's studio, she sent her Major Domo ahead to cover all the nude statues with sheets. The heavy Prussian régime made it impossible for me any longer to dream of Germany as the country for my work. I then thought of Russia for there I had found such responsive enthusiasm that I had made a fortune. Keeping in mind a possible school in St. Petersburg, I journeyed there again in January, 1907, accompanied by Elizabeth, with a group of twenty of my little pupils. This experiment was not successful. Although the public received with enthusiasm my pleadings for a renaissance of the real dance, the Imperial Ballet was too firmly rooted in Russia to make any change possible.

I took my little pupils to witness the training of the children of the Ballet School. These latter looked at them as canary birds in a cage might view the circling swallows in the air. But the day had not yet come for a school of free human movement in Russia. The Ballet, which was the intrinsic expression of Tsaristic etiquette, still exists, alas! The only hope for my school in Russia, a school for a greater, freer human expression, would have been from the efforts of Stanislavsky. But, although he did all in his power to help me, he did not have the means to install us in his great Art Theatre, which was what I should have liked.

So, failing to find support for the School either in Germany or Russia, I decided to try England. In the summer of 1908 I took my flock to London. Under the management of the famous impresarios, Joseph Schumann and Charles Frohman, we danced for several weeks at the Duke of York's Theatre. London audiences looked upon me and my School as a charming amusement, but I could find no real aid for the foundation of a future School.

Seven years had passed since I had first danced at the New Gallery. I had the joy of renewing my former friendships with Charles Hallé and Douglas Ainslie, the poet. The great and beautiful Ellen Terry came often to the theatre. She loved the children. Once she took them all to the Zoo, to their intense delight. The gracious Queen Alexandra honoured our performances twice by her presence in a box, and many ladies of the English nobility, among them the famous Lady de Grey, who was afterwards Lady Ripon, came quite unpretentiously behind the scenes and greeted me most sweetly.

It was the Duchess of Manchester who suggested that my idea might take root in London and that I might find support for my school there. To that end, she invited us all to her country house on the Thames, where we danced again for Queen Alexandra and King Edward. For a short time

I was buoyed up with hopes of a school in England, but in the end—disillusion once more! Where was the building, where the land or the income sufficient to realise my dreams on the large scale that I pictured them?

As always, the expenses of my little flock were enormous. Once more my bank account was nil, and so, in the end, my School was forced to return to Grünewald, while I signed a contract with Charles Frohman for an American tour.

It cost me many pangs to part from my School, from Elizabeth, and Craig, but, most of all, to forego the big bond between myself and my baby, Deirdre, who was now almost a year old, and grown into a blonde, rosy-cheeked child, with blue eyes.

And so it happened that one day in July, I found myself all alone on a big ship bound for New York—just eight years since I had left there on a cattle boat. I was already famous in Europe. I had created an Art, a School, a Baby. Not so bad. But, as far as finances went I was not much richer than before.

Charles Frohman was a great manager, but he failed to realise that my Art was not of the nature of a theatrical venture. It could only appeal to a certain restricted public. He presented me in the heat of August, and as a Broadway attraction, with a small and insufficient orchestra, attempting to play the "Iphigenia" of Gluck, and the Seventh Symphony of Beethoven. The result was, as might have been expected, a flat failure. The few people who wandered into the theatre on those torrid nights, when the temperature was ninety degrees, and more, were bewildered, and, most of them, not pleased with what they saw. The critics were few, and wrote badly. On the whole I could not but feel that my return to my native country was a great mistake.

One evening when I was sitting in my dressing-room, feeling particularly discouraged, I heard a fine, hearty voice greeting me, and saw, standing in the doorway, a man, not tall, but of beautiful frame, with a shock of brown curly hair and a winning smile. He held out his hand to me in spontaneous affection and said so many beautiful things about the effect that my Art had upon him, that I felt recompensed for all I had suffered since my arrival in New York. This man was George Grey Barnard, the great American sculptor. Thereafter he came every night to the performance, and often brought with him artists, poets and other friends of his, among them David Belasco, the genial theatrical producer, the painters Robert Henri and George Bellows, Percy MacKaye, Max Eastman—in fact all the young revolutionaries of Greenwich Village. I remember, too, the three inseparable poets who lived together in a tower below Washington Square—E. A. Robinson, Ridgeley Torrence and William Vaughn Moody.

This friendly greeting and enthusiasm from the poets and artists cheered me immensely, and made up for the meagreness and coldness of the New York audiences.

At that time George Grey Barnard conceived the idea of making of me a dancing statue, to be called "America Dancing." Walt Whitman has said, "I hear America singing," and one fine October day, in such weather as is only known in New York in autumn, out at his studio on Washington Heights, we stood together on a hill overlooking the country and, spreading out my arms, I said "I see America dancing." That is how Barnard conceived the statue.

I used to arrive at his studio every morning, bringing a lunch basket. We spent many delightful hours talking of new plans for art inspiration in America.

In his studio I remember a charming torso of a young girl, for which, he told me, Evelyn Nesbit had posed, before she met Harry K. Thaw, when she was a simple girl. Her beauty enraptured all the artists.

Naturally, these studio conversations, these mutual ecstasies over beauty had their effect. I, for one, was willing to give myself body and soul to the task of inspiring the great statue of "America Dancing," but George Grey Barnard was one of those men who carried virtue to fanaticism. None of my young tender fancies could affect his religious fidelity. The marble of his statues was not any colder nor more severe. I was the ephemeral, he the eternal. What wonder, then, that I desired to be moulded and immortalised by his genius? With every atom of my being I longed to become the mobile clay under his sculptor's hands.

Ah, George Grey Barnard, we will grow old, we will die, but not those magic moments we spent together, I the Dancer, you the Magician who could have seized this dance through its fluid reflection—you the Master Power to send the lightning stroke of the moment down to Eternity. Ah, where is my masterpiece—my chef d'œuvre—"America Dancing"? I look up and encounter the gaze of Human Pity—of his colossal statue of Abraham Lincoln dedicated to America—the great brow, the furrowed cheeks, furrowed by flowing tears of Human Pity and Great Martyrdom— and I the slight, futile figure dancing before this ideal of superhuman faith and virtue.

But at least I was not Salome. I wanted the head of no one: I was never a Vampire, but always an Inspirational. If you refused me "your lips, Johannes," and your love, I had the intelligent grace of "Young America" to wish you God-speed on your journey of virtue. Godspeed, but not Adieu, because your friendship has been one of the most beautiful and sacred things of my life. So is the Occidental perhaps wiser than the Oriental sister. "I want your mouth, Johannes—your mouth," and not your head on a charger, for that is the Vampire, not the Inspirational. "Take me!"

—"Ah, you won't? Then au revoir, and think of me, and from thoughts of me great future works may come."

The statue of "America Dancing" had a wonderful beginning, but, alas, no development. Shortly afterwards, on account of the sudden illness of his wife, the posing had to be abandoned. I had hoped to be his masterpiece, but it was not I who inspired Barnard's masterpiece for America, but Abraham Lincoln, whose statue now stands in the sombre garden before Westminster Abbey.

Charles Frohman, finding that the stay on Broadway was disastrous, attempted a tour in the smaller towns, but this tour was also so badly arranged that it was even more of a failure than the New York performances. Finally I lost patience, and went to see Charles Frohman. I found him in a very disconcerted state, thinking over all the money he had lost. "America does not understand your Art," he said. "It is considerably over the heads of Americans, and they will never understand it. It would be better for you to return to Europe."

I had a contract with Frohman, calling for a six months' tour, with a guarantee, whether or not it made a success. Nevertheless, from a feeling of hurt pride, and also out of contempt for his lack of sportsmanship, I took this contract and tore it up before his eyes, saying, "At any rate this leaves you free from all responsibility."

Following the counsels of George Barnard, who told me repeatedly that he was proud of me, as a product of American soil, and that it would be a great sorrow to him if America did not appreciate my Art, I decided to stay in New York. So I took a studio in the Beaux Arts Building, fitted it up with my blue curtains and my carpet, and proceeded to create some new work, dancing every evening for the poets and artists.

In the Sunday *Sun* of November 15, 1908, there was a description of one of these evenings:

"She (Isadora Duncan) is swathed from the waist down in a wonderful bit of Chinese embroidery. Her short, dark hair is rolled and coiled in a loose knot at the nape of her neck, parted simply, Madonna like, about her face . . . and upturned nose and greyish-bluey eyes. Many of her press notices speak of her as being tall and statuesque—a triumph of art, for she is in reality but five feet six, and weighs one hundred and twenty-five pounds.

"Amber border lights are turned on, and a yellow disk in the centre of the ceiling glows softly, completing the colour effects. Miss Duncan apologises for the incongruity of the piano music.

" 'There should be no music for such a dance as this,' she says, 'except such music as Pan might make on a reed cut from the river bank, a flute perhaps, a shepherd's pipe—that is all. The other arts—painting, sculpture, music, poetry —have left dancing far behind. It has been practically one of the lost arts, and to try to harmonise it with one so far ahead as music, is difficult and inconsistent. It is to revive that lost art of dancing that I have devoted my life.'

"She has been standing near her parterre of poets when she begins to talk, and when she finishes, she is at the other side of the room. You do not know how she got there, but you think of her friend Ellen Terry as she does it, and the latter's nonchalant way of ignoring space.

"She is no longer a fatigued, sad-faced hostess, but a pagan spirit, stepping naturally from a bit of broken marble as if that were the most obvious thing in the world to do. A Galatea, perhaps, for certainly Galatea danced in the first few moments of her release. She is Daphne with loosened hair, escaping the embraces of Apollo in that Delphic Grove. Her own hair falls as that simile comes to your mind.

"No wonder she was tired of standing on that piece of Elgin marble all these years for the delectation of British lorgnettes, and the half-disapproving eyes behind them. A long series of Tanagra figurines, the processions of the Parthenon frieze, the garlanded grief of urn and tablet, the abandon of the Bacchantes, pass before your eyes, which seem to be watching her, but are in reality watching that whole panorama of human nature before artifice stepped in.

"Miss Duncan admits that her whole life has been an effort to go back, to discover that simplicity which has been lost in the maze of many generations.

" 'In those far-off days which we are pleased to call Pagan, every emotion had its corresponding movement,' she says. 'Soul, body, mind worked together in perfect harmony. Look at those Hellenic men and maidens caught and imprisoned by sculpture's lure, rather than hacked and chiselled from opposing marble—you can almost tell what they will say to you when they open their lips, and, if they do not open them, what matter, for you know just the same.'

"Then she stops short and is again a dancing sprite, an amber figurine offering you wine from an uplifted cup, throwing roses at Athene's shrine, swimming on the crest of the purple waves of the Ægean Sea, while the poets look on and the Prophet strokes his beard prophetically and one of them quotes softly from John Keats' 'Ode on a Grecian Urn':

" '*Who are these coming to the sacrifice?*

. . . . .

Beauty is truth, truth beauty—that is all
Ye know on earth, and all ye need to know.'

"The Editor of an Art Magazine (Mary Fanton Roberts) speaks ecstatically what Miss Duncan admits has been the most pleasing summing up of her work that she has read:

" 'It is far back, deep down the centuries, that one's spirit passes when Isadora Duncan dances; back to the very morning of the world, when the greatness of the soul found free expression in the beauty of the body, when rhythm of motion corresponded with rhythm of sound, when the movements of the human body were one with the wind and the sea, when the gesture of a woman's arm was as the unfolding of a rose petal, the pressure of her foot upon the sod as the drifting of a leaf to earth. When all the fervour of religion, of love, of patriotism, sacrifice or passion expressed itself to the measure of the cythara, the harp or the timbrel, when men and women danced before their hearthstones and their gods in religious ecstasy, or out in the forests and by the sea because of the joy of life that was in them, it had to be that every strong, great or good impulse of the human soul poured from the spirit to the body in perfect accord with the rhythm of the Universe.' "

George Grey Barnard had counselled me to stay in America, and I was glad I had listened to him. For, one day, there arrived in the studio a man who was to be instrumental in gaining for me the enthusiasm of the American public. This was Walter Damrosch. He had seen me dancing an interpretation of the Seventh Symphony of Beethoven at the Criterion Theatre, with a small, bad orchestra, and he had had the understanding to realise what would be the effect of this dancing when inspired by his own fine orchestra and glorious conducting.

My studies of the piano and of the theory of orchestral composition, as a child, must have remained in my subconsciousness. Whenever I lie quiet and shut my eyes, I can hear the whole orchestra as plainly as if they were playing before me, and for each instrument I see a god-like figure in movement of fullest expression. This orchestra of shadows danced always in my inner vision.

Damrosch proposed to me a series of representations at the Metropolitan Opera House for the month of December, to which I joyfully assented.

The result was just as he had predicted. At the first performance, Charles Frohman, who had sent for a box, was astonished to learn that not a seat remained in the theatre. This experience proves that, no matter how great the artist, without the proper setting even the greatest art can be lost. This was the case with Eleanora Duse on her first tour in America, when, because of poor management, she played to almost empty houses and felt that America could never appreciate her. Whereas, when she returned in 1924, she was greeted from New York to San Francisco with one continual ovation, simply because, this time, Morris Gest had had the artistic intelligence to understand her.

I was very proud to travel with an orchestra of eighty men, conducted by the great Walter Damrosch. This tour was particularly successful, as there reigned throughout the orchestra such a feeling of good-will towards the chief and towards myself. Indeed, I felt such sympathy with Walter Damrosch that it seemed to me when I stood in the centre of the stage to dance, I was connected by every nerve in my body with the orchestra and with the great conductor.

How can I describe the joy of dancing with this orchestra? It is there before me—Walter Damrosch raises his baton—I watch it, and, at the first stroke there surges within me the combined symphonic chord of all the instruments in one. The mighty reverberation rushes over me and I become the Medium to condense in unified expression the joy of Brünnhilde awakened by Siegfried, or the soul of Isolde seeking in Death her realisation. Voluminous, vast, swelling like sails in the wind, the movements of my dance carry me onward—onward and upward, and I feel the presence of a mighty power within me which listens to the music and then reaches out through all my body, trying to find an outlet for this listening. Sometimes this power grew furious, sometimes it raged and shook me until my heart nearly burst from its passion, and I thought my last moments on earth had surely arrived. At other times it brooded heavily, and I would suddenly feel such anguish that, through my arms stretched to the Heavens, I implored help from where no help came. Often I thought to myself, what a mistake to call me a dancer—I am the magnetic centre to convey the emotional expression of the Orchestra. From my soul sprang fiery rays to connect me with my trembling, vibrating Orchestra.

There was a flutist who played so divinely the solo of the Happy Spirits in "Orpheus" that I often found myself immobile on the stage with the tears flowing from my eyes, just from the ecstasy of listening to him, and the singing of the violins and the whole orchestra soaring upwards, inspired by the wonderful conductor.

Louis of Bavaria used to sit alone listening to the orchestra at Bayreuth, but if he had danced to this orchestra, he would have known an even greater delight.

There was a marvellous sympathy between Damrosch and me, and to each one of his gestures I instantly felt the answering vibration. As he augmented the crescendo in volume, so the life in me mounted and overflowed in gesture—for each musical phrase translated into a musical movement, my whole being vibrated in harmony with his.

Sometimes when I looked down from the stage and saw the great brow of Damrosch bent over the score, I felt that my dance really resembled the birth of Athena, springing full-armed from the head of Zeus.

This tour in America was probably the happiest time of my life, only, naturally, I suffered from homesickness, and when I danced the Seventh Symphony, I pictured about me the forms of my pupils when they should have grown to an age to interpret it with me. So it was not a complete joy, but the hope of a future, greater joy. Perhaps there is no complete joy in life, but only hope. The last note of Isolde's love song seems complete, but that means Death.

In Washington I was met by a perfect storm. Some of the Ministers had protested against my dance in violent terms.

And then, suddenly, to the astonishment of every one, who should appear in the stage box on the afternoon of a matinée, but President Roosevelt himself. He seemed to enjoy the performance and led the applause after every item of the programme. He afterwards wrote to a friend:

"What harm can these Ministers find in Isadora's dances? She seems to me as innocent as a child dancing through the garden in the morning sunshine and picking the beautiful flowers of her fantasy."

This saying of Roosevelt's, which was quoted in the newspapers, considerably abashed the preachers, and aided our tournée. In fact, the entire tournée was most happy and propitious in every way, and no one could have asked for a kinder director or more charming comrade than Walter Damrosch, who had the temperament of a really great artist. In his moments of relaxation he could enjoy a good supper and play upon the piano for hours, never tired, always genial, light-hearted and delightful.

When we returned to New York, I had the satisfaction of hearing from my bank that I had a goodly deposit to my account.   If it had not been for the pulling at my heart-strings to see my Baby and my School, I would never have left America.   But one morning I left a little group of friends on the pier—Mary and Billy Roberts, my poets, my artists, and returned to Europe.

CHAPTER TWENTY-TWO

ELIZABETH brought twenty pupils of the School and my Baby to meet me in Paris. Imagine my joy—I had not seen my Baby for six months! When she saw me she looked at me in the queerest fashion, and then began to cry. Naturally I began to cry too—it was so strange and wonderful to hold her in my arms again. And that other child—my School. They had all grown so tall. It was a splendid reunion, and we danced and sang together the whole afternoon.

That great artist Lugné Poe had taken charge of my representations in Paris. He was responsible for bringing to Paris Eleanora Duse, Susanne Desprès and Ibsen. He noted that my work needed a certain setting, and engaged for me the Gaiété Lyrique, and the Colonne Orchestra, with Colonne to direct it. The result was that we took Paris by storm. Such poets as Henri Lavedan, Pierre Mille, Henri de Régnier wrote of me enthusiastically.

Paris turned a smiling countenance.

Each representation I gave was crowded with the élite of the artistic and intellectual world. Then I seemed very near to accomplishing my dream, and the School I desired seemed within easy reach.

I had taken two large apartments at No. 5 Rue Danton. I lived on the first floor and on the second I had all the children of the School with their governesses.

One day, just before a matinée, I had a bad fright. My baby suddenly, without warning, began to choke and cough. I thought it might be the dreaded croup and, taking a taxi,

I flew about Paris trying to find a doctor at home. Finally I found a noted children's specialist who kindly came back with me and soon reassured me that it was nothing serious, only a cough.

I arrived at the matinée half an hour late. Colonne had filled in the interval with music. All the afternoon, as I danced, I trembled with apprehension. Naturally I adored my child and felt that if anything should happen to her I could not survive.

How strong, egotistical and ferocious a possession is Mother Love. I do not think it is very admirable. It would be infinitely more admirable to be able to love all children.

Deirdre was now running about and dancing. She was particularly lovely, and a perfect miniature of Ellen Terry, which was certainly due to my thoughts and admiration of Ellen. When Humanity advances, all mothers will be isolated before the birth of their children in some protected place where they shall be surrounded by statues, pictures and music.

The event of the season was the Brisson Ball, to which all the artists and literary lights of Paris were invited. Every one was to go as the title of a different work. I went as the Bacchante of Euripides, and, being a Bacchante, I found Mounet-Sully in Greek robes, who might have personified Dionysus himself. I danced with him all the evening—or at least I danced about him, for the great Mounet disdained modern dance steps, and it was bruited about that our conduct was extremely scandalous. But it was really innocent enough, and I gave this great artist some hours of diversion which he merited. It seemed so strange that, with my American innocence, I should have so shocked Paris that night!

The recent discoveries of mental telepathy have proven that brain-waves part through those air-passages that are sympathetic to them and reach their destination, sometimes even without the consciousness of the sender.

I had arrived at a point where breakdown was indicated. It was impossible to meet all the expenses of my growing school out of my resources. With the money which I had made myself I had adopted and cared for and educated forty children, of whom twenty were in Germany and twenty in Paris, and I was helping other people besides. One day, in joke, I said to my sister Elizabeth:

"This can't go on! My banking account is overdrawn. If the School is to continue, we must find a millionaire."

Once I had voiced this wish, it obsessed me.

"I must find a millionaire!" I repeated a hundred times a day, first in a joke and then, finally, according to the Coué system, in earnest.

One morning after an especially successful performance at the Gaiété Lyrique, I was sitting in a dressing-gown before my mirror. I remember I had my hair in curling papers for the afternoon matinée, and it was covered with a little lace cap. My maid came to me with a visiting card on which I read a well-known name, and suddenly there sang in my brain: "Here is my millionaire!"

"Let him enter!"

He entered, tall and blond, curling hair and beard. My first thought was: Lohengrin. *Wer will mein Ritter sein?* He spoke in a charming voice, but he seemed shy. "He is like a big boy disguised in a beard," I thought.

"You do not know me, but I have often applauded your wonderful art," he said.

Then a curious feeling came over me. I had met this man before. Where? As in a dream, I remembered the funeral of the Prince de Polignac: I, a young girl, crying bitterly, primitively unused to a French funeral; the long row of relatives in the side aisle of the church. Some one pushed me forward. "Il faut serrer la main!" they whispered. And I, overcome with genuine grief for my dear friend gone, gave my hand to one after another of the relatives. And I remembered suddenly looking into the eyes of one. It was the tall man before me.

We had met first in a church before a coffin. No prophecy of happiness, that! Nevertheless. from that moment I realised that this was my millionaire, for whom I had sent my brain-waves seeking, and that, for whatever fate, it was *Kismet*.

"I admire your art, your courage in the ideal of your school. I have come to help you. What can I do? Would you like, for instance, to go with all these dancing children to a little villa on the Riviera, by the sea, and there compose new dances? The expense you don't need to worry about. I will bear it all. You have done a great work; you must be tired. Now let it rest on my shoulders."

In a week's time all my little troop were in a first-class carriage, speeding towards the sea and the sunshine. Lohengrin met us at the station. He was radiant; dressed all in white. He took us to a lovely villa by the sea, from whose terraces he pointed out to us his white-winged yacht.

"It is called the Lady Alicia," he said. "But perhaps now we will change the name to Iris."

The children danced about under the orange trees in their light blue tunics, their hands filled with blossoms and fruit. Lohengrin was most kind and charming to the children, thoughtful of every one's comfort. His devotion to them added a new element of trust to the feeling of gratitude with which I already regarded him and which, through daily contact with his charm, was soon to deepen to something much stronger. At that time, though, I merely regarded him as my knight, to be worshipped at a distance, in an almost spiritual fashion.

The children and I were in a villa in Beaulieu, but Lohengrin lived in a fashionable hotel in Nice. Now and then he asked me to dine with him. I remember I went in my simple Greek tunic and was embarrassed to find there a woman in a wonderful coloured gown covered with diamonds and pearls. I knew at once that she was my enemy. She filled me with dread, which was afterwards justified.

One evening, with characteristic generosity, Lohengrin had invited a large party to a Carnival Ball at the Casino. He provided Pierrot costumes for every one, made in flowing Liberty satin. It was the first time I had ever donned a Pierrot costume, the first time I had ever attended a public masked ball. It was a joyous festivity. For me there was only one cloud. The lady of the diamonds—also provided with a Pierrot costume—came to the ball. When I looked at her, I suffered tortures. But, afterwards, I remember dancing with her with frenzy—so much is love akin to hate—until the major-domo touched us on the shoulder and informed us it was not allowed.

In the midst of all this fooling, I was suddenly called to the telephone. Some one told me from the villa at Beaulieu that Erica, the baby of the School, was taken suddenly with croup—very serious—perhaps dying. I rushed from the telephone to the supper table, where Lohengrin was entertaining his guests. I told him to come, quick, to the telephone. We must 'phone for a doctor. And it was there, in the proximity of that telephone box, under the stress of that common panic for one dear to us both, that our defences broke down and our lips met for the first time. But we wasted not a second. Lohengrin's automobile was at the door. Just as we were, as two Pierrots, we went and picked up the doctor, then sped on to Beaulieu. We found little Erica suffocating, her face quite black. The doctor did his work. We waited beside the bed, two frightened Pierrots, for the verdict. Two hours later, with the dawn creeping in at the window, the doctors pronounced that the baby was saved. The tears were racing down our cheeks and melting the grease-paint, but Lohengrin took me in his arms: "Courage, darling! Let us go back to our guests." And all the way back, in the automobile, he held me close, whispering, "Dearest, if it were only for this one night, this one memory, I would love you always."

At the Casino, time had flown so rapidly that most of the guests had hardly noticed our absence.

One, however, had counted every minute of it. The little lady of the diamonds had watched our departure with jealous eyes and, as we re-entered, she snatched a knife from the table and darted up to Lohengrin. Fortunately, he realised her intention in time and, gripping her by the wrist, swung her in a trice high above his head. In this wise he carried her off to the ladies' room as though the whole incident were a joke, a pre-arranged part of the Carnival. There, he delivered her over to the attendants, with the simple remark that she appeared a little hysterical and was apparently in need of a drink of water! After which he returned to the ballroom, entirely unmoved, and in reckless good spirits. And indeed, from then on, the gaiety of the whole party increased, until it reached its climax at five A.M. when I danced all the wild and conflicting emotions of the evening into a Tango Apache with Max Dearley.

When the party broke up at sunrise, the lady of the diamonds went back to her hotel alone, and Lohengrin remained with me. His generosity towards the children, his anxiety and genuine pain at little Erica's illness—all this had won my love.

Next morning he proposed a flight on the yacht, now rechristened. We took my little girl with us, and, leaving the

School in the care of the governesses, we sailed away towards Italy.

* * *

All money brings a curse with it, and the people who possess it cannot be happy for twenty-four hours.

If I had only realised that the man I was with had the psychology of a spoilt child, that every word and every action of mine should have been carefully prepared to please, all might have been well. But I was too young and too naïve to know this, and I prattled on, explaining to him my ideas of life, Plato's "Republic," Karl Marx, and a general reform of the world, without the least notion of the havoc I was creating. This man, who had declared that he loved me for my courage and generosity, became more and more alarmed when he found what sort of a red-hot revolutionary he had taken aboard his yacht. He gradually comprehended that he could not reconcile my ideals with his peace of mind. But the climax came when, one evening he asked me what was my favourite poem. Delighted, I brought him my *livre de chevet* and read to him the "Song of the Open Road" by Walt Whitman. Carried away by my enthusiasm, I did not notice what effect this was having, and when I looked up I was astonished to find his handsome face congested with rage.

"What rot!" he exclaimed. "That man could never have earned his living!"

"Can't you see," I cried, "he had the vision of Free America?"

"Vision be damned!"

And suddenly I realised that *his* vision of America was that of the dozens of factories which made his fortune for him. But such is the perversity of woman that, after this and similar quarrels, I threw myself into his arms, forgetting everything under the brutality of his caresses. Also, I consoled myself with the idea that soon he would open his eyes and see, and that then he would help me to make that great School for the children of the people.

And, in the meantime, the magnificent yacht sailed on through the blue Mediterranean.

I can see it all as if it were yesterday: the broad deck of the yacht; the table set with crystal and silver for lunch, and Deirdre, in her white tunic, dancing about. Certainly I was in love and happy. And yet, all the time I was unpleasantly aware of the stokers, stoking in the engine-room; the fifty sailors on the yacht; the Captain and the Mate—all this immense expenditure for the pleasure of two people. Subconsciously I was uneasy of mind at the passing of these days, each a loss from the mark. And sometimes I contrasted unfavourably the ease of this life of luxury, the continual feasting, the nonchalant giving up of one's being to pleasure, with the bitter struggle of my early youth. Then quickly I would react to the impression on my body and mind of the glory of the dawn as it melted into the heat of a dazzling noon. My Lohengrin, my Knight of the Grail, should come, too, to share the great idea!

We spent a day at Pompeii, and Lohengrin had the romantic idea that he would like to see me dance in the Temple of Pæstum by moonlight. He straightway engaged a small Neapolitan orchestra and arranged that they should proceed to the temple and await our coming. But just that day there was a summer storm and a deluge of rain. All that day and the next the yacht was unable to leave the harbour, and when we finally arrived at Pæstum, we found the orchestra, drenched through and very miserable, sitting on the steps of the temple, where they had waited for twenty-four hours.

Lohengrin ordered dozens of bottles of wine and a lamb la Pélicaire, which we ate Arab fashion with our fingers.

The famished orchestra ate and drank so much and were so fatigued from their waiting in the temple, that they were quite unable to play. As it began to drizzle slightly again, we all went to the yacht and set sail for Naples. The orchestra made a brave attempt to play for us on the deck, but as the boat began to rock, one by one they turned green and retired to the cabins. . . .

And that was the end of the romantic idea of dancing by moonlight in the Temple of Pæstum!

Lohengrin wanted to continue to sail in the Mediterranean, but I remembered I had a contract with my impresario in Russia and, deaf to all pleadings, and even though it was very difficult for me, I decided to keep my contract. Lohengrin brought me back to Paris. He would have come to Russia with me, but feared passport difficulties. He filled my compartment with flowers, and we said a tender good-bye.

It is a strange fact that when parting from a loved one, although we may be torn by the most terrible grief, we experience at the same time a curious sensation of liberation.

That tournée in Russia was as successful as were the others, but it was marked by an event that might have been tragic, though it turned out rather comic. One afternoon Craig walked in to see me, and for a short moment I was on the verge of believing that nothing mattered—neither the School, nor Lohengrin, nor anything—but just the joy of seeing him again. However, a dominant trait in my character is fidelity.

Craig was in high spirits, in the midst of creating his Hamlet for the Stanislavsky Art Theatre. All the actresses of the Stanislavsky troupe were in love with him. The actors were delighted with his beauty, geniality and extraordinary vitality. He would harangue them by the hour on the art of the theatre and they did their best to follow all his fantasies and imaginings.

When I saw him I felt again all the old charm and fascination, and things might have ended differently had it not been that I had with me a very pretty secretary. On the last evening, when we were just leaving for Kieff, I gave a little dinner to Stanislavsky, Craig and the secretary. In the middle of dinner Craig asked me if I meant to remain with him or not. As I could not answer, he flew into one of his old-time rages, lifted the secretary from her chair, carried her into the other room and locked the door. Stanislavsky was terribly shocked, and did his best to persuade Craig to open the door, but when we found that persuasion had no effect, we could do nothing but go to the station, where we found the train had left ten minutes before.

I returned with Stanislavsky to his apartment, and we tried to talk mournfully of modern art, and to avoid the subject of Craig but I could see that Stanislavsky was distressed and shocked by Craig's behaviour.

The next day I took the train to Kieff. There I was joined some days later by a rather pale and somewhat shaken secretary. When I asked her if she did not want to stay in Russia with Craig, she said emphatically that she did not, so we returned to Paris, where L. met us.

He had a strange, gloomy apartment in the Place des Vosges. He took me there—into a Louis XIV bed, where he fairly smothered me with caresses. There, for the first time, I knew what the nerves and sensations can be transformed to. It seemed to me that I came to life in a new and exhilarating manner which I had never known before.

Like Zeus he transformed himself into many shapes and forms, and I knew him now as a Bull, now as a Swan, and again as a Golden Shower, and I was by this love carried over the waves, caressed with white wings delicately, and strangely seduced and hallowed in a Golden Cloud.

Then, too, I learned to know all the really good restaurants in the city of Paris, where L. was kowtowed to and treated like a king. All the Maîtres d'Hotel and all the cooks vied with one another to please him—and no wonder for he distributed money in a truly royal manner. For the first time, too, I learnt the difference between a *poulet cocotte* and a *poulet simple*—the different values of ortolans, truffles and mushrooms. In fact, nerves lying dormant in my tongue and palate awoke, and I learned to know the vintage of wines and just what year and what *crû* was the most exquisite to the sense of smell and taste, besides many things that I had hitherto ignored.

And now, for the first time, I visited a fashionable dressmaker, and fell to the fatal lure of stuffs, colours, form—even hats. I, who had always worn a little white tunic, woolen in winter, linen in summer, succumbed to the enticement of ordering beautiful gowns, and wearing them. Only I had one excuse. The dressmaker was no ordinary one, but a genius—Paul Poiret, who could dress a woman in such a way as also to create a work of art. Yet this was for me the change from sacred to profane art.

All these gratifications had their reactions, and there were days when we spoke of that weird sickness—neurasthenia.

I remember, during an exquisite morning walk in the Bois de Boulogne, with Lohengrin, seeing a far-away, tragic expression (that I learned in time to dread) coming over his face. When I asked the reason, he replied:

"Always my mother's face in her coffin; wherever I am I see her dead face. What use to live, since it all ends only in death?"

And I realised that riches and luxury do not create contentment! It is certainly more difficult for rich people to accomplish anything serious in life. Always that yacht in the harbour inviting one to sail on Azure Seas.

CHAPTER TWENTY-THREE

THAT summer we spent in the yacht off Brittany. Often it was so rough that I got off and followed the yacht along the coast in an auto. L. stuck to the ship, but he was not a very good sailor, and often he turned very dark green. Such are the pleasures of the rich!

In September I went to Venice with my baby and the nurse. For some weeks I was alone with them. One day I went into the Cathedral of St. Marco and was sitting there alone, gazing at the blue and gold of the dome when suddenly it seemed to me that I saw the face of a little boy, but it was also the face of an angel with great blue eyes and an aureole of golden hair.

I went to the Lido, and sitting there, with little Deirdre playing on the sands, I spent some days in meditation. What I had dreamed in the Cathedral of St. Marco filled me at the same time with joy and disquietude. I loved, but I now knew something of the fickleness and selfish caprice of what men call love, and this sacrifice coming for my Art—perhaps fatal for my Art—my work—and suddenly I began to suffer an intense nostalgia for my Art—my work—my School. This human life seemed so heavy beside my dreams of Art.

I believe that in each life there is a spiritual line, an upward curve, and all that adheres to and strengthens this line is our real life—the rest is but as chaff falling from us as our souls progress. Such a spiritual line is my Art. My life has known but two motives—Love and Art—and often Love destroyed Art, and often the imperious call of Art put a tragic end to Love. For these two have no accord, but only constant battle.

In this state of indecision and mental anguish I went to

Milan to meet a doctor friend whom I had summoned there, and laid my problem before him.

"Why, it is preposterous!" he exclaimed, "you a unique artist, to again risk depriving the world for ever of your Art. It is quite impossible. Pray take my advice and prevent such a crime against humanity."

I listened to him undecided, in a state of anguished indecision—one moment filled with revolt that such a deformation should again come to my body, which was the instrument of my Art, again tortured by the call, the hope, the vision of that angel's face, the face of my son.

I asked my friend to leave me for an hour to decide. I remember the bedroom of the hotel—a rather gloomy room—and facing me I suddenly saw a picture, a strange woman in eighteenth century gown, whose lovely, but cruel eyes looked straight into mine. I stared at her eyes and they seemed to mock me. "Whatever you may decide," she seemed to say, "it is the same. Look at my loveliness, that shone so many years ago. Death swallows all—all—why should you suffer to again bring life into the world, only to be swallowed up by death?"

Her eyes became more cruel, more sinister, my anguish more terrible. I hid my eyes from hers with my hands. I tried to think, to decide. I implored those eyes, through the mist of my troubled tears, but they seemed to show no pity: relentless they mocked me. Life or Death, poor creature, you are in the relentless trap.

Finally I rose and spoke to the eyes. "No, you shall not trouble me. I believe in Life, in Love, in the sanctity of Nature's Law."

Was it imagination, or did there suddenly shine in those hard eyes a gleam of terrible, mocking laughter?

When my friend returned I told him my decision, and after that nothing would alter it.

I returned to Venice, and, taking Deirdre in my arms, I whispered to her: "You will have a little brother."

"Oh," laughed Deirdre, and clapped her hands with glee. "How sweet, how sweet."

"Yes, yes, it will be sweet."

I sent a telegram to L. and he came rushing down to Venice. He seemed delighted—full of joy, love, tenderness. The demon Neurasthenia completely disappeared for a time.

I had signed a second contract with Walter Damrosch and in October I sailed for America.

L. had never seen America and was wild with excitement, remembering he had American blood. Of course he took the largest suite on the boat and we had a special menu printed every night and travelled like Royal personages. Travelling with a millionaire does simplify things, and we had a most magnificent apartment in the Plaza, with every one bowing down right and left.

I believe there is some law and convention in the U. S. A. that does not allow two lovers to travel together. Poor Gorky and his mistress of seventeen years' standing, were hunted from pillar to post and their lives made a torment to them, but of course when one is so very rich, these little disagreeablenesses are all smoothed away.

The tour in America was most happy, successful and prosperous, for money attracts money, until one day in January a very nervous lady came into my loge and exclaimed, "But, my dear Miss Duncan, it's plainly visible from the front row. You can't continue like this."

And I replied, "Oh, but, my dear Mrs. X., that's just what I mean my dancing to express—Love—Woman—Formation —Springtime. Botticelli's picture, you know—the fruitful Earth—the three dancing Graces *enceinte*—the Madonna—

the Zephyrs *enceinte* also. Everything rustling, promising New Life. That is what my Dance means—"

At this Mrs. X. looked quizzical, but we thought it was better to let the tour stop, and return to Europe, for my blessed state was really becoming quite visible.

I had a great joy in that Augustin and his little girl returned with us. He had separated from his wife, and I thought the trip would distract him.

* * *

"How would you like to travel up the Nile on a dahabeah all winter—to fly from grey and sullen skies to where is brilliant sunshine: to visit Thebes, Denderah, all that you have longed to see? The yacht is ready to take us to Alexandria, the dahabeah fitted out with thirty native sailors, and a first-class cook; there are sumptuous cabins—bedrooms with baths—"

"Ah, but my School, my work—"

"Your sister Elizabeth tends the School very well, and you are so young that you have plenty of time for your work."

So we spent the winter sailing up the Nile, and it would have been a dream of happiness—it almost was—if it had not been for that same monster Neurasthenia, which appeared from time to time like a black hand covering the sun.

As the dahabeah voyages slowly up the Nile the soul travels back a thousand—two thousand—five thousand years; back, through the mists of the Past to the Gates of Eternity.

How calm and beautiful was this voyage to me at that time, carrying, as I did, within me the promise of a new life. Temples that spoke of Ancient Kings of Egypt penetrating through the golden desert sands, down to the profound mysteries of the Tombs of the Pharaohs. The little life within me seemed to vaguely surmise this journey to the land of darkness and death. One moonlight night, in the Temple of Denderah, it seemed to me that all the eyes in the battered faces of the Goddess Hathor, the Egyptian Aphrodite, repeated with hypnotic insistence throughout the Temple, were turned toward my unborn child.

Especially wonderful is the Valley of the Dead, and most of all, to me, the grave of a little Prince who never grew to be a great Pharaoh or King. Dead at such a tender age—remaining through the centuries the dead child—and one thought of the six thousand years he had lain there. But, if he had lived, he would have been six thousand years old!

What do I remember of that trip in Egypt? The purple sunrise, the scarlet sunset, the golden sands of the desert, the temples. The sunny days spent in the courtyard of a temple dreaming of the life of the Pharaohs—dreaming of my baby to come. The peasant women walking on the banks of the Nile with vases poised on their beautiful heads, their voluminous bodies swaying under their black draperies; the slight figure of Deirdre dancing on the deck; Deirdre walking in the ancient streets of Thebes. The little child looking up at the battered ancient gods.

When she saw the Sphinx she said, "Oh, Mama, this Dolly is not very pretty, but how imposing!"

She was just learning words of three syllables.

The little child before the Temples of Eternity—the little Prince in the tombs of the Pharaohs—the Valley of the Kings, and the caravans passing over the desert—the wind moving the sand in waves across the desert—whither?

The sunrise in Egypt came with an extraordinary intensity about four o'clock in the morning. After that it was impossible to sleep, as there began the steady, continuous wail of the *sakieh*, drawing water from the Nile. Then, too, began the procession of labourers on the shore, drawing water, tilling the fields, driving camels, and this continued until sunset in living and moving frescoes.

The dahabeah moved slowly to the singing of the sailors as their bronzed bodies rose and fell with the oars, we watching idly and enjoying all this as spectators.

The nights were beautiful. We had with us a Steinway piano and a very talented young English artist who played for us every night Bach and Beethoven, whose solemn measures harmonize so well with the space and the temples of Egypt.

We reached Wadi Halfa a few weeks later, and penetrated into Nubia, where the Nile is so narrow that one can almost touch the banks on either side. Here the men of the party left to go on to Khartoum, and I remained alone on the dahabeah with Deirdre and spent the most peaceful time of my life, for two weeks, in that marvellous country where worry and trouble seem quite futile. Our boat seemed to be rocked by the rhythm of the ages. For those who can afford it, a trip up the Nile in a well-appointed dahabeah is the best rest cure in the world.

Egypt is a land of dreams for us—a land of labour for the poor fellah—but, in any case, it is the only land that I know where labour can be beautiful. The fellah, who lives mainly on a soup of lentils, and unleavened bread, has a beautiful, supple body, and whether stooping in the fields, or drawing water from the Nile, presents always a bronze model to delight the heart of a sculptor.

*　　*　　*

We returned to France and landed at Villefranche, and L. rented for the season a magnificent villa at Beaulieu, with terraces sloping down to the sea. With his characteristic impetuousness, he amused himself buying up land on Cap Ferrat, where he intended to build a great Italian castle.

We made auto trips to visit the towers of Avignon, and

ISADORA DUNCAN
From a photograph by Otto, Paris

the walls of Carcassonne, which were also to serve as models for this castle. A castle stands now on Cap Ferrat, but, alas, like so many of his other fancies, it has never been finished.

At this time he was obsessed by an abnormal restlessness. When he was not rushing off to Cap Ferrat to buy land, he was taking the Rapide to Paris on a Monday and returning on Wednesday. I remained calmly in the garden by the blue sea, pondering on the strange difference which divides life from Art, and often wondering if a woman can ever really be an artist, since Art is a hard task-master who demands everything, whereas a woman who loves gives up everything to life. At any rate, here I was, for the second time, completely separated and immobilised from my Art.

On the first of May, a morning when the sea was blue, the sun burning and all Nature bursting into blossom and joy, my son was born.

Unlike the stupid peasant doctor of Nordwyck, intelligent Dr. Bosson knew how to alleviate the suffering with wise doses of morphia, and this second experience was quite different from the first.

Deirdre came into my room with her charming little face filled with a precocious maternity.

"Oh, the sweet little boy, Mother; you need not worry about him. I will always hold him in my arms and take care of him."

The words came back to me when she was dead, and held him in her little stiff white arms. Why do people call upon God, Who, if He exists, must be unconscious of all this?

So, once again, I found myself lying by the sea with a baby in my arms—only instead of the little white, wind-tossed Villa Maria, it was a palatial mansion, and instead of the sullen, restless North Sea, the blue Mediterranean.

CHAPTER TWENTY-FOUR

WHEN I returned to Paris, L. asked me if I would not like to give a fête for all my friends, and told me to draw up a programme for it, for which we would be delighted to give *carte blanche*. It seems to me that rich people never know how to amuse themselves. If they give a dinner-party, it is not very different from a dinner given by a poor concierge, and I had always thought how marvellous a fête one could give, if only one had enough money. And this is how I managed.

The guests were invited to arrive at four o'clock in the afternoon at Versailles, and there, in the park, were marquees with every sort of refreshment, from caviar and champagne to tea and cakes. After this, on an open space where tents had been erected, the Colonne orchestra, under the direction of Pierné, gave us a programme of the works of Richard Wagner. I remember how wonderful was the Siegfried idyll under the shade of the great trees on that beautiful summer afternoon, and how solemn, just as the sun was setting, the tones of the Siegfried Funeral March.

After the concert, a magnificent banquet invited the guests to more material pleasures. This banquet, of varied and wonderful courses, lasted until midnight, when the grounds were illuminated, and, to the strains of a Vienna orchestra, every one danced until the small hours.

This was my idea of how, if a rich man must spend money on entertaining his friends, it should be done. To this fête came all the élite and all the artists of Paris, and they really appreciated it.

But the strange part of it all was that, although I had

arranged it all to please L., and it had cost him 50,000 francs (pre-war francs too!) he was not present.

About an hour before the fête, I received a telegram saying that he had had a stroke and was too ill to come, but that I was to receive the guests without him.

No wonder that I felt inclined to become a Communist when I so often had exemplified for me the fact that for a rich man to find happiness was like Sisyphus trying to roll his stone up-hill from Hell.

That same summer L. took it into his head that we should be married, although I protested to him that I was against marriage.

"How stupid for an artist to be married," I said, "and as I must spend my life making tours round the world, how could you spend your life in the stage-box admiring me?"

"You would not have to make tours if we were married," he answered.

"Then what should we do?"

"We should spend our time in my house in London, or at my place in the country."

"And then what should we do?"

"Then there is the yacht."

"But then what should we do?"

L. proposed that we should try the life for three months. "If you don't like it, I shall be much astonished."

So that summer we went to Devonshire, where he had a wonderful château which he had built after Versailles and the Petit Trianon, with many bedrooms and bathrooms, and suites, all to be at my disposition, with fourteen automobiles in the garage and a yacht in the harbour. But I had not reckoned on the rain. In an English summer it rains all day long. The English people do not seem to mind it at all. They rise and have an early breakfast of eggs and bacon, and ham and kidneys and porridge. Then they don mackintoshes and go forth into the humid country till lunch, when they eat many courses, ending with Devonshire cream.

From lunch to five o'clock they are supposed to be busy with their correspondence, though I believe they really go to sleep. At five they descend to their tea, consisting of many kinds of cakes and bread and butter and tea and jam. After that they make a pretence of playing bridge, until it is time to proceed to the really important business of the day—dressing for dinner, at which they appear in full evening dress, the ladies very décolleté and the gentlemen in starched shirts, to demolish a twenty-course dinner. When this is over they engage in some light political conversation, or touch upon philosophy until the time comes to retire.

You can imagine whether this life pleased me or not. In the course of a couple of weeks I was positively desperate.

Now, in the château, there was a wonderful ballroom with Gobelins tapestry and a picture of the coronation of Napoleon by David. It seems that David made two such pictures, one of which is in the Louvre, and the other in the ballroom of L.'s house in Devonshire.

Noticing my increasing despair, L. said, "Why don't you dance again—in the ballroom?"

I thought of the Gobelins tapestry and the David picture.

"How can I make my simple gestures before these, on the oily, waxed floor?"

"If that is all that troubles you," he said, "send for your curtains and your carpet."

So I sent for my curtains, which were hung over the tapestry, and I placed the carpet over the waxed floor.

"But I must have a pianist."

"Send for a pianist," said Lohengrin.

So I telegraphed to Colonne: "Spending summer in England, must work, send pianist."

In the Colonne orchestra there had been a first violinist,

a strange-looking man with a very large head which oscillated on a badly-made body. This first violinist also played the piano and Colonne had brought him to me. But this person was so unsympathetic to me that he gave me a sense of absolute physical revulsion whenever I looked at him or touched his hand, and I had begged Colonne not to bring him to see me. Colonne had said he adored me, but I told him I could do nothing against this feeling of repulsion, and I simply could not stand him. One evening when Colonne was ill and could not direct for me at the Gaiété Lyrique, he sent this man as his substitute. I was very angry and said, "I cannot dance if he directs for me."

He came into the dressing-room to see me, and, looking at me with tears in his eyes, he said: "Isadora, I adore you, do let me direct this once."

I looked at him coldly:

"No: I must explain that you are physically abhorrent to me."

Upon which he burst into tears.

The audience was waiting, so Lugné Poe persuaded Pierné to conduct instead.

On a particularly rainy day I received a telegram from Colonne: "Sending pianist. Arriving such an hour and such a day."

I went to the station, and what was my astonishment to see this man X. descending from the train.

"How is it possible that Colonne has sent you? He knows I hate and detest you."

"Je vous demande pardon, Madame, le cher Maître m'a envoyé——" he stammered.

When L. learned who the pianist was, he said: "At least I have no cause for jealousy."

L. was still suffering from the effects of what he always considered to have been a stroke, and had with him in the château a doctor and a trained nurse. They were very emphatic as to my line of conduct. I was placed in a far-away room at the other end of the house, and told that on no account was I to disturb L., who had to spend hours every day in his room on a diet of rice, macaroni, and water, and every hour the doctor came to take his blood pressure. At certain times L. was led down to a sort of cage which had been brought over from Paris, in which he sat while thousands of volts of electricity were turned on him, and he would sit there looking extremely pathetic and saying:

"I hope this will do me good."

All this added considerably to my condition of restlessness, and, combined with the ceaseless rain, may perhaps explain the extraordinary events which followed.

To drown my ennui and dissipate my annoyance, I began to work with X., much as I disliked him, but whenever he played for me I placed a screen around him, saying:

"You are so unspeakably offensive to me that I cannot bear to look at you."

Staying at the château was the Countess A., an old friend of L.'s.

"How can you treat the poor pianist in such a way?" she said, and one day she insisted that I should invite him to come with us in the closed auto in which we took a drive every day after lunch.

So, very reluctantly, I invited him. The auto had no *strapontins*, so we had to sit all on the same seat, I in the centre with the Countess on my right and X. on the left. As usual, it poured with rain. When we had gone a little way into the country, a feeling of such disgust for X. came over me that I rapped on the glass and told the chauffeur to turn and go home. He nodded, and, wishing to please me, took a sharp turn. The country road was full of ruts and, as the car turned, I was thrown into the arms of X. He closed his arms around me. I sat back and looked at him, and suddenly felt my whole being going up in flames like a pile of lighted straw. I have never felt anything so violent. And, all of a sudden, as I looked at him, I was aghast. How had I not seen it before? His face was perfectly beautiful, and in his eyes there was a smothered flame of genius. From that moment I knew that he was a great man.

All the way back to the house I gazed at him in a kind of passionate trance, and as we entered the hall of the château, he took my hand, and still keeping his eyes upon mine, drew me gently behind the screen in the ballroom. How was it possible that from such violent antipathy could be born such violent love?

The only stimulant allowed to L. at that time was the famous discovery, now being sold by thousands of bottles, which is supposed to stimulate the phagocytes, and the butler was ordered to present this stimulant to the guests every day with L.'s compliments, and, although I found out afterwards that the dose should be only a teaspoonful, L. insisted that we should drink it by the wine-glass.

From that day in the auto, we had one obsession, to be alone—in the conservatory, in the garden, even taking long walks in the muddy country lanes—but these violent passions have violent ends, and there came a day when X. had to leave the château, never to return. We made this sacrifice to save the life of a man who was supposed to be dying.

Long afterwards, when I listened to the beautiful music of "The Mirror of Jesus," I realised that I was right in feeling that this man was a genius—and genius has always had a fatal attraction for me.

But this episode proved to me that I certainly was not suited to domestic life, and so, in the autumn, somewhat wiser and sadder, I sailed for America to fulfil a third contract. Then, for the hundredth time, I made a firm decision that hereafter I would give my entire life to Art, which though a hard task-master, is a hundred per cent more grateful than human beings.

While on this tour I made a definite appeal to America to help me to found my School. My three years' experience of the life of the rich had convinced me that it was hopeless, barren and selfish, and had proved to me that we can find no real joy except in a universal expression. That winter I harangued the audience in the tier boxes of the Metropolitan, and the newspapers brought it out as a headline scandal, "Isadora Insults the Rich." I said something like this:

"It has been quoted that I have said unkind things about America. Perhaps I have—that does not mean that I do not love America. Perhaps it means that I love America too much. I once knew a man who was passionately in love with a woman who would have nothing to say to him, and treated him badly. Every day he wrote her an insulting letter. When she asked him, 'Why do you write me such rude things?' he replied, 'Because I love you so madly.'

"A psychologist will tell you the explanation of this story, and probably it is the same with me and America. Of course I love America. Why, this School, these children, are we not all the spiritual offspring of Walt Whitman? And this dancing, that has been called 'Greek.' It has sprung from America, it is the dance of the America of the future. All these movements—where have they come from? They have sprung from the great Nature of America, from the Sierra Nevada, from the Pacific Ocean, as it washes the coast of California; from the great spaces of the Rocky Mountains—from the Yosemite Valley—from the Niagara Falls.

"Beethoven and Schubert were children of the people all their lives. They were *poor* men, and their great work was inspired by and belongs to Humanity. The people need great drama, music, dancing.

"We went over to the East Side and gave a performance for nothing. Some people said to me: 'If you play a symphony of Schubert on the East Side, the people will not care for it.'

"Well, we gave a free performance (the theatre without a box-office—so refreshing), and the people sat there transfixed, with tears rolling down their cheeks; that is how they cared for it. Funds of life and poetry and art are waiting to spring from the people of the East Side. Build for them a great Amphitheatre, the only democratic form of theatre, where every one has an equal view, no boxes or balconies and—look at that gallery up there—do you think it is right to put human beings on the ceiling, like flies, and then ask them to appreciate Art and Music?

"Build a simple, beautiful theatre. You don't need to gild it; no need of all those ornaments and fal-lals. Fine art comes from the Human Spirit and needs no externals. In our School we have no costumes, no ornaments—just the beauty that flows from the inspired human soul, and the body that is its symbol, and if my Art has taught you anything here, I hope it has taught you that. Beauty is to be looked for and found in children; in the light of their eyes and in the beauty of their little hands outstretched in their lovely movements. Hand in hand, across the stage, you have seen them, more beautiful than any string of pearls belonging to any of the women who generally sit in the boxes here. These are my pearls and my diamonds: I want no others. Give beauty and freedom and strength to the children. Give art to the people who need it. Great music should no longer be kept for the delight of a few cultured people, it should be given free to the masses: it is as necessary for them as air and bread, for it is the Spiritual Wine of Humanity."

During this trip to America I had much happiness from the friendship of that artist-genius, David Bispham. He came to all my representations and I went to all his recitals and afterwards, in my suite at the Plaza, we would have supper and he would sing to me, "On the Road to Mandalay," or "Danny Deever," and we laughed and embraced and were delighted with each other.

This chapter might be called "An Apology for Pagan Love," for now that I had discovered that Love might be a pastime as well as a tragedy, I gave myself to it with pagan innocence. Men seemed so hungry for Beauty, hungry for that love which refreshes and inspires without fear or responsibility. After a performance, in my tunic, with my hair crowned with roses, I was so lovely. Why should not this loveliness be enjoyed? Gone were the days of a glass of hot milk and Kant's "Critique of Pure Reason." Now it seemed to me more natural to sip champagne and have some charming person tell me how beautiful I was. The divine pagan body, the passionate lips, the clinging arms, the sweet refreshing sleep on the shoulder of some loved one—these were joys which seemed to me both innocent and delightful. Some people may be scandalised, but I don't understand why, if you have a body in which you are born to a certain amount of pain—cutting of teeth, pulling out of teeth, filling of teeth; and every one, however virtuous, is subject to illness, grippe, etc.—why should you not, when the occasion presents, draw from this same body the maximum of pleasure? A man who labours all day with his brain, sometimes torn with heavy problems and anxiety—why should he not be taken in those beautiful arms and find comfort for his pain and a few hours of beauty and forgetfulness? I hope that those to whom I gave it will remember it with the same pleasure as I do. I have not time to write about them all in these memoirs, any more than I can tell in one volume all the beautiful hours I have spent in forests or in the fields, or all the marvellous happiness I have had from symphonies of Mozart or Beethoven, of the exquisite hours given me by such artists as Isaye, Walter Rummel, Hener Skene and others.

"Yes," I continually cried, "let me be Pagan, be Pagan!" but I was probably never much more advanced than to be a Pagan Puritan, or a Puritanical Pagan.

I shall never forget my return to Paris. I had left my children at Versailles with a governess. When I opened the door, my little boy came running towards me, with golden curls making an aureole about his lovely face. I had left him a little baby in the cradle.

In 1908 I had bought Gervex's studio at Neuilly, which had a music room like a chapel, and I now went to live there with my children, and in this studio I used to work all day, and sometimes all night too, with my faithful friend Hener Skene, who was a pianist of great talent and indefatigable energy for work. We used often to begin to work in the morning, and as the daylight never penetrated into this studio, which was hung round with my blue curtains and lit by arc lamps, we had no idea of the passing of time. Sometimes I used to say, "Don't you feel hungry? I wonder what time it is?" And we would look at the clock and find that it was four o'clock next morning! We were so interested in our work that we got into what the Hindus call "a state of static ecstasy."

I had a house in the garden for my children, governess and nurse, so that the music could never disturb them. There was a beautiful garden and in the spring and summer we danced with the doors of the studio wide open.

And in this studio we not only worked but played. L. delighted to give dinner parties and fêtes, and often the vast studio was turned into a tropical garden or a Spanish Palace, and there came all the artists and celebrated people in Paris.

One evening, I remember, Cécile Sorel, Gabriel d'Annunzio and myself improvising a pantomime, in which D'Annunzio showed great histrionic talent.

*　　*　　*

For many years I was prejudiced against him on account of my admiration for Duse, whom I imagined he had not treated well, and I refused to meet him. A friend had said to me, "May I bring D'Annunzio to see you?" and I replied, "No, don't, for I shall be very rude to him if I see him." But in spite of my wishes, he entered one day, followed by D'Annunzio.

Although I had never seen him before, when I saw this extraordinary being of light and magnetism I could only exclaim, "Soyez le bienvenu; comme vous êtes charmant!"

When D'Annunzio met me in Paris in 1912, he decided he would make my conquest. This was no compliment, as D'Annunzio wanted to make love to every well-known woman in the world and string them round his waist as the Indian strings his scalps. But I resisted on account of my admiration for Duse. I thought I would be the only woman in the world who would resist him. It was a heroic impulse.

When D'Annunzio wants to make love to a woman, every morning he sends a little poem to her with a little flower expressing the poem. Every morning at 8 o'clock I received this little flower, and yet I held to my heroic impulse!

One night (I had a studio then in the street near the Hotel Byron), D'Annunzio said to me with a peculiar accent: "I will come at midnight."

All day long I and a friend of mine prepared the studio.

We filled it with white flowers, with white lilies: all the flowers that one brings to a funeral. And we lit myriads of candles. D'Annunzio was *ébloui* at the sight of this studio, which was like a Gothic chapel, with all those candles burning and all those white flowers. He came in and we received him and led him to a divan heaped with cushions. First I danced for him. Then I covered him with flowers and put candles all round him, treading softly and rhythmically to the strains of Chopin's Funeral March. Gradually, one by one, I extinguished all the candles, leaving alight only those at his head and feet. He lay as if hypnotised. Then, still moving softly to the music, I put out the light at his feet. But when I advanced solemnly towards the one at his head, with a tremendous effort of will-power he sprang to his feet and with a loud shriek of terror rushed from the studio, while the pianist and I, helpless with laughter, collapsed in each other's arms.

The second time I resisted D'Annunzio was at Versailles. I invited him to dinner at the Trianon Palace Hotel. This was about two years later. We went out there in my automobile.

"Don't you want to come for a walk in the forest before déjeuner?"

"Oh, certainly, that would be lovely."

We took the automobile to the Forest of Marly, then left it in order to enter the woods. D'Annunzio was most ecstatic.

We strolled for awhile and then I suggested:

"Now let us go back to the déjeuner."

But we couldn't find the automobile. So we tried to find the Hotel Trianon and the déjeuner on foot. We walked and we walked and we walked, but we couldn't find the gate! Finally, D'Annunzio began to cry like a child: "I want my lunch! I want my lunch! I have a brain, and that brain wants to be fed. When I am famished, I can't go on!"

I comforted him as best I could, and finally we found the gate and got back to the hotel, where D'Annunzio ate a magnificent lunch.

The third time I resisted D'Annunzio was years afterwards during the war. I came to Rome and stayed at the Hotel Regina. By a strange chance, D'Annunzio had the room next to me. Every night he used to go and dine with the Marquesa Casatti. One night she invited me to dine. I went to the palace and walked into the antechamber. It was all done out in Grecian style and I sat there awaiting the arrival of the Marquesa, when I suddenly heard a most violent tirade of the most vulgar language you could possibly imagine directed at me. I looked round and saw a green parrot. I noticed he was not chained. I got up and leaped into the next salon. I was sitting there awaiting the Marquesa, when I suddenly heard a noise—brrrrr—and I saw a white bulldog. *He* wasn't chained, so I leaped into the next salon, which was carpeted with white bear rugs and had bear skins even on the walls. I sat down there and waited for the Marquesa. Suddenly I heard a hissing sound. I looked down and saw a cobra in a cage sitting up on end and hissing at me. I leaped into the next salon, all lined with tiger skins. *There* was a gorilla, showing its teeth. I rushed into the next room, the dining room, and there I found the secretary of the Marquesa. Finally the Marquesa descended for dinner. She was dressed in transparent gold pyjamas. I said:

"You love animals, I see."

"Oh, yes, I adore them,—especially monkeys," she replied, looking at her secretary.

Strange to say, after this exciting apéritif, the dinner passed off with the utmost formality.

After dinner we went back into the salon with the orangutan and the Marquesa sent for her fortune-teller. She arrived in a high, pointed hat and witch's cloak, and began to tell our fortunes with the cards.

And then D'Annunzio came in. (And pray how was the devil dressed? . . .)

D'Annunzio is very superstitious and believes in all fortune-tellers. This one told him the most extraordinary story. She said:

"You will fly in the air and do terrific deeds. You will fall and be at the gates of death. But you will go through death and go by death and will live to great glory."

To me she said:

"You are going to awaken the nations to a new religion and found great temples all over the world. You have most extraordinary protection, and whenever an accident is going to happen to you, great angels guard you. You will live to be a great age. You will live for ever."

After that we went back to the hotel. D'Annunzio said to me:

"Every night I am coming to your room at twelve o'clock. I have conquered all the women in the world, but I have yet to conquer Isadora."

And every night he came to my room at twelve o'clock.

And I said to myself:

"I am just going to be unique. I am going to be the only woman in the world to resist D'Annunzio."

He told me the most wonderful things about his life, his youth and his art.

"Isadore, je n'en peux plus! Prends moi, prends moi!"

I was so *bouleversée* by his genius that at this moment I never knew what to do, so I used to lead him gently out of my room into his own. This went on for about three weeks and then I was so mad that I simply rushed to the station and took the first train away.

He used to ask:

"Pourquoi ne peux-tu pas m'aimer?"

"A cause d'Eleanore."

At the Hotel Trianon D'Annunzio had a gold-fish which he loved. It was in a wonderful crystal bowl and D'Annunzio used to feed it and talk to it. The gold-fish would agitate its fins and open and shut its mouth as though to answer him.

One day when I was staying at the Trianon, I said to the maître d'hotel:

"Where is the gold-fish of D'Annunzio?"

"Ah, madame, sorrowful story! D'Annunzio went to Italy and told us to take care of it. 'This gold-fish,' he said, 'is so near to my heart. It is a symbol of all my happiness!' And he kept telegraphing: *How is my beloved Adolphus?* One day Adolphus swam a little more slowly round the bowl and ceased to ask for D'Annunzio. I took it and threw it out of the window. But there came a telegram from D'Annunzio: *Feel Adolphus is not well.* I wired back: *Adolphus dead. Died last night.* D'Annunzio replied: *Bury him in the garden. Arrange his grave.* So I took a sardine and wrapped it in silver paper and buried it in the garden and I put up a cross: Here lies Adolphus! D'Annunzio returned:

" 'Where is the grave of my Adolphus?'

"I showed him the grave in the garden and he brought many flowers to it and stood for a long time weeping tears upon it."

But one fête had a tragic dénouement. I had arranged the studio as a tropical garden with tables for two hidden among thick foliage and rare plants. By this time I was somewhat initiated into the different intrigues of Paris, so I was able to put together couples who I knew wished it, thus causing tears on the part of some of the wives. The guests were all in Persian costumes and we danced to a Gypsy orchestra. Among the guests were Henri Bataille and Berthe Bady, his celebrated interpreter, my friends of many years.

As I have said before, my studio was like a chapel, and hung round for about fifteen metres high with my blue curtains. But there was a little apartment on the high balcony which had been transformed by the art of Poiret into a veritable domain of Circe. Sable black velvet curtains were reflected on the walls in golden mirrors; a black carpet, and a divan with cushions of Oriental textures, completed this apartment, the windows of which had been sealed up and the doors of which were strange, Etruscan tomb-like apertures. As Poiret himself said on its completion, "Voilà des lieux où on ferait bien d'autres actes et on dirait bien d'autres choses que dans des lieux ordinaires."

This was true. The little room was beautiful, fascinating and, at the same time, dangerous. Might there not be some character in furniture which makes all the difference between virtuous beds and criminal couches, respectable chairs and sinful divans? At any rate, what Poiret had said was right. In that apartment one felt differently and spoke differently than was the case in my chapel-like studio.

On this particular evening the champagne flowed as freely as it always did when L. gave a fête. At two o'clock in the morning I found myself sitting on a divan in the Poiret room with Henri Bataille and, although he had always been to me as a brother, this evening, filled with the fascination of the place, he spoke and acted differently. And then, who should appear but L. When he saw Henri Bataille and me on the golden divan reflected in the endless mirrors, he flew to the studio, began to apostrophise the guests about me, and said that he was going away, never to return.

This had a somewhat damping effect upon the guests, but in a moment turned my mood from comedy to tragedy.

"Quick," I said to Skene, "play the Death of Iseult, or the evening will be spoilt."

Rapidly I discarded my embroidered tunic and changed into a white robe, while Skene at the piano played even more marvellously than usual, and then I danced until the dawn.

But that evening was to have a tragic sequel. In spite of our innocence, L. was never convinced of it, and swore he would never see me again. I pleaded in vain, and Henri Bataille, who was much disturbed over the incident, went so far as to send L. a letter. It was of no avail.

L. only consented to see me in an automobile. His curses fell upon my ears with the empty clanging of demon bells. Suddenly he stopped cursing, and opening the door of the auto, pushed me into the night. Alone I walked along the street for hours in a daze. Strange men made grimaces at me and murmured equivocal propositions. The world seemed suddenly transformed to an obscene Hell.

Two days later I heard that L. had left for Egypt.

CHAPTER TWENTY-FIVE

MY best friend and greatest comforter in those days was the musician, Hener Skene. He had a strange character, in that he despised success or personal ambition. He adored my art and was only happy when playing for me. He had the most extraordinary admiration for me of any one I have ever met. A marvellous pianist, with nerves of steel, he often played all night for me, Beethoven's Symphonies one night, on another the whole cycle of the Ring, from "Rheingold" to the "Götterdämmerung."

In January, 1913, we made a tournée in Russia together. A strange incident marked this trip. Arriving at Kieff one morning at daybreak, we took a sleigh to the hotel. Hardly awakened from sleep, suddenly I saw on either side of the road quite clearly, two rows of coffins, but they were not ordinary coffins, they were the coffins of children. I clutched Skene's arm.

"Look," I said, "all the children—all the children are dead!"

He reassured me.

"But there is nothing."

"What? Can't you see?"

"No: there is nothing but the snow—the snow heaped up on either side of the road. What a strange hallucination—it is fatigue."

That day, to rest me and calm my nerves, I went to a Russian bath. In Russia the baths are arranged with tiers of long wooden shelves in the hot rooms. I was lying upon one of these shelves and the attendant was out of the room, when suddenly the heat overcame me and I fell from the shelf to the marble floor beneath.

The attendant found me lying unconscious and they had to carry me back to the hotel. A doctor was sent for and diagnosed a slight concussion of the brain.

"You cannot possibly dance to-night—high fever—"

"But I have a horror of disappointing the public," and I insisted upon going to the theatre.

The programme was Chopin. Quite unexpectedly at the end of the programme I said to Skene:

"Play the Funeral March of Chopin."

"But why?" he asked. "You have never danced it."

"I don't know—play it."

I insisted so earnestly that he acceded to my wish and I danced to the March. I danced a creature who carries in her arms her dead, with slow, hesitating steps, towards the last resting place. I danced the descent into the grave and finally the spirit escaping from the imprisoning flesh and rising, rising towards the Light—the Resurrection.

When I finished and the curtain fell, there was a curious silence. I looked at Skene. He was deathly pale and trembling. He took my hands in his. They were icy.

"Never ask me to play that again," he pleaded. "I experienced death itself. I even inhaled the odour of white flowers—funeral flowers—and I saw coffins of children—coffins—"

We were both shaken and unnerved, and I believe that some spirit gave us that night a singular premonition of what was to come.

When we returned to Paris in April, 1913, Skene played this March again for me at the Trocadero at the end of a long performance. After a religious silence, the public remained awed, and then applauded wildly. Some women were weeping—some almost hysterical.

Probably the past, the present and the future are like a long road. Beyond each turn the road exists, only we cannot see it, and we think this is the future, but the future is there already waiting for us.

After the vision of the Funeral March in Kieff I began to experience a strange sense of coming evil, which depressed me. I gave some representations upon my return to Berlin, and again I was under a certain spell to compose a dance of one going forward in the world suddenly crushed by a terrible blow, and the wounded rising after this cruel stroke of Fate to, perhaps, a new hope.

My children, who had been staying with Elizabeth during my tour in Russia, were brought to me in Berlin. They were in wonderful health and spirits, and danced about, the very expression of joy. Together we returned to Paris, to my vast house in Neuilly.

Once again I was at Neuilly, living with my children. Often I stood upon the balcony, unknown to her, and watched Deirdre composing dances of her own. She also danced to poems of her own composition—the little childish figure in the great blue studio, with the sweet, childish voice saying, "Now I am a bird, and I fly so, so high among the clouds"; and, "Now I am a flower looking up to the bird and swaying, so, so." Watching her exquisite grace and beauty, I dreamed that she, perhaps, would carry on my School as I imagined it. She was my best pupil.

Patrick was also beginning to dance, to a weird music of his own. Only he would never allow me to teach him. "No," he would say solemnly, "Patrick will dance Patrick's own dance alone."

Living there at Neuilly, working in the studio, reading for hours in my library, playing in the garden with my children or teaching them to dance, I was quite happy, and dreaded any more tours which would separate me from the children.

As they became more beautiful each day, so it became more difficult for me to have the courage to leave them. I had always prophesied a great Artist to come who would combine the two gifts of creating music and dancing simultaneously, and when my little boy danced, it seemed to me that he might become the one who would create the new dance born from the new music.

Not only was I allied to these two adorable children by the poignant tie of flesh and blood, but I also had with them a higher bond to an almost superhuman degree, the tie of Art. They were both passionately fond of music and would beg to remain in the studio when Skene played or I worked, when they would sit so quiet, with such intense faces, that I was sometimes frightened that beings so young should exhibit so serious an attention.

I remember one afternoon that great artist Raoul Pugno was playing Mozart. The children entered on tip-toe and stood on either side of the piano as he played. When he had finished they each, with one accord, put their blonde heads under his arms and gazed at him with such admiration that he was startled and exclaimed:

"From whence come these angels—Mozart's angels—" at which they laughed and climbed on his knees and hid their faces on his beard.

I gazed at the beautiful group with tender emotion, but what if I had known then how near were all three to that shadowy land "from whence no traveller returns."

This was the month of March. I was dancing alternately at the Châtelet and the Trocadero, but in spite of the fact that every relative touchstone of my life bespoke happiness, I suffered continually from a strange oppression.

Again one night at the Trocadero I danced Chopin's Funeral March with Skene playing the organ, and again I felt over my forehead that icy breath and smelt the same

strong scent of white tuberoses and funeral flowers.
Deirdre, a lovely white figure in the central box, when she
saw me dancing this, suddenly wept as if her little heart
would break, and cried out, "Oh, why should my Mama be
so sad and sorry?"

This was the first faint note of the Prelude of the Tragedy
which presently was to end all hopes of any natural, joyous
life for me—for ever after. I believe that although one may
seem to go on living, there are some sorrows that kill. One's
body may drag along its weary way on earth, but one's
spirit is crushed—for ever crushed. I have heard people
speak of the ennobling influence of sorrow. I can only say
that those last few days of my life, before the blow fell, were
actually the last days of my spiritual life. Ever since then
I have had only one desire—to fly—to fly—to fly from the
Horror of it, and my life has been but a series of weird
flights from it all, resembling the sad Wandering Jew, the
Flying Dutchman; and all life has been to me but as a
phantom ship upon a phantom ocean.

By some strange coincidence, the psychic happening often
finds its reflection in material objects. Poiret, when he
designed for me that exotic and mysterious apartment of
which I have spoken, had placed on each golden door a
double black cross. At first I found this design only original
and bizarre, but little by little these black double crosses
began to affect me in a curious manner.

As I have said, notwithstanding all the seemingly fortunate circumstances of my life, I had been living under a
strange oppression—a sort of sinister foreboding, and now
I suddenly found myself at night awaking with a start and
a feeling of fright. I kept a night light burning, and one
night, by its dim glow I saw emerging from the double black
cross which faced my bed a moving figure, draped in black,
which approached the foot of the bed and gazed at me with

pitiful eyes. For some moments I was transfixed with horror, then I turned on the lights full, and the figure vanished; but this curious hallucination—the first of the kind that I had ever had—occurred again and then again, at intervals.

I was so troubled by this that one night at a dinner given by my kind friend, Mrs. Rachel Boyer, I confided in her. She was alarmed, and, with her usual good-heartedness, insisted on telephoning at once for her doctor. "For," she said, "you must have some sickness of the nerves."

The young and handsome Dr. René Badet arrived. I told him of these visions.

"Your nerves are evidently over-strained: you must go for some days into the country."

"But I am giving recitals under contract in Paris," I replied.

"Well, go to Versailles—it is so near you will be able to motor in, and the air will do you good."

The next day I told this to the children's dear nurse, who was very pleased. "Versailles will be so good for the children," she said.

So we packed a few valises and were about to start forth when there appeared at my gate, and slowly advanced up the path, a slender figure draped in black. Was it my overwrought nerves, or was this the same figure that emerged nightly from the double cross? She came up to me.

"I have run away," she said, "only to see you. I have been dreaming of you lately and felt I must see you."

Then I recognised her. It was the ancient Queen of Naples. Only a few days before I had taken Deirdre to see her. I said:

"Deirdre, we are going to see a Queen."

"Oh, then, I must wear my robe de fête," said Deirdre, for so she called a little dress Poiret had made for her, an elaborate thing with many embroidered ruffles.

I had spent some time in teaching her to make a real Court curtsey and she was delighted, only at the last moment she burst into tears and said, "Oh, Mama, I am afraid to go and see a real Queen."

I believe poor little Deirdre thought she would be obliged to enter a real Court, as in a Fairy Pantomime, but when, in the great little house on the edge of the Bois she was presented to the slight, exquisite woman with her white hair braided in a crown, she made a brave attempt to do her Court curtsey, and then laughing, flew into the outstretched Royal arms. She had no fear of the Queen, who was all goodness and grace.

This day when she came in her mourning veil, I explained to her that we were departing for Versailles, and the reason. She said she would be very pleased to come with us—it would be an adventure. On the way, with a sudden tender gesture, she took my two little ones in her arms and held them to her bosom, but when I saw those two blonde heads enshrouded in black, again I experienced that strange oppression that had so often affected me lately.

At Versailles we had a merry tea with the children and then I escorted the Queen of Naples back to her dwelling. I have never met a sweeter, more sympathetic or more intelligent spirit than the sister of the ill-fated Elizabeth.

Awaking in the lovely park of the Trianon Hotel next morning, all my fears and forebodings were dissipated. The doctor was right, it was the country I needed. Alas, if the Chorus of the Greek Tragedy had been there! They might have cited an instance that often by taking the opposite road to avoid misfortune, we walk straight into it, as was the case of the unhappy Œdipus. If I had never gone to Versailles to escape the prophetic vision of Death that was over me, the children would not, three days later, have met their death on that same road.

I remember that evening so well, for I danced as never before. I was no longer a woman, but a flame of joy—a fire—the sparks that rose, the smoke whirling from the hearts of the public— And, as a farewell, after a dozen encores, I danced last of all the "Moment Musical," and as I danced it seemed to me that something sang within my heart "Life and Love—the Highest Ecstasy—and all are mine to give—are mine to give to those who need them." And suddenly it seemed as if Deirdre were sitting on one of my shoulders and Patrick on the other, perfectly balanced, in perfect joy, and as I looked from one side to another in my dance, I met their laughing, bright baby faces—baby smiles—and my feet were never tired.

* * *

After that dance I had a great surprise. Lohengrin, whom I had not seen from the time of his departure for Egypt, some months before, came into my loge. He seemed deeply affected by my dancing that evening and by our meeting, and proposed to join us at supper at Augustin's apartment in the Champs Elysées Hotel. We returned and waited before the spread table. Moments passed—an hour passed—he did not come. This attitude threw me into a state of cruel nervousness. In spite of the fact that I knew he had not taken that Egyptian trip alone, I had been deeply glad to see him, for I loved him always and longed to show him his own son, who had grown strong and beautiful in his father's absence. But when three o'clock came and he had not arrived, bitterly disappointed I left to rejoin the children at Versailles.

After the emotion of the performance and the wearing nervousness of waiting, I was worn out and, throwing myself into my bed, I slept profoundly.

I was awakened early next morning when the children came in, as was their custom, to leap upon my bed with shouts of laughter. Then, as was our habit, we had breakfast together.

Patrick was more than usually boisterous, and amused himself by turning over the chairs and as each chair fell he shouted with joy.

Then a singular thing happened. The night before some one, whose identity I have never known, sent me two beautifully bound copies of the works of Barbey d'Aurevilly. I reached out my hand and took up one of these volumes from the table beside me. I was about to chide Patrick for making over-much noise, when, by hazard, I opened the book, and my eye fell on the name "Niobe," and then these words:

Belle, et mère d'enfants dignes de toi, tu souriais quand on te parlait de l'Olympe. Pour te punir, les flèches des Dieux atteignirent les têtes dévouées de tes enfants, que no protégea pas ton sein découvert.

Even the nurse said, "Please, Patrick, don't make such a noise; you annoy Mama."

She was a sweet, good woman, the most patient in the world, and she adored both children.

"Oh, let him be," I cried, "think what life would be, nurse, without their noise."

And the direct thought came to me—How empty and dark would life be without them, for more than my Art and a thousand times more than the love of any man, they had filled and crowded my life with happiness. I read further:

Quand il ne resta plus de poirine à percer que la tienne, tu la tournas avidement du côté d'où venaient les coups . . . et tu attendis! Mais en vain, noble et malheureuse femme. L'arc des Dieux était détendu et se jouait de toi.—

Tu attendis ainsi,—toute la vie,—dans un désespoir tranquille et sombrement contenu. Tu n'avais pas jeté les cris familiers aux poitrines humaines. Tu devins inerte, et l'on raconte que tu fus changée en rocher pour exprimer l'inflexibilité de ton cœur;—

And then I closed the book, for a sudden fear caught me at the heart. I opened my arms and called both children to me and, as my arms closed about them, I felt sudden tears—for I remember every word and gesture of that morning. How often on sleepless nights I have gone over and over each moment of it, and wondered hopelessly why some vision had not warned me, to prevent what was to come.

It was a mild grey morning. The windows were open on the park, where the trees were putting on their first blossoms. I felt for the first time that year the peculiar rush of joy which comes over us in the first soft spring days, and between the delight of spring and the sight of my children, so rosy and lovely and happy, I had such a great emotion of joy that I suddenly jumped out of bed and began to dance with them, all three of us bubbling with laughter. The nurse looked on smiling, too.

Suddenly the telephone rang. It was L.'s voice, asking me to come to town to meet him and bring the children. "I want to see them." He had not seen them for four months.

I was delighted to think this would bring about the reconciliation I longed for, and I whispered the news to Deirdre.

"Oh, Patrick," she cried, "where do you think we are going to-day?"

How often I hear the childish voice, "Where do you think we are going to-day?"

My poor, fragile, beautiful children, if I had known that day what a cruel fate would find you. Where, where did you go that day?

And then the nurse said, "Madame, I think it's going to rain—perhaps they had better stay here."

How often, as in a horrible nightmare, I have heard her warning and cursed my unconsciousness of it. But I thought the meeting with L. would be so much simpler if the children were there.

On the way in the automobile on that last ride from Versailles to Paris, holding the little forms in my arms, I was filled with new hope and confidence in life. I knew that when L. saw Patrick he would forget all his personal feelings against me and I dreamed that our Love might go on to create some really great purpose.

Before leaving for Egypt, L. had bought an important piece of land in the centre of Paris and meant to build there a Theatre for my School. A Theatre that would be a meeting place and a haven for all the great Artists of the world. I thought that Duse would find there a fitting frame for her divine art, and that here Mounet-Sully would be able to realise his long cherished ambition to play the trilogy of "Œdipus," "Rex Antigone" and "Œdipus at Colonnus" in sequence.

All this I thought of on that drive to Paris and my heart was light with great hopes of Art. That Theatre was fated never to be built, nor Duse to find the Temple worthy of her, and Mounet-Sully died without ever realising his wish to give the trilogy of Sophocles. Why is it that the Artist's hope is almost always an unfulfilled dream?

It was as I thought. L. was delighted to see his little boy again, and Deirdre, whom he tenderly loved. We had a very gay luncheon at an Italian restaurant, where we ate much spaghetti, drank Chianti and talked of the future of the wonderful theatre.

"It will be Isadora's Theatre," L. said.

"No," I replied, "it will be Patrick's Theatre, for Patrick

is the Great Composer, who will create the Dance to the Music of the Future."

When the lunch was finished L. said, "I feel so happy to-day, why not go to the Salon des Humoristes?"

But I had an engagement to rehearse, so L. took our young friend H. de S., who was with us, while I, with the children and the nurse, returned to Neuilly. When we were before the door I said to the nurse:

"Will you come in with the children and wait?"

But she said, "No, Madame, I think we had better return. The little ones need rest."

Then I kissed them and said, "I will also return soon." And then, in leaving, little Deirdre put her lips against the glass window. I leaned forward and kissed the glass on the spot where her lips were at that moment. The cold glass gave me an uncanny impression.

I entered my great studio. It was not yet time for the rehearsal. I thought to rest a while and mounted to my apartment, where I threw myself down on the couch. There were flowers and a box of bonbons that some one had sent me. I took one in my hand and ate it lazily, thinking— "Surely, after all, I am very happy—perhaps the happiest woman in the world. My Art, success, fortune, love, but, above all, my beautiful children."

I was thus lazily eating sweets and smiling to myself, thinking, "L. has returned, all will be well," when there came to my ears a strange, unearthly cry.

I turned my head. L. was there, staggering like a drunken man. His knees gave way—he fell before me—and from his lips came these words:

"The children—the children—are dead!"

*   *   *

I remember a strange stillness came upon me, only in my throat I felt a burning, as if I had swallowed some live coals.

But I could not understand. I spoke to him very softly; I tried to calm him; I told him it could not be true.

Then other people came, but I could not conceive what had happened. Then entered a man with a dark beard. I was told he was a doctor. "It is not true," he said, "I will save them."

I believed him. I wanted to go with him, but people held me back. I know now that this was because they did not wish me to know that there was indeed no hope. They feared the shock would make me insane, but I was, at that time, lifted to a state of exaltation. I saw every one about me weeping, but I did not weep. On the contrary, I felt an immense desire to console every one. Looking back it is difficult for me to understand my strange state of mind. Was it that I was really in a state of clairvoyance, and that I knew that death does not exist—that those two little cold images of wax were not my children, but merely their cast-off garments? That the souls of my children lived in radiance, but lived for ever?

Only twice comes that cry of the mother which one hears as without one's self—at birth and at death. For when I felt in mine those little cold hands that would never again press mine in return, I heard my cries—the same cries as I had heard at their births. Why the same? Since one is the cry of supreme joy and the other of sorrow. I do not know why, but I know they are the same. Is it not that in all the Universe there is but one great cry containing Sorrow, Joy, Ecstasy, Agony—the Mother Cry of Creation?

* * *

How many times we go forth in the morning on some light errand and, passing the black, sinister procession of a Christian burial, we shudder and think of all our loved ones, and will not let the thought creep in that one day we shall be the mourners in such a black procession.

From my earliest childhood I have always felt a great antipathy for anything connected with churches or Church dogma. The readings of Ingersoll and Darwin, and Pagan philosophy had strengthened this antipathy. I am against the modern code of marriage, and I think the modern idea of a funeral is ghastly and ugly to a degree of barbarism. As I had the courage to refuse marriage and to refuse to have my children baptised, so now I refused to admit in their death the mummery of what one calls Christian burial. I had one desire—that this horrible accident should be transformed into beauty. The unhappiness was too great for tears. I could not weep. Crowds of friends came to me weeping. Crowds of people stood in the garden and the street weeping, but I would not weep, only I expressed a strong will that these people who came to show their sympathy in black should be transformed to beauty. I did not put on black. Why change one's dress? I have always held the wearing of mourning to be absurd and unnecessary. Augustin, Elizabeth and Raymond sensed my wish and they built in the studio a huge mound of flowers, and when I was conscious the first thing I heard was the Colonne orchestra playing the beautiful lament of Gluck's "Orphée."

But how difficult it is in one day to change ugly instincts and to create beauty. If I had had my wish there would have been no sinister black-hatted men, no hearses, none of the useless ugly mummery which makes of Death a macabre horror instead of exaltation. How splendid was the act of Byron in burning Shelley's body on the pyre by the sea! But I could only find in our civilisation the less beautiful alternative of the Crematorium.

How I wanted when parting from the remains of my children and their sweet nurse some gesture, some last radiance. Surely the day will come when the Intelligence of the World will finally revolt at these ugly rites of the Church, and create and participate in some final ceremony of beauty for their dead. Already the Crematorium is a great advance on the ghastly habit of putting bodies in the ground. There must be many who feel as I do, but of course my endeavour to express this was criticised and resented by many orthodox religionists, who considered that because I wanted to say farewell to my loved ones in Harmony, Colour, Light and Beauty, and because I brought their bodies to the Crematorium instead of putting them in the earth to be devoured by worms, I was a heartless and terrible woman. How long must we wait before some intelligence will prevail among us in Life, in Love—in Death?

I arrived at the dismal crypt of the Crematorium and saw before me the coffins which entombed the golden heads, the clinging, flower-like hands, the swift little feet of all I loved —now to be consigned to the flames—to remain hereafter but a pathetic handful of ashes.

I returned to my Neuilly studio. I had some definite plan to end my own life. How could I go on—after losing the children? Only it was the words of the little girls of my School, who stood around me—"Isadora, live for us. Are we not also your children?"—that awakened me to the task of soothing the grief of these other children, who stood there weeping their hearts out for the death of Deirdre and Patrick.

If this sorrow had come to me much earlier in life, I might have overcome it; if much later, it would not have been so terrible, but at that moment, in the full power and energy of life, it completely shattered my force and power. If a great love had then enveloped me and carried me away— but L. did not respond to my call.

Raymond and his wife Penelope were leaving for Albania

to work among the refugees. He persuaded me to join them there. I left with Elizabeth and Augustin for Corfu. When we arrived in Milan to spend the night, I was shown into the same room in which I had spent such hours of conflict four years before, debating the birth of little Patrick, and now he had been born, had come with the angel face of my dream in St. Marco, and had gone.

When I looked again into the sinister eyes of the lady of the portrait, who seemed to say, "Is it not as I predicted —all leads to death?"—I experienced such a violent horror that I rushed down the corridor and begged Augustin to take me to another hotel.

We took the boat from Brindisi and shortly after, one lovely morning, arrived in Corfu. All nature was glad and smiling, but I could find no comfort in it. Those who were with me say that for days and weeks I sat only staring before me. I took no account of time—I had entered a dreary land of greyness where no will to live or move existed. When real sorrow is encountered there is for the stricken, no gesture, no expression. Like Niobe turned to stone, I sat and longed for annihilation in death.

L. was in London. I thought if he would only come to me perhaps I could escape from this ghastly, death-like coma. Perhaps if I could feel warm, loving arms about me I might come to life.

One day I asked that no one should disturb me. In my room with the windows darkened I lay flat on my bed with my hands clasped on my breast. I had arrived at the last limit of despair, and I repeated over and over again a message to L.

"Come to me. I need you. I am dying. If you do not come I will be following the children."

I repeated this like a sort of Litany, over and over again.

When I rose I found it was midnight. After that I slept painfully.

The next morning Augustin awakened me with a telegram in his hand.

"For God's sake send news of Isadora. Will start at once for Corfu. L."

The days that followed I waited with the first glimmer of hope I had had out of the darkness.

One morning L. arrived, pale and agitated.

"I thought you were dead," he said.

And then he told me that on the afternoon that I had sent him the message I had appeared to him, a vaporous vision at the foot of his bed and told him in just the words of my message, so oft repeated—"Come to me—Come to me—I need you—if you do not come I will die."

When I had the proof of this telepathic bond between us, I had the hope also that by a spontaneous love gesture the unhappiness of the past might be redeemed to feel again that stirring in my bosom; that my children might return to comfort me on earth. But it was not to be. My intense yearning—my sorrow—were too strong for L. to stand. One morning he left abruptly, without warning. I saw the steamer receding from Corfu, and knew that he was on board. I saw the steamer receding over the blue waters and I was left once more alone.

Then I said to myself—Either I must end life at once, or I must find some means to live in spite of the constant gnawing anguish that day and night devour me. For every night—awake or asleep—I lived over that terrible last morning, heard Deirdre's voice, "Guess where we are going to-day"—heard the nurse say: "Madame, perhaps they had better not go out to-day," and heard my frenzied reply, "You are right. Keep them, good Nurse, keep them, do not let them go out to-day."

Raymond came from Albania. He was, as usual, filled with enthusiasm. "The whole country is in need. The villages devastated; the children starving. How can you stay here in your selfish grief? Come and help to feed the children—comfort the women."

His pleading was effective. Again I put on my Greek tunic and sandals and followed Raymond to Albania. He had the most original methods of organising a camp for the succour of the Albanian refugees. He went to the market-place in Corfu and bought raw wool. This he loaded on a little steamer he had hired, and carried it to Santi Quaranta, the chief port for the refugees.

"But Raymond," I said, "how are you going to feed the hungry with raw wool?"

"Wait," said Raymond, "you will see. If I brought them bread it would only be for to-day; but I bring them wool, which is for the future."

We landed on the rocky coast of Santi Quaranta where Raymond had organised a centre. A sign said, "Who wants to spin wool, will receive a drachma a day."

A line of poor, lean, famished women was soon formed. With the drachma they would receive yellow corn, which the Greek Government was selling in the port.

Then Raymond piloted his little boat again to Corfu. There he commanded carpenters to make for him weaving looms, and returning to Santi Quaranta, "Who wants to weave spun wool in patterns for one drachma a day?"

Crowds of the hungry applied for the task. These patterns Raymond furnished them from ancient Greek vase designs. Soon he had a line of weaving women by the sea and he taught them to sing in unison with their weaving. When the designs were woven they turned out to be beautiful couch covers, which Raymond sent to London to be sold at 50 per cent profit. With this profit he started a bakery

ISADORA DUNCAN
With her children Deirdre and Patrick
From a photograph by Otto, Paris.

and sold white bread 50 per cent cheaper than the Greek Government was selling yellow corn, and so he started his village.

We lived in a tent by the sea. Each morning at sunrise we dipped in the sea and swam. Now and then Raymond had a surplus of bread and potatoes, so we went over the hills to the villages and distributed the bread to the hungry.

Albania is a strange, tragic country. There was the first altar to Zeus the Thunderer. He was called Zeus the Thunderer because in this country—winter and summer— are continual thunder storms and violent rains. Through these storms we trudged in our tunics and sandals, and I realised that to be washed by the rain is really more exhilarating than to walk in a mackintosh.

I saw many tragic sights. A mother sitting under a tree with her baby in her arms and three or four small children clinging to her—all hungry and without a home; their house burnt, the husband and father killed by the Turks, the flocks stolen, the crops destroyed. There sat the poor mother with her remaining children. To such as these Raymond distributed many sacks of potatoes.

We returned to our camp weary, yet a strange happiness crept into my spirit. My children were gone, but there were others—hungry and suffering—might I not live for those others?

It was in Santi Quaranta, where there were no coiffeurs, that I first cut off my hair and threw it into the sea.

When my health and strength came back, this life among the refugees became impossible for me. No doubt there is a great difference between the life of the artist and that of the Saint. My artist life awoke within me. It was quite impossible, I felt, with my limited means, to stop the flood of misery represented by the Albanian refugees.

CHAPTER TWENTY-SIX

ONE day I felt that I must leave this country of many mountains, great rocks and storms. I said to Penelope:

"I feel I can no longer look at all this misery. I have a longing to sit in a mosque with one quiet lamp—I long for the feeling of Persian carpets beneath my feet. I am tired of these roads. Will you come with me on a little flight to Constantinople?"

Penelope was delighted. We changed our tunics for quiet dresses and took the boat for Constantinople. During the day I remained in my cabin on deck, and at night, when the other passengers were asleep, I slipped a scarf over my head and stepped out of my door into the moonlit night. Leaning over the side of the ship, also moon-gazing, was a figure dressed entirely in white, even to white kid gloves— the figure of a young man, holding in his hand a little black book, from which he appeared from time to time to read, then murmur what seemed to be an invocation. His face, white and drawn, was lit by two magnificent dark eyes, and crowned by jet black hair.

On my approach the stranger spoke to me.

"I dare to address you," he said, "because I have a sorrow as great as your own, and I am returning to Constantinople to comfort my mother, who is in great affliction. A month ago she had the news of the tragic suicide of my eldest brother and, barely two weeks later, followed another tragedy—the suicide of my second brother. I am the only one remaining to her. But how can I be of any consolation to her? I who am myself in so desperate a mood that I feel the happiest thing would be to follow my brothers."

We talked together and he told me he was an actor, and the little book in his hand was a copy of "Hamlet," which part he was then studying.

We met again upon the deck the next evening, and like two unhappy ghosts, each immersed in his own thoughts, yet each finding some comfort in the presence of the other, we remained there till the dawn.

When we reached Constantinople he was met and embraced by a tall, handsome woman in deepest mourning.

Penelope and I descended at the Peira Palace Hotel and spent the first two days of our visit wandering about Constantinople, chiefly in the old town among the narrow streets. On the third day I had an unexpected visitor. It was the mother of my sorrowful friend of the boat, the woman who had met him. She came to me in the greatest anguish. She showed me the pictures of her two beautiful sons whom she had lost and said, "They are gone, I cannot bring them back, but I have come to beg you to help me save the last—Raoul. I feel he is following his brothers."

"What can I do," I said, "and in what way is he in danger?"

"He has left the city and is at the little village of San Stefano, quite alone in a villa, and from his desperate expression as he left I can only fear the worst. You made such a deep impression on him that I think you might make him see the wickedness of his action, make him pity his mother and return to life."

"But what is the reason of his desperation?" I asked.

"I do not know, any more than I know the reason for the suicide of his brothers. Beautiful, young, fortunate, why did they only seek death?"

Very much touched by the mother's appeal, I promised to go to the village of San Stefano and do what I could to bring Raoul to reason. The hall porter told me the road was rough and almost impossible for an auto. So I went down to the Port and hired a little tug-boat. There was a wind and the waters of the Bosporus were very choppy, but we arrived safely at the little village. By his mother's directions I found Raoul's villa. It was a white house standing in a garden in a lonely spot near the ancient cemetery. There was no bell. I knocked, but received no answer. I tried the door, and finding it open, I entered. The room on the ground floor was empty, so I ascended a short flight of stairs and, opening another door, found Raoul in a little white-washed room, with white walls and floors and doors. He was lying on a white-covered couch, dressed as I had seen him on the boat, in his white suit, with immaculate white gloves. Near the couch was a small table upon which stood a crystal vase in which was a white lily and, beside it, a revolver.

The boy himself, who, I believe, had not eaten for two or three days, was in a far-away land where my voice could hardly reach him. I tried to shake him into life, telling him of his mother, how her heart had been lacerated by the death of his brothers, and finally I managed to take him by the hand and pull him by sheer force down to my little waiting boat—carefully leaving the revolver behind.

On the way back he wept continuously and refused to go back to his mother's house, so I persuaded him to come to my rooms at the Peira Palace, where I tried to draw from him the reason of his extreme grief, for it seemed to me that even the death of his brothers could not account for his state. At last he murmured:

"No, you are right: it is not the death of my brothers: it is Sylvio."

"Who is Sylvio? Where is she?" I asked.

"Sylvio is the most beautiful being in the world," he

replied. "He is here in Constantinople with his mother."

On learning that Sylvio was a boy, I was rather aghast; but, as I have always been a student of Plato and, indeed, consider his "Phædrus" the most exquisite love song ever written, I was not as shocked as some people might have been. I believe the highest love is a purely spiritual flame which is not necessarily dependent on sex.

But I was determined at any cost to save the life of Raoul, so instead of making any further remark I simply asked:

"What is Sylvio's telephone number?"

Soon I heard Sylvio's voice on the wire—a sweet voice which seemed to me to come from a sweet soul. "You must come here at once," I said.

Shortly after he appeared. He was a lovely youth of about eighteen. So might Ganymede have looked when he disturbed the emotions of the mighty Zeus himself.

And when this feeling continues and he is nearer to him and embraces him, in gymnastic exercises and at other times of meeting, then the fountain of that stream, which Zeus when he was in love with Ganymede named Desire, overflows upon the lover, and some enters into his soul, and some when he is filled flows out again; and as a breeze or an echo rebounds from the smooth rocks and returns whence it came, so does the stream of beauty, passing through the eyes, which are the windows of the soul, come back to the beautiful one; there arriving and quickening the passages of the wings, watering them and inclining them to grow, and filling the soul of the beloved also with love. And thus he loves, but he knows not what; he does not understand and cannot explain his own state; he appears to have caught the infection of blindness from another; the lover is his mirror in whom he is beholding himself, but he is not aware of this.

(Jowett)

We dined and spent the evening together. Later, on the

balcony overlooking the Bosporus, I had the pleasure of seeing Raoul and Sylvio in soft, confidential conversation, which assured me that the life of Raoul was saved for the moment. I telephoned to his mother and told her of the success of my efforts. The poor woman was overcome with joy and could hardly express her gratitude to me.

That night when I bade my friends good-night, I felt that I had done a good deed in saving the life of this beautiful boy, but a few days later the distracted mother again came to me.

"Raoul is back at the villa in San Stefano. You must save him once more."

I thought that this was rather a tax on my good nature, but I could not resist the appeal of the poor mother. This time, however, as I had found the boat rather rough, I risked the road and took an auto. Then I called up Sylvio and told him he must come with me.

"Now what is the reason of all this dementia?" I asked him.

"Well, it is like this," said Sylvio. "I certainly love Raoul, but I cannot say I love him as much as he loves me, so he says he would rather not live."

We set out at sunset and after many bumps and shakings arrived at the villa. We took it by storm and again carried the melancholy Raoul back to the Hotel where, with Penelope, we discussed until long into the night how to find an effective remedy for the strange sickness which affected Raoul.

The next day as Penelope and I wandered in the old streets of Constantinople, in a dark, narrow lane, Penelope pointed to a sign. It was written in Armenian, which she could translate, and said that here lived a fortune-teller.

"Let us consult her," said Penelope.

We entered an old house and, after ascending a winding

stair and traversing many passages of ancient, crumbling
filth, in a back room we found a very old woman crouched
over a cauldron from which arose strange odours. She was
an Armenian but spoke some Greek so Penelope could understand her, and she told us how, in the last massacre by
the Turks, she had, in this room, witnessed the dreadful
slaughter of all her sons, daughters and grandchildren,
even to the last little baby, and from that moment she had
become clairvoyant and could see into the future.

"What do you see in my future?" I asked her, through
Penelope.

The old woman looked for a while into the smoke of the
cauldron, then uttered some words which Penelope translated for me.

"She greets you as the daughter of the Sun. You have
been sent on earth to give great joy to all people. From
this joy will be founded a religion. After many wanderings,
at the end of your life, you will build temples all over the
world. In the course of time you will return to this city
where, too, you will build a temple. All these temples will
be dedicated to Beauty and Joy because you are the daughter
of the Sun."

At the time, this poetical prophecy seemed curious to me,
considering my then condition of sorrow and despair.

Then Penelope asked: "What will be my future?"

She spoke to Penelope, and I noticed that the latter turned
pale and seemed terribly frightened.

"What has she said to you?" I asked.

"What she says is very disquieting," Penelope answered.
"She says I have a little lamb, she means my boy Menalkas.
She says, 'You wish for another little lamb,' that must be
the daughter I am always hoping for. But she says this
wish will never be realised. She also says that I shall soon
receive a telegram telling me that one I love is very ill and

another I love is near death. And after this," continued Penelope, "she says that my life will not be of long duration, but, in a high place, overlooking the world, I shall have my last meditation and leave this sphere."

Penelope was very much upset. She gave the old woman some money and, bidding her farewell, she took my hand and fairly ran along the passages, down the stairs and into the narrow street until we found a cab which took us back to the hotel.

As we entered, the porter came forward with a telegram. Penelope leaned upon my arm almost fainting. I had to lead her up to her room, where I opened the telegram. It read: "Menalkas very ill, Raymond very ill. Return at once."

Poor Penelope was distracted. Hurriedly we threw our things into the trunks and I asked when there would be a boat for Santi Quaranta. The porter said that one was leaving at sunset. But, even in our haste, I remembered the mother of Raoul and I wrote to her: "If you wish to save your boy from the danger that threatens him, he must leave Constantinople at once. Do not ask me why but, if possible, bring him to the boat upon which I am leaving this afternoon at five o'clock."

I received no answer and it was only as the boat left that Raoul, carrying a valise and looking more dead than alive, hurried up the gangway and came on board. I asked him if he had a ticket or a cabin, but he had thought of neither. However, these boats of the Orient are amiable and accommodating and I was able to arrange with the Captain that, as there was no cabin available, Raoul should sleep in the sitting-room of my suite, for I really felt for this boy a mother's anxiety.

On arriving at Santi Quaranta we found Raymond and Menalkas stricken with fever. I did my best to persuade

Raymond and Penelope to leave this gloomy land of Albania and come back with me to Europe. I brought the ship's doctor to use his influence, but Raymond refused to leave his refugees or his village, and Penelope would not, of course, leave him. So I was forced to leave them on that desolate rock, with only a little tent to protect them, over which a perfect hurricane was blowing.

The steamer went on towards Trieste and both Raoul and I were very unhappy, his tears never ceasing to flow. I had telegraphed for my car to meet us at Trieste as I dreaded the contact of other passengers on the train, and we motored northward through the mountains to Switzerland.

Here we stopped for a while on the Lake of Geneva. We were a curious couple, each immersed in his own sorrow and, perhaps, for that reason we found each other good company. We spent days in a little boat on the lake, and finally I extracted from Raoul a sacred promise that, for his mother's sake, he would never again think of attempting suicide.

So, one morning, I saw him off on the train, to return to his theatre, and I have never seen him since. But I heard later that he had a very successful career, making a great impression by his characterisation of Hamlet, and that I could understand; for who could say those lines, "To be or not to be," with more understanding of them than poor Raoul? However, he was so very young that I hope he has found happiness since.

Left by myself in Switzerland, I was overcome by a feeling of great weariness and melancholy. I could no longer stay in one place for any time, but, devoured by restlessness, I travelled all through Switzerland in my motor-car and, finally, following an irresistible impulse, drove back to Paris. I was quite alone, for the society of any one else had become impossible for me. Even the company of my brother Augustin, who had joined me in Switzerland, had no power to break the spell which bound me. At last I arrived at such a pitch that even the sound of a human voice had become obnoxious to me, and when people came into my room they seemed to be far away and unreal. So I arrived in Paris one night at the door of my house in Neuilly. The place was deserted except for an old man who looked after the garden and lived in the porter's lodge at the gate.

I entered my great studio and, for a moment, the sight of my blue curtains recalled my Art and my work and I resolved to endeavour to come back to it. To this end I sent for my friend Hener Skene to play for me, but the sound of the familiar music only had the effect of throwing me into fits of weeping. Indeed, I now cried for the first time. Everything about the place brought back only too keenly days when I had been happy. Soon I had the hallucination of hearing the children's voices in the garden, and when, one day, I chanced to enter the little house in which they had lived, and saw their clothes and toys scattered about, I broke down completely and realised that it would be impossible for me to stay in Neuilly. Still I made some efforts and called some of my friends to me.

But at night I could not sleep and I knew that the river was too perilously near to the house, so one day, unable to stand this atmosphere any longer, I again took my auto and set forth on my way to the South. Only when I was in the car and going at seventy or eighty kilometres an hour could I get any relief from the indescribable anguish of the days and nights.

I went over the Alps and down into Italy and continued my wanderings, sometimes finding myself in a gondola on the canals of Venice, asking the gondolier to row all night, another time in the ancient town of Rimini. I spent one night in Florence where I knew that C. was living, and I felt a great desire to send for him, but knowing that he was now married and settled down to a domestic life, I thought his presence would only cause discord and I refrained.

One day, in a little town by the sea, I received a telegram which read, "Isadora, I know you are wandering through Italy. I pray you come to me. I will do my best to comfort you." It was signed Eleanora Duse.

I have never known how she discovered my whereabouts to send the telegram, but when I read the magic name, I knew that Eleanora Duse was the one person whom I might wish to see. The telegram was sent from Viareggio, just on the opposite side of the promontory from where I was. I started at once in my auto, after sending a grateful reply to Eleanora to announce my arrival.

The night I reached Viareggio there was a great storm. Eleanora was living in a little villa far out in the country, but she had left a message at the Grand Hotel asking me to come to her.

CHAPTER TWENTY-SEVEN

THE next morning I drove out to see Duse, who was living in a rose-coloured villa behind a vineyard. She came down a vine-covered walk to meet me, like a glorious angel. She took me in her arms and her wonderful eyes beamed upon me such love and tenderness that I felt just as Dante must have felt when, in the "Paradiso," he encounters the Divine Beatrice.

From then on I lived at Viareggio, finding courage from the radiance of Eleanora's eyes. She used to rock me in her arms, consoling my pain, but not only consoling, for she seemed to take my sorrow to her own breast, and I realised that if I had not been able to bear the society of other people, it was because they all played the comedy of trying to cheer me with forgetfulness. Whereas Eleanora said:

"Tell me about Deirdre and Patrick," and made me repeat to her all their little sayings and ways, and show her their photos, which she kissed and cried over. She never said, "Cease to grieve," but she grieved with me, and, for the first time since their death, I felt I was not alone. For Eleanora Duse was a super-being. Her heart was so great it could receive the tragedy of the world, her spirit the most radiant that has ever shone through the dark sorrows of this earth. Often when I walked with her by the sea, it seemed to me that her head was among the stars, her hands reached to the mountain tops.

Looking up to the mountain, she once said to me:

"See the stern rough sides of the Croce, how sombre and forbidding they seem beside the tree-covered slopes of the Ghilardone, the sunny vines and lovely flowering trees. But if you look to the top of the dark rough Croce you will perceive a gleam of white marble waiting for the sculptor to give it Immortality, whereas the Ghilardone produces only the wherewithal for man's earthly needs—the other his dream. Such is the Artist's life—dark, sombre, tragic but giving the white marble from which spring Man's aspirations."

Eleanora loved Shelley and sometimes at the end of September, in the frequent storms, when a flash of lightning broke over the sullen waves, she would point to the sea, saying:

"Regard—the ashes of Shelley flash—he is there, walking over the waves."

As I was pestered by strangers always staring at me in the Hotel, I took a villa. But what made me choose such a place? A large, red brick house set far back in a forest of melancholy pine trees, and enclosed within a great wall. And if the outside was sad, the interior was of a melancholy that defies description. It had been inhabited, so the village legend ran, by a lady who, after an unhappy passion for a personage of high rank at the Austrian Court—some said Franz Joseph himself—had the further misfortune of seeing the son of their union go mad. At the top of the villa there was a small room with barred windows, the walls painted in fantastic designs and a small, square aperture in the door through which food had evidently been handed to the poor young madman when he became dangerous. On the roof was a great open loggia, looking over the sea on one side and the mountains on the other.

This gloomy abode, which contained at least sixty rooms, it was my fancy to rent. I think it was the enclosed pine forest and the wonderful view from the Loggia that attracted me. I asked Eleanora if she would not like to live there with me but she refused politely, and moving in from her summer villa, took a little white house near by.

Now Duse had the most extraordinary peculiarity as to correspondence. If you were in another country she might only send you a long telegram from time to time in three years, but, living near by, she sent a charming little word almost every day and sometimes two or three in the day, and then we would meet and often walk by the sea, when Duse would say, "The Tragic Dance promenades with the Tragic Muse."

One day Duse and I were walking by the sea when she turned to me. The setting sun made a fiery halo about her head. She gazed at me long and curiously.

"Isadora," she said in a choking voice, "don't, don't seek happiness again. You have on your brow the mark of the great unhappy ones of the earth. What has happened to you is but the Prologue. Do not tempt Fate again."

Ah, Eleanora, if I had but heeded your warning! But Hope is a hard plant to kill and no matter how many branches are knocked off and destroyed, it will always put forth new shoots.

Duse was then a magnificent creature, in the full power of her life and intelligence. When she walked along the beach she took long strides, walking unlike any other woman I have ever seen. She wore no corset, and her figure, at that time very large and full, would have distressed a lover of fashion, but expressed a noble grandeur. Everything about her was the expression of her great and tortured soul. Often she read to me from the Greek tragedies, or from Shakespeare, and when I heard her read certain lines of Antigone I thought what a crime it was that this splendid interpretation was not being given to the world. It is not true that Duse's long retirement from the stage in the fulness and ripeness of her Art was due, as some people prefer to think, to an unhappy love or some other sentimental reason, nor even to ill-health, but she had not the help or the capital necessary to carry out her ideas of Art as she wished—that is the simple, shameful truth. The world that "loves Art" left this greatest actress of the world to eat her heart out in solitude and poverty for fifteen long years. When Morris Gest finally came to the realisation of this and arranged a tournée for her in America, it was too late, for she died on that last tour, pathetically endeavouring to amass the money necessary for her work, for which she had waited all those long years.

* * *

I hired a grand piano for the villa, and then I sent a telegram to my faithful friend Skene, who joined me at once. Eleanora was passionately fond of music and every evening he played for her Beethoven, Chopin, Schumann, Schubert. Sometimes she would sing in a low, exquisitely toned voice, her favourite song, "In questa tomba oscura, lascia mia pianga," and, at the last words—"Ingrata—Ingrata"—her tone and looks took on such a deeply tragic and reproachful expression that one could not look at her without tears.

One day at dusk, I rose suddenly, and asking Skene to play, I danced for her the Adagio from the Sonata Pathétique of Beethoven. It was the first gesture I had made since the 19th of April, and Duse thanked me by taking me in her arms and kissing me.

"Isadora," she said, "what are you doing here? You must return to your Art. It is your only salvation."

Eleanora knew that I had received, a few days before, an offer of a contract to tour South America.

"Accept this contract," she urged me, "if you knew how short life is and how there can be long years of ennui, ennui —nothing but ennui! Escape from the sorrow and ennui— escape!"

"Fuir, fuir," she said, but my heart was too heavy. I could make some gestures before Eleanora, but to go again before a public seemed to me impossible. My whole being was too tortured—every heart-beat only crying out for my children. As long as I was with Eleanora I was comforted, but the night in this lonesome villa, with the echoes from all its empty, gloomy rooms, I passed in waiting for the morning. Then I would rise and swim out into the sea. I thought I would swim so far that I should be unable to return, but always my body of itself turned landward—such is the force of life in a young body.

One grey, autumn afternoon, I was walking alone along the sands when, suddenly, I saw going just ahead of me the figures of my children Deirdre and Patrick, hand in hand. I called to them but they ran laughing ahead of me just out of reach. I ran after them—followed—called—and suddenly they disappeared in the mist of the sea-spray. Then a terrible apprehension came upon me. This vision of my children—was I mad? I had for some moments the distinct feeling that I was then with one foot over the line which divides madness from sanity. I saw before me the Asylum—the life of dreary monotony, and in bitter despair I fell upon my face and cried aloud.

I don't know how long I had lain there when I felt a pitying hand on my head. I looked up and saw what I thought to be one of the beautiful contemplation figures of the Sistine Chapel. He stood there, just come from the sea, and said:

"Why are you always weeping? Is there nothing I can do for you—to help you?"

I looked up.

"Yes," I replied. "Save me—save more than my life—my reason. Give me a child."

That night we stood together on the roof of my villa.

The sun was setting beyond the sea, the moon rising and flooding with sparkling light the marble side of the mountain, and when I felt his strong youthful arms about me and his lips on mine, when all his Italian passion descended on me, I felt that I was rescued from grief and death, brought back to light—to love again.

The next morning when I recounted all this to Eleanora, she did not seem at all astonished. Artists live so continally in a land of Legend and Fantasy that, for the youth of Michael Angelo to come from the sea to comfort me, seemed to her quite natural and, although she hated meeting strangers, she even graciously consented that I should present to her my young Angelo, and we visited his studio—for he was a sculptor.

"You really think he is a genius?" she asked me, after viewing his work.

"Without a doubt," I replied, "and probably he will be a second Michael Angelo."

Youth is wonderfully elastic. Youth believes in everything, and I almost believed that my new love would conquer sorrow. Then I was so tired of the constant horrible pain. There was a poem of Victor Hugo's that I used to read constantly, and I finally persuaded myself, "Yes, they will come back; they are only waiting to return to me." But alas! this illusion did not last long.

It seemed that my lover belonged to a strict Italian family and he was engaged to a young girl who also belonged to a strict Italian family. He had not told me this, but one day he explained it to me in a letter and then said farewell. But I was not at all angry with him. I felt he had saved my reason, and then I knew I was no longer alone; and from this moment I entered into a phase of intense mysticism. I felt that my children's spirits hovered near me—that they would return to console me on earth.

As the autumn approached, Eleanor moved to her apartment in Florence and I also abandoned my gloomy villa. I went first to Florence and then to Rome, where I planned to spend the winter. I spent Christmas in Rome. It was sad enough, but I said to myself: "Nevertheless I am not in the tomb or the mad-house—I am here." And my faithful friend Skene remained with me. He never questioned, never doubted—only gave me his friendship and adoration—and his music.

Rome is a wonderful city for a sorrowful soul. At a time when the dazzling brightness and perfection of Athens would have made my pain more acute, Rome, with its great ruins, tombs and inspired monuments, witness of so many dead generations, was an anodyne. Especially I liked to wander in the Appian Way at early morning when, between the long rows of tombs the wine carts came in from Frascati with their sleeping drivers like tired fauns reclining on the wine barrels. Then it seemed to me that time ceased to exist. I was as a ghost who had wandered on the Appian Way for a thousand years, with the great spaces of the Campagna and the great arch of Raphael's sky above. Sometimes I lifted my arms to this sky and danced along—a tragic figure between the rows of tombs.

At night Skene and I wandered forth and stopped often by the many fountains that never cease to flow from the prodigal springs of the mountain. I loved to sit by the fountain and hear the water rippling and splashing. Often I would sit there weeping silently, my gentle companion holding my hands in sympathy.

From these sad wanderings I was awakened one day by a long telegram from L. beseeching me in the name of my Art to return to Paris, and under the influence of this message I took the train for Paris. On the way we passed Viareggio. I saw the roof of the red brick villa among the pines and thought of the months of alternate despair and hope I had spent there and of my divine friend Eleanora, whom I was leaving.

L. had ready for me a magnificent suite of rooms at the Crillon, overlooking the Place de la Concorde, and filled with flowers. When I told him of my Viareggio experience and my mystic dream of the children's reincarnation and return to earth, he hid his face in his hands and after what seemed a struggle, he said:

"I came to you first in 1908 to help you but our love led us to tragedy. Now let us create your School, as you wish it, and some beauty on this sad earth for others."

Then he told me he had bought the great Hotel at Bellevue with its terrace overlooking all Paris and its gardens sloping to the river and rooms for a thousand children. It only depended on me for the School to exist for all time.

"If you are willing to leave all personal feeling aside and, for the time being, to exist only for an idea," he said.

Seeing what a tangled mesh of sorrow and catastrophe this life had brought me, in which only my Idea always shone bright and untarnished above it all, I consented.

The next morning we visited Bellevue and, from then on, decorators, furnishers were busy under my direction, transforming this rather banal hotel to a Temple of the Dance of the Future.

There were fifty new aspirants chosen from a concours in the centre of Paris, there were the pupils of the first school, the governesses.

The dancing-rooms were the dining-rooms of the old hotel, hung with my blue curtains. In the centre of the long room I built a platform with stairs leading down from it, and this platform could be used for the spectators or by the authors who sometimes tried their works there. I had come to the conclusion that the monotony and languor of life

in an ordinary school is partly caused by the floors being
all on the same level. Therefore, between many of the
rooms I made little passages leading up on one side and
again leading down. The dining-room was arranged like
the English House of Commons in London, with rows of
seats in tiers going up on either side, the older pupils and
teachers on the higher seats and the children below.

In the midst of this moving, bubbling life I once more
found the courage to teach, and the pupils learned with the
most extraordinary rapidity. In three months from the
opening of the school, they had made such progress that
they were the wonder and admiration of all the artists who
came to see them. Saturday was the Artists' Day. A public
lesson for artists was given in the morning from eleven to
one o'clock and then, with L.'s usual prodigality, there was
a great lunch served for the artists and children together.
As the weather grew finer it was served in the garden, and
after lunch there was music, poetry and dancing.

Rodin, whose house was on the opposite hill, at Meudon,
paid us frequent visits. He would sit in the dancing-room
making sketches of the young girls and children as they
danced. Once he said to me:

"If I had only had such models when I was young!
Models who can move, and move according to Nature and
Harmony! I have had beautiful models, it is true, but never
one who understood the science of movement as your pupils
do."

I bought for the children many-coloured capes and when
they left the School to walk in the woods, as they danced and
ran, they resembled a flock of beautiful birds.

I believed that this school at Bellevue would be permanent
and that I should spend there all the years of my life, and
leave there all the results of my work.

In the month of June we gave a Festival at the Trocadero.

I sat in a loge watching my pupils dance. At certain parts of the programme the audience rose and shouted with enthusiasm and joy. At the close they applauded at such length that they would not leave. I believe that this extraordinary enthusiasm for children who were in no wise trained dancers or artists, was enthusiasm for the hope of some new movement in humanity which I had dimly foreseen. These were indeed the gestures of the Vision of Nietzsche:

"Zarathustra the dancer, Zarathustra the light one, who beckoneth with his pinions, one ready for flight, beckoning unto all birds, ready and prepared, a blissfully light-spirited one."

These were the future dancers of the Ninth Symphony of Beethoven.

CHAPTER TWENTY-EIGHT

LIFE at Bellevue began in the morning with a burst of joy. One heard little feet rushing along the corridors —children's voices singing together. When I descended I found them in the dancing-room, and when they saw me they shouted "Good morning, Isadora." Who could be morose in such an atmosphere? And though often, when I looked among them for two little missing faces, I went to my room to weep alone, still I found the courage each day to teach them, and the lovely grace of their dancing encouraged me to live.

In 100 A.D. there stood on one of the hills of Rome a school, known as the "Seminary of Dancing Priests of Rome." The pupils of this school were chosen from the most aristocratic families, and not only that, but they had to possess an ancestral lineage dating back many hundreds of years, during which no stain had fallen upon it. Although they were taught all the arts and philosophies, dancing was their chief expression. They would dance in the theatre at the four seasons of the year, Spring, Summer, Autumn and Winter. On these occasions they descended from their hill to Rome, where they took part in certain ceremonies and danced before the people for the purification of those who beheld them. These boys danced with such happy ardour and purity, that their dance influenced and elevated their audience as medicine for sick souls. It was of such expression that I dreamed when I first formed my School, and I believed that Bellevue, standing on an Acropolis near Paris might have the same significance to that city and its artists as the School of the Dancing Priests of Rome.

A band of artists came every week to Bellevue with their sketch-books, for the School was already proving to be a source of inspiration from which hundreds of sketches and many models of dancing figures, which exist to-day, were inspired. I dreamed that through this School there might come a new ideal for the relation between the artist and his model, and through the influence of the forms of my pupils moving to the music of Beethoven and César Franck, dancing the Chorus of the Greek Tragedy, or reciting Shakespeare, the model would no longer be that poor little dumb creature one sees sitting in the studios of artists, but a living, moving ideal of the highest expression of life.

To further these hopes, L. now visualised the possibility of building the theatre which had been so tragically interrupted, on the hill of Bellevue, of making it a Festival Theatre to which the people of Paris would come on great fête days, and of endowing it with a Symphonic Orchestra.

Once more he called to him the Architect Louis Sue, and the models of the theatre, which had been abandoned, were again set up in the library, and the foundations were already marked out. In this theatre I hoped to realise my dream of again bringing together the arts of music, tragedy and dancing, in their purest forms. Here Mounet-Sully, Eleanora Duse or Suzanne Desprès would play Œdipus or Antigone, or Electra, while the pupils of my school would dance the Chorus. Here, too, I hoped to celebrate the Centenary of Beethoven with the Ninth Symphony and a thousand of my pupils. I pictured a day when the children would wend their way down the hill like Pan Athene, would embark on the river and, landing at the Invalides, continue their sacred Procession to the Panthéon and there celebrate the memory of some great statesman or hero.

I spent hours every day teaching my pupils, and when I was too tired to stand, I reclined on a couch and taught them by the movements of my hands and arms. My powers of teaching seemed indeed to border on the marvellous. I had only to hold out my hands towards the children and they danced. It was not even as though I taught them to dance, but rather as if I opened a way by which the Spirit of the Dance flowed over them.

We were planning a performance of the "Bacchæ" of Euripides, and my brother Augustin, who was to play the part of Dionysus, and who knew it by heart, would read it to us every night, or one of Shakespeare's plays, or Byron's "Manfred"; and D'Annunzio, who was enthusiastic about the School, often lunched or dined with us.

The small group of the pupils from the first school, who were now tall young girls, aided me in teaching the little ones, and it was a very touching sight for me to see the great change that had taken place in them, and with what confidence and knowledge they passed on my teachings.

But in the month of July of that year 1914, a strange oppression came over the earth. I felt it, and the children felt it too. When we were on the terrace overlooking the city of Paris, the children were often silent and subdued. Huge black clouds gathered in the sky. An uncanny pause seemed to hang over the land. I sensed it, and it seemed to me that the movements of the babe I bore were weaker, not so decided as those of the others had been.

I suppose I was also very tired from the effort I had made to change grief and mourning into new life, and as the month of July advanced L. suggested that he should send the School to England to spend the vacation at his house in Devonshire, So one morning they all trooped in, two by two, to say good-bye to me. They were to spend August by the sea and return in September. When they had all gone, the house seemed strangely empty and in spite of all my struggles, I fell a prey to a deep depression. I was very

tired, and would sit for long hours on the terrace overlooking Paris, and it seemed to me more and more that
some danger loomed from the East.

Then one morning, came the sinister news of the assassina-
tion of Calmette, which threw the whole of Paris into a state
of disquietude and apprehension. It was a tragic event—
the forerunner of the greater tragedy. Calmette had always
been a good friend to my Art and my School, and I was much
shocked and saddened by this news.

I felt restless and full of fears. Now that the children
were gone, Bellevue seemed so vast and quiet, and the great
dancing-room seemed so melancholy. I tried to calm my
fears with the thought that the baby would soon be born,
the children would return and Bellevue be again a centre
of life and joy, but the hours dragged along, until one
morning my friend Dr. Bosson, who was our guest at the
time, came in with a very white face, holding a newspaper
in his hand where I read the headlines telling of the assassi-
nation of the Archduke. Then came rumours, and, shortly
after, the certainty of war. How true it is that coming
events cast their shadows before them. Now I knew that
the dark shadow I had felt hanging over Bellevue for the
last month, was the war. While I had been planning the
renaissance of the Art of the Theatre, and festivals of great
human joy and exaltation, other forces had been planning
war, death and disaster, and alas! what was my small force
against the onrush of all this?

It was on the first of August that I felt the first pangs of
childbirth. Beneath my windows they were calling the news
of the mobilisation. It was a hot day and the windows were
open. My cries, my sufferings, my agony were accompanied
by the rolling of the drums and the voice of the Crier.

My friend Mary brought a cradle into the room, all
hung with white muslin. I kept my eyes on the cradle. I

was convinced that Deirdre or Patrick was coming again to me. The drums continued. Mobilisation—War—War. Is there War? I wondered. But my child must be born and it was so hard for him to come into the world. A stranger doctor took the place of my friend Bosson who had received his orders to join the army and had left. The doctor kept on saying, "Courage, Madame." Why say "Courage" to a poor creature torn with horrible pain? It would have been much better if he had said to me, "Forget that you are a woman; that you should bear pain nobly, and all that sort of rot, forget everything, scream, howl, yell—" or better still if he had been humane enough to give me some champagne. But this doctor had his system, which was to say "Courage, Madame." The nurse was upset and kept on saying, "Madame, c'est la guerre—c'est la guerre." I thought, "My baby will be a boy, but he will be too young to go to the war."

Finally I heard the baby's cry—he cried—he lived. Great as had been my fear and horror in that terrible year, it was now all gone in one great shock of joy. Mourning and sorrow and tears, long waiting and pain all made up for by one great moment of joy. Surely if there is a God He is a great stage director. All those long hours of mourning and fear were transformed to joy when they placed a beautiful boy baby in my arms.

But the drums continued, "Mobilisation—War—War."

"Is there War?" I wondered. "What do I care? My baby is here, safe in my arms. Now let them make war— What do I care?"

So egotistical is human joy. Outside my window and door was a running to and fro and voices—the weeping of women—calls—discussions as to the mobilisation, but I held my child and dared, in the face of this general disaster, to feel gloriously happy, borne up to the Heavens with the transcendental joy of again holding my own child in my arms.

Evening came. My room was filled with people rejoicing about the baby who lay on my arm. "Now you will be happy again," they said.

Then, one by one they left, and I was alone with the baby. I whispered, "Who are you, Deirdre or Patrick? You have returned to me." Suddenly the little creature stared at me and then gasped, as if choking for breath, and a long whistling sigh came from his icy lips. I called the nurse—she came, looked, and snatched the baby up in her arms in alarm, and from the other room I heard calls for oxygen—hot water—

After an hour of anguished waiting, Augustin came in and said:

"Poor Isadora—your baby—has died—"

I believe that in that moment I reached the height of any suffering that can come to me on earth, for in that death it was as if the others died again—it was like a repetition of the first agony—with something added.

My friend Mary came, and, weeping, took the cradle away. In the next room I heard hammer taps closing the little box which was my poor baby's only cradle. These hammer taps seemed to strike on my heart the last notes of utter despair. As I lay there, torn and helpless, a triple fountain of tears, milk and blood flowed from me.

A friend came to see me and said: "What is your personal sorrow? Already the war is claiming hundreds—already the wounded and dying are being sent back from the Front." So it seemed only natural to me to give Bellevue for a Hospital.

For in those days of the war every one felt the same enthusiasm. That marvellous message of defiance, the wonderful enthusiasm that was to lead to miles of devastated

country and graveyards, who can say whether it was right
or wrong? Certainly at the present moment it seems to
have been rather useless, but how can we judge? And
Romain Rolland sitting in Switzerland, above it all, calling
upon his pale and thoughtful head the curses of some and
the blessings of others.

At any rate, from that moment, we were all flame and
fire, and even the artists said, "What is Art? The boys are
giving their lives, the soldiers are giving their lives—what
is Art?" And if I had had any intelligent sense at that
time, I should have said, "Art is greater than life," and
would have remained in my studio creating Art. But I
went with the rest of the world and said, "Take all these
beds, take this house that was made for Art, and make a
hospital to nurse the wounded."

One day two stretcher-bearers came to my room and asked
me if I would like to see my hospital. As I could not walk,
they carried me on a stretcher from room to room. In each
room I saw that my bas-reliefs of Bacchantes and Dancing
Fauns and Nymphs and Satyrs had been taken down from
the walls, as well as all my draperies and curtains, and, in
the place of the bas-reliefs were cheap effigies of a black
Christ on a golden cross, supplied by one of the Catholic
Stores which turned out thousands of these during the war.
I thought of the poor wounded soldiers on their first awakening, and how much more cheerful for them to have seen the
rooms as they were before. Why should they see this poor,
black Christ stretched upon a golden cross? What a melancholy sight for them.

In my wonderful dancing-room the blue curtains had disappeared and there were endless rows of cots waiting for
the suffering men. My library, where poets had stood on
the shelves for the initiated, was now turned into an operat-
ing theatre, waiting for the martyrs. In my then weakened

state all these sights affected me deeply. I felt that Dionysus had been completely defeated. This was the reign of Christ after the Crucifixion.

Shortly after this, one day I heard the first heavy steps of the stretcher-bearers, bringing in the wounded.

Bellevue! My Acropolis, that was to have been a fountain of inspiration, an Academy for the higher life inspired by philosophy, poetry and great music. From that day Art and Harmony vanished, and within your walls were heard my first cries—the cries of the wounded Mother and of the baby who had been frightened from this world by the War Drum. My Temple of Art was turned into a Calvary of Martyrdom and, in the end, into a charnel house of bloody wounds and death. Where I had thought of strains of heavenly music, there were only raucous cries of pain.

Bernard Shaw says that as long as men torture and slay animals and eat their flesh, we shall have war. I think all sane, thinking people must be of his opinion. The children of my School were all vegetarians and grew strong and beautiful on a vegetable and fruit diet. Sometimes during the war when I heard the cries of the wounded I thought of the cries of the animals in the slaughter house, and I felt that as we torture these poor defenceless creatures so the gods torture us. Who loves this horrible thing called War? Probably the meat eaters, having killed, feel the need to kill —kill birds, animals—the tender stricken deer—hunt foxes.

The butcher with his bloody apron incites bloodshed, murder. Why not? From cutting the throat of a young calf to cutting the throat of our brothers and sisters is but a step. While we are ourselves the living graves of murdered animals, how can we expect any ideal conditions on the earth?

* * *

When I could be moved, Mary and I left Bellevue for the

sea. We went through the War Zone and, when I gave my name, were treated with the greatest courtesy. When a sentry on duty said, "It is Isadora, let her pass," I felt it was the greatest honour I had ever received.

We went to Deauville and found rooms at the Hotel Normandie. I was very tired and ill, and glad to find this haven of rest. But weeks passed and I remained in a discouraging state of languor, and so weak that I could hardly walk out on the beach to breathe the fresh breeze of the ocean. At last, feeling that I was really ill, I sent to the hospital for the doctor.

To my astonishment he did not come, but sent back an evasive answer, and having no one to attend to me, I remained at the Hotel Normandie too ill to make any plans for my future.

At that time the hotel was a refuge for many distinguished Parisians. Next to our rooms were those of the Comtesse de la Beraudiére who had as her guest the poet Comte Robert de Montesquiou and after dinner we often heard his light falsetto voice reciting his poems, and, amidst the constant news of war and carnage that reached us, it was wonderful to listen to him proclaiming with ecstasy the power of Beauty.

Sacha Guitry was also a guest at the Normandie and every evening in the hall he entertained a delighted audience with his irrepressible fund of stories and anecdotes.

Only as every courier from the Front reached us with news of the World Tragedy, there was a sinister hour of realisation.

But this life soon became distasteful to me, and, as I was too ill to travel, I rented a furnished villa. This villa was called "Black and White," and in it everything, rugs, curtains, furniture, was black and white. When I took it, I thought it very chic, and did not realise until I tried to live in it, how depressing it could be.

So here I was, transported from Bellevue, with all its hope of my School, Art, Future New Life, to this little black and white house by the sea, alone, sick, desolate. But probably the worst of all was the illness. I could hardly find strength for a short walk on the beach. Autumn came with September storms. L. wrote me that they had taken my School to New York, hoping to find there a refuge during the war.

One day, feeling more than usually desolate, I went to the Hospital to seek the doctor who had refused to come to me. I found a short man with a black beard and, was it my imagination, or did he turn as if to fly when he saw me? I approached and said:

"Why, Doctor, what have you against me that you will not come to see me when I ask you? Don't you know that I am really ill and need you?"

He stammered some excuses, still with that haunted look, and promised to come the next day.

The next morning the autumn storms began. The sea was high, the rain poured down. The doctor came to the Villa "Black and White."

I was sitting there, vainly trying to light a wood fire, but the chimney smoked badly. The doctor felt my pulse and asked me the usual questions. I told him of my sorrow at Bellevue—of the baby who would not live. He continued to stare at me in the same hallucinated manner.

Suddenly he clutched me in his arms and covered me with caresses.

"You are not ill," he exclaimed, "only your soul is ill—ill for love. The only thing that can cure you is Love, Love, and more Love."

Alone, weary and sorrowful, I could only feel very grate-

ful for this passionate and spontaneous burst of affection.
I looked into the eyes of this strange doctor and found love,
and I returned it with all the dolorous force of my wounded
soul and body.

Each day, after his work at the Hospital, he came to
my villa. He told me of the terrible experiences of the day,
of the sufferings of the wounded, the often hopeless operations—all the horrors of the horrible War.

Sometimes I went with him on night duty when the vast
Hospital at the Casino slept and only the central night light
burned. Here and there a wakeful martyr turned with weary
sighs and groans, and he went from one to another, giving
a word of comfort or something to drink, or a God-given
anæsthetic.

And after these hard days and pitiful nights this strange
man had need of love and passion, at the same time pathetic
and ferocious, and from these fiery embraces and hours of
maddening pleasure my body emerged healed and well, so
that now I could again walk beside the sea.

One night I asked this strange doctor why he had refused
to come to me at my first summons. He did not answer my
question, and a look of such pain and tragedy crept into his
eyes that I was afraid to pursue the subject. But my curiosity grew. There was some mystery. I felt that my past
was in some way connected with his refusal to answer my
question.

On the first of November, the Day of the Dead, I was
standing at the window of the villa when I noticed that the
garden plot, laid out in black and white stones had exactly
the aspect of two graves. This appearance of the garden
became a sort of hallucination, until I could not look at it
without shuddering. Indeed I seemed caught in a net of
suffering and death, alone all day in the villa or wandering
on the now cold and desolate sands. Train after train

arrived at Deauville with its tragic freight of wounded or dying. The once fashionable Casino, which, the season before, had resounded with Jazz Band and laughter, was transformed into a huge caravansary of suffering. I became more and more a prey to melancholy, and the passion of André became each night more sombre in its fantastic intensity. Often when I encountered that desperate regard of his, as of a man haunted by a terrible memory, he would respond to my questions, "When you know all, it will mean our separation. You must not ask me."

I awoke one night to find him bending over me, watching me in my sleep. The despair in his eyes was too terrible for me to suffer any longer.

"Tell me what it is," I begged. "I can no longer bear this sinister mystery."

He moved a few steps from me and stood with bent head gazing at me—a short, square man, with a black beard.

"Don't you know me?" he asked.

I looked. The mist cleared away. I gave a cry. I remembered. That terrible day. The doctor who came to me to bid me hope. He who had tried to save the children.

"Now you know," he said, "what I suffer. When you sleep you look so like your little girl as she lay there. And I tried so hard to save her—for hours from my mouth I endeavoured to give her my breath—my life—through her poor little mouth—to give her my life—"

His words caused ne such terrible pain that I cried helplessly the rest of the night, and his unhappiness seemed to equal my own.

From that night I realised that I loved this man with a passion I had myself ignored, but as our love and desire for one another increased, so also increased his hallucination, until again one night I awoke and found those terrible eyes of sorrow gazing at me, and I knew that the obsession that possessed him might lead us both to insanity.

The next day I walked along the beach, farther and farther, with a terrible desire never to return either to the melancholy Villa "Black and White" or to the death-like love that encompassed me there. I walked so far that it became dusk, and then quite dark, before I realised that I must return. The tide was coming in fast, and often I walked through the incoming waves. Although it was very cold, I felt a great desire to face them and walk straight into the sea, to end for ever the intolerable grief from which I could find no relief either in Art, in the rebirth of a child, or in love. In every effort to escape, I found only destruction, agony, death.

Half way to the villa, André met me. He had become very anxious, for, finding my hat, which I had dropped in my distraction on the beach, he had also thought that I had sought to end my pain in the waves. When after walking for miles, he saw me approaching, alive, he cried like a child. We walked back to the villa and tried to comfort one another, but we realised that our separation was absolutely necessary if we wished to retain our sanity, for our love, with its terrible obsession, could only lead to death or a madhouse.

And another thing happened to make my desolation even more intense. I had sent to Bellevue for a trunk of warm clothes. One day a trunk arrived at the villa, but the senders had made a mistake and, when I opened it, I found it contained the clothes of Deirdre and Patrick. When I saw them there, before my eyes once more—the little dresses they had last worn—the coats and shoes and little caps—I heard again that cry which I had heard when I saw them lying dead—a strange, long, wailing cry, which I did not recognise as my own voice—but as if some cruelly-hurt animal called its death-cry from my throat.

André found me there, unconscious, when he returned—lying over the open trunk with all the little garments clutched in my arms. He carried me into the next room and took the trunk away and I never saw it again.

CHAPTER TWENTY-NINE

WHEN England entered the war, L. transformed his château in Devonshire into a hospital and, to safeguard the children of my School, who were of all nationalities, he embarked them all for America. Augustin and Elizabeth, who were with the School in New York, sent me frequent telegrams to join them, so at last I decided to go.

André took me to Liverpool and put me on board a great Cunard liner bound for New York.

I was so sad and tired that all the way over I never left my cabin except at night, when I would emerge on deck while all the other passengers were sleeping, and when Augustin and Elizabeth met me in New York, they were shocked to see how changed and ill I was.

I found my School installed in a villa—a happy band of War Refugees. Taking a huge studio on Fourth Avenue and Twenty-third Street, I hung it about with my blue curtains, and we began work anew.

Coming from bleeding, heroic France, I was indignant at the apparent indifference of America to the War, and one night, after a performance at the Metropolitan Opera House, I folded my red shawl around me and improvised the "Marseillaise." It was a call to the boys of America to rise and protect the highest civilisation of our epoch—that culture which has come to the world through France. The next morning the newspapers were enthusiastic. One of them said:

"Miss Isadora Duncan earned a remarkable ovation at the close of her programme with an impassioned rendition of 'The Marseillaise,' when the audience stood and cheered her for several minutes. . . . Her exalted poses were imitative of the classic figures on the Arc de Triomphe in Paris. Her shoulders were bare, and also one side, to the waist line, in one pose, as she thrilled the spectators with representation of the beautiful figures (of Rude) on the famous arch. The audience burst into cheers and bravas at the living representation of noble art."

My studio soon became a rendezvous for all the poets and artists. From this moment my courage came back, and finding the newly built Century Theatre free, I leased it for the season and proceeded to create there my "Dionysion."

But the snobbish shape of this theatre angered me. In order to transform it into a Greek Theatre, I removed all the orchestra seats, and placed there a blue carpet on which the Chorus could circulate. I covered the ugly boxes with great blue curtains, and with a troupe of thirty-five actors, eighty musicians and a hundred singing voices, put on the tragedy of "Œdipus," with my brother Augustin in the title rôle and my School and myself as the Chorus.

My audience consisted mostly of people from the East Side who, by the way, are among the real lovers of Art in America to-day. The appreciation of the East Side so touched me that I went over there with my entire School and an orchestra, and gave a free performance in the Yiddish Theatre, and, if I had had the means, I would have remained there dancing for these people whose very soul is made for music and poetry. But alas! this great venture of mine proved a costly experiment, and landed me in complete bankruptcy. Appealing to some of New York's millionaires, I only received the answer: "But why do you wish to give representations of Greek Tragedy?"

At that moment all New York had the "jazz" dance craze. Women and men of the best society, old and young, spent their time in the huge salons of such hotels as the Biltmore, dancing the fox trot to the barbarous yaps and cries of the Negro orchestra. I was invited to one or two gala dances at the time, and could not restrain my indignation that this should be going on while France was bleeding and needing the help of America. In fact the whole atmosphere in 1915 disgusted me, and I determined to return with my School to Europe.

But now I lacked the wherewithal to pay for our tickets. I had reserved berths on the return boat, the *Dante Alighieri*, but had no money to pay for them. Three hours before the boat was to sail, I still lacked the necessary funds, when there entered my studio a young American woman, quietly dressed, who asked if we were leaving for Europe that day.

"You see," I said, pointing to the children in their travelling cloaks, "we are all ready but we have not yet found the money to complete payment for the tickets."

"How much do you need?" she asked.

"About two thousand dollars," I replied, at which this extraordinary young woman took out a pocketbook, counted out two notes of a thousand dollars each, and placed them on the table, saying:

"I am very delighted to help you in this small matter."

I looked in amazement at this stranger, whom I had never seen before, and who without asking for any acknowledgment even, placed this large sum of money at my disposal. I could only imagine that she must be some unknown millionaire. But afterwards I found that this was not true. Indeed, in order to place this money at my disposal, she had sold out her entire capital of stocks and bonds the day before.

With many others, she came to see us off at the boat. Her name was Ruth—Ruth who said: "Thy people shall be my people; thy ways as my ways." And such a Ruth she has been to me ever since.

Having been forbidden any further manifestations of the "Marseillaise" in New York, we all stood on the deck, each child with a little French flag hidden up its sleeve, and I had given the word that when the whistle blew and the ship left the shore, we should all wave our flags and sing the "Marseillaise," which we did with great joy to ourselves and to the great trepidation of the officials on the dock.

My friend Mary, who had come to see me off, could not, at the last moment, bear to part from me, and, without luggage or a passport, she leapt on to the deck and joined us in singing, and said, "I am coming with you."

And so, to the singing of the "Marseillaise" we left the rich, pleasure-loving America of 1915, and set sail for Italy, with my now nomadic school. We reached Naples on a day of great enthusiasm. Italy had decided to enter the war. We were all delighted to be back and had a charming fête in the country, and I remember that I addressed a crowd of staring peasants and working people surrounding us, "Thank God for your beautiful country and don't envy America. Here, in your wonderful land of blue skies and vines and olive trees, you are richer than any American millionaire."

In Naples we had a discussion as to our next destination. I wished very much to go to Greece with the idea of camping on Kopanos until the end of the war. But this idea frightened my elder pupils, as they were travelling on German passports, so I decided to seek refuge in Switzerland, where it would be possible to give a series of performances.

For this purpose we went to Zurich. Stopping at the Hôtel Bar du Lac, was the daughter of a well-known American millionaire. I thought this a wonderful opportunity to interest her in my school and one afternoon had the children dance for her on the lawn. They were such a lovely sight that I thought surely she would be touched, but when I approached her on the subject of helping my school, she replied, "Yes, they may be lovely, but they do not interest me. I am only interested in the analysis of my own soul." She had been studying for years with Dr. Jung, the disciple of the celebrated Freud, and she spent hours every day writing down the dreams she had had the night before.

That summer, in order to be near my pupils, I was at the Hôtel Beau Rivage in Ouchy. I had pretty rooms with a balcony on the lake. I took a sort of huge barrack which had served as a restaurant, and hanging around it the never-failing inspiration of my blue curtains, transformed it into a Temple where I taught the children, and danced every afternoon and evening.

One day we had the joy to receive Weingartner and his wife, and danced for him all the afternoon and evening Gluck, Mozart, Beethoven and Schubert.

From my balcony I used to see every morning assembled on another large balcony overlooking the lake a group of beautiful boys in shining silk kimonos. They seemed to centre about an older man—large, blond, with a form resembling Oscar Wilde. They used to smile at me from their balcony and one night they invited me to supper. I found them charming and gifted boys—war refugees, among whom at this supper was the handsome young Duke of S.

On other nights they took me in a motor boat on the romantic Lake Leman. The boat was effervescent with champagne. We generally landed at 4 o'clock in the morning at Montreux, where a mysterious Italian Count gave a four o'clock supper. This handsome, but rather hard, macabre beauty slept all day and only rose at night. Often he would take out of his pocket a little silver syringe and every one pretended not to notice while he deliberately injected it in his white thin arm. Afterwards his wit and gaiety knew no bounds, but they said he endured horrible sufferings in the daytime.

The amusing society of these charming youths diverted me in my otherwise sad and lonely state, but their evident indifference to feminine charms rather piqued my pride. I decided to put my powers to the test, and succeeded so well that one night, accompanied only by a young American friend, I started off with the leader of the band in a superb Mercedes car. It was a wonderful night. We sped along the shores of Lake Leman, flew past Montreux. I called out "Further, further," until finally, at dawn, we found ourselves at Viege. Still I cried "Further, further," and we sped up through the eternal snows and over the St. Gotthard Pass.

I laughed to think of my friend's charming band of young beauties when they found to their consternation in the morning that their Sultan was gone, and with one of the abhorred sex, and I exerted all my powers of seduction, and soon we were descending into Italy. We did not stop until we arrived in Rome, and from Rome we went on to Naples. Then, when I glimpsed the sea, I had a burning desire to see Athens again.

We took a little Italian steamer, and one morning I found myself again ascending the white marble steps of the Propylæa, toward the temple of the divine and wise Athena. I remembered so vividly the last time I was there, and could not help feeling ashamed when I thought how terribly I had lapsed from wisdom and harmony in the interval, and alack! with what a price of suffering I had paid for the passion that had entranced me.

The modern town was in a tumult. The fall of Venezelos was proclaimed on the day after our arrival, and it was thought probable that the Royal Family would be on the side of the Kaiser. That night I gave a charming dinner-party, my guests including the Secretary of the King, M. Melas. In the centre of the table I had heaped red roses, and under them was hidden a little gramophone. In the same room was a group of high officials from Berlin. Suddenly we heard from their table the toast, "Hoch der Kaiser," at which I brushed aside the roses and started my gramophone, which began to play "The Marseillaise." At the same moment I proposed the toast, "Vive la France."

The King's secretary looked somewhat alarmed, but was really delighted, as he warmly espoused the cause of the Allies.

By this time a large crowd had assembled in the square before our open windows. Holding high above my head the picture of Veniselos and bidding my young American friend follow me with the gramophone, always bravely playing "The Marseillaise," we proceeded to the centre of the square where, to the music of the little instrument and the singing of the now enthusiastic crowd, I danced the Hymn of France. Afterwards I harangued the crowd:

"You have a second Pericles, the great Veniselos—why do you allow him to be troubled? Why do you not follow him? He only will lead Greece to its greatness."

We then formed a procession to the house of Veniselos and, standing under his windows sang alternately the Greek Hymn and "The Marseillaise," until soldiers with fixed bayonets unkindly dispersed our meeting.

After this episode, which had really delighted me, we took the boat back to Naples, and continued our journey to Ouchy.

From then on, until the end of the war, I made desperate efforts to keep my School together, thinking that the war would end and we should be able to return to Bellevue. But the war went on and I was obliged to borrow money from money-lenders at fifty per cent to pay for the upkeep of the School in Switzerland.

In 1916, for this purpose, I accepted a contract to go to South America, and set sail for Buenos Aires.

As I advance in these memoirs, I realise more and more the impossibility of writing one's life—or rather, the lives of all the different people I have been. Incidents which seemed to me to last a lifetime have taken only a few pages: intervals that seemed thousands of years of suffering and pain and through which, in sheer self-defence, in order to go on living, I emerged an entirely different person, do not appear at all long here. I often ask myself desperately, What reader is going to be able to clothe with flesh the skeleton that I have presented? I am trying to write down the truth, but the truth runs away and hides from me. How find the truth? If I were a writer, and had written of my life twenty novels or so, it would be nearer the truth. And then, after I had written these novels, I should have to write the story of the Artist, which would be a story quite apart from all the others. For my artist life and thoughts of Art have grown quite aloof, and grow still, like a separate organism, seemingly quite independent of what I call my Will.

Still here I am, trying to write the truth of all that happened to me and I greatly fear that it will turn out an awful mess. But there you are—I have begun the impossible task of putting this record of my life on paper and will go on with it to the end, although I can already hear the voices of all the so-called good women of the world saying: "A most disgraceful history." "All her misfortunes are only a just requital of her sins." But I am not conscious of having sinned. Nietzsche says, "Woman is a mirror," and I have only reflected and reacted to the people and forces that have seized me and, like the heroines of the "Metamorphoses" of Ovid, have changed form and character according to the decree of the immortal gods.

As the boat stopped at New York, Augustin, who did not like the idea of my travelling alone so far in wartime, joined me, and his company was a great comfort to me. On the boat there were also some young boxers, headed by Ted Lewis, who used to get up at six o'clock every morning to train, and then swim in the big salt-water swimming bath on board. I trained with them in the morning and danced for them at night, so the voyage was very gay and did not seem at all long. Maurice Dumesnil, the pianist, accompanied me on this voyage.

Bahia was my first experience of a semi-tropical town, and it seemed very soft, green and wet. Although it poured continually, the women walking along the streets in calico dresses soaked through and clinging to their forms, appeared to be quite oblivious to the rain, and did not seem to care whether they were wet or dry. This was also the first time that I had seen the mixture of black and white races taken with nonchalance. At one restaurant where we lunched, there was a black man at a table with a white girl, and at another table a white man with a black girl. In the small church were women carrying little naked mulatto babies to be christened.

In every garden bloomed the red hibiscus, and the whole town of Bahia teemed with the promiscuous love of black and white races. In some quarters of the town black, white and yellow women leaned lazily out of the windows of the houses of ill-fame, and seemed here to have none of the haggard or furtive looks which usually characterise the prostitutes of large cities.

* * *

A few nights after our arrival in Buenos Aires, we went to a Students' Cabaret. It was the usual long, low-ceilinged, very smoky room, overcrowded with dark young men interlaced with equally brunette girls, all dancing the tango. I had never danced the tango but the young Argentine who was our cicerone persuaded me to try. From my first timid steps I felt my pulses respond to the enticing languorous rhythm of this voluptuous dance, sweet as a long caress, intoxicating as love under southern skies, cruel and dangerous as the allurement of a tropical forest. All this I felt as the arm of this dark-eyed youth guided me with confidential pressure and now and then thrust the glance of his bold eyes into mine.

I was suddenly recognised and surrounded by the students, who explained that it was the night of the celebration of the Freedom of Argentina, and he begged me to dance their Hymn. As I always love to please students, I consented and after hearing the translation of the words of the Argentine Hymn, I wrapped the Argentine flag about me and endeavoured to represent for them the suffering of their once enslaved colony and its freeing itself from the Tyrant. My success was electric. The students, who had never seen this sort of dance before, shouted with enthusiasm and asked me to repeat the Hymn over and over again while they sang.

I returned to the hotel flushed with my success and delighted with Buenos Aires, but, alas! I rejoiced too soon. The next morning my Manager was furious at reading a sensational account of my performance in the papers, and informed me that according to law he considered my contract broken. All the best families in Buenos Aires were withdrawing their subscriptions, and would boycott my performances, and thus the soirée which had so delighted me was the ruin of my Buenos Aires tournée.

Art gives form and harmony to what in life is chaos and discord. A good novel works up artistically to a certain climax, and has no anti-climax. Love in Art ends, as for

Isolde, with a tragic and beautiful closing note, but Life is full of anti-climaxes, and a love affair in real life generally ends with a discord, and that in the very middle of a musical phrase, leaving a strident, clamorous dissonance. And often in real life a love affair after its culmination revives again only to die a miserable death on the tomb of financial reclamations and lawyers' fees.

I had started on this tournée in the hope of obtaining sufficient funds to keep my School during the war. Imagine my consternation on receiving a cable from Switzerland to say that my cable sending money had, owing to war restrictions, been held up. As the directress of the boarding school in which I had left the girls was unable to keep them without payment, they were in danger of being turned out of doors. With my usual impulsiveness, I insisted that Augustin should start at once for Geneva with the necessary funds to save my pupils—not realising that this left me without enough money to pay the hotel bill, and, as my irate manager had departed for Chili with a Comic Opera troupe, my pianist, Dumesnil, and I were left stranded in Buenos Aires.

The audiences were cold, heavy, unappreciative. In fact, the only success I had in Buenos Aires was that night in the cabaret when I danced the Hymn of Freedom. We were obliged to leave our trunks at the hotel and continue our journey to Montevideo. Fortunately, my dancing tunics have no value with hotel proprietors!

And at Montevideo we found the audiences exactly the opposite to the Argentines—wild with enthusiasm—so we were able to continue our tournée to Rio de Janeiro. We arrived there without money, without baggage, but the Director of the Municipal Theatre was so kind as immediately to book performances, and here I found audiences so intelligent, so quick and responsive as to bring out the best in any artist who appeared before them.

Here I met the poet, Jean de Rio, who was beloved by all
the young men of Rio, for every youth in Rio is a poet himself. When we walked together we were followed by all these
young men crying, "Viva Jean de Rio, Viva Isadora."

*   *   *

Leaving Dumesnil in Rio, for he had made such a sensation there that he did not wish to leave, I returned to New
York. The journey was sad and lonely, for I was anxious
about my School. Some of the boxers also who had gone
out with me came back on the same ship as stewards, having
had no success and made no money.

Among the passengers was an American named Wilkins,
who was always drunk, and every night at dinner he would
say, "Take this bottle of Pommery 1911 to the table of
Isadora Duncan," to the consternation of every one.

When we reached New York no one came to meet me, as
my cable had not been delivered owing to war difficulties.
By chance I called up a great friend, Arnold Genthe. He
is not only a genius but a wizard. He had left painting for
photography but this photography was most weird and
magical. It is true he pointed his camera at people and
took their photographs, but the pictures were never photographs of his sitters but his hypnotic imagination of them.
He has taken many pictures of me which are not representations of my physical being but representations of conditions
of my soul, and one of them is my very soul indeed.

He had always been my greatest friend, so finding myself
on the dock alone I called him up on the telephone. What
was my surprise at being answered by a familiar voice, but
not the voice of Arnold. It was Lohengrin, who, by a
strange coincidence, had just gone in to see Genthe that
morning. When he heard that I was alone at the docks
without funds, and without friends, he at once said he would
come to my aid.

Some minutes later he arrived. When I saw his tall, commanding figure again I had a curious feeling of confidence and safety, and I was as delighted to see him as he was to see me.

As a parenthesis, you may notice in this autobiography that I have always been faithful to my loves, and in fact would probably never have left any of them if they had been faithful to me. For just as I once loved them, I love them still and for ever. If I have parted from so many, I can only blame the fickleness of men and the cruelty of Fate.

And so, after these disastrous voyages, I was rejoiced to see my Lohengrin once more coming to the rescue. With his customary commanding manner, he soon released my luggage from the Customs and then we went to Genthe's studio and all three went out to lunch on Riverside Drive, overlooking Grant's tomb.

We were all delighted to be together again and drank much champagne and I felt that my return to New York was of happy augury. L. was in one of his kindest and most generous moods. After lunch he rushed down and engaged the Metropolitan Opera House and spent the afternoon and evening sending out invitations to every artist for a great free gala performance. This performance was one of the most beautiful experiences of my life. There were present all the artists, actors and musicians of New York and I had the joy of dancing without the oppression of the box office. Of course at the close of the performance, as I always did during the war, I ended with the "Marseillaise," and received a tremendous ovation for France and the Allies.

I told L. how I had sent Augustin to Geneva, and my anxiety about the School and, with his extraordinary generosity, he cabled the funds necessary to bring the School over to New York. But, alas, for part of the School the money was too late. All of the little pupils had been claimed by their parents and taken home. This dispersing of the School to which I had sacrificed years of work, cost me much pain, but I was somewhat comforted by the arrival of Augustin and the six elder children shortly afterwards.

L. continued to be in the best and most generous moods, and there was nothing too good for the children or for me. He rented a great studio at the top of Madison Square Garden, where we worked every afternoon. In the morning he would take us for long motor drives by the Hudson. He gave gifts to every one. In fact, for the time being life became wonderful through the magic power of money.

But as the rigorous New York winter advanced, my health failed, and L. suggested that I should take a trip to Cuba. He sent his secretary to accompany me.

I have the most delightful memories of Cuba. L.'s secretary was a young Scotchman and a poet. My health did not permit me to give any performances, but we spent three weeks in Havana driving along the coast, enjoying the picturesque surroundings. I remember one tragic-comic incident of our stay there.

About two kilometres from Havana there was an ancient Leper House, surrounded by a high wall. But the wall was not high enough to prevent us from seeing at times a mask of horror looking over it. The authorities realised the incongruity of this place next door to a fashionable winter resort and decided to move it. But the lepers refused to go. They clung to the doors, to the walls, some got on to the roofs and clung there, and it was even rumoured that some of them had escaped into Havana and were hiding there. The removal of this leper house always seemed to me like a queer, uncanny play of Maeterlinck.

Another house where I visited, was inhabited by a member of one of the oldest families who had a fancy for monkeys and gorillas. The garden of the old house was filled with cages in which this lady kept her pets. Her house was a point of interest to all visitors, whom she entertained with the most lavish hospitality, receiving her guests with a monkey on her shoulder and holding a gorilla by the hand. These were the tamest of her collection, but some were not so mild, and, as one passed their cages they would shake the bars and utter shrieks and make faces. I asked if they were not dangerous and she replied nonchalantly that apart from getting out of their cages and killing a gardener now and then, they were quite safe. This information made me rather anxious and I was glad when the time came to depart.

The strange part of the story is that this woman was very beautiful, with large expressive eyes, well-read and intelligent, and was wont to gather together in her house the brightest lights in the world of literature and art. How, then, explain her fantastic affection for apes and gorillas? She told me that in her Will she had left her entire collection of monkeys to the Pasteur Institute for experimental work in connection with cancer and tuberculosis, which seemed to me a peculiar form of showing post-mortem love.

I have another interesting recollection of Havana. On a festival night, when all the cabarets and cafés were teeming with life, after our usual tour by the sea and the pampas land, we arrived at a typical Havana café, somewhere about three o'clock in the morning. Here we found the usual assortment of morphimaniacs, cocainists, opium smokers, alcoholists, and other derelicts of life. Taking our places at a small table in the low-ceilinged, dimly-lit, smoky room, my attention was drawn to a white-faced, hallucinated-looking man, with cadaverous cheeks and ferocious eyes. With his long thin fingers he touched the keys of a piano and to my astonishment there came forth Chopin's Preludes, played with marvellous insight and genius. I listened for some time, then approached him, but he could only speak a few incoherent words. My movement had riveted the attention of the café upon me, and realising that I was absolutely incognito, there came over me a fantastic desire to dance for this strange audience. Wrapping my cape about me, directing the pianist, I danced to the music of several of the Preludes. Gradually the drinkers in the little café lapsed into silence, and, as I continued to dance, not only did I gain their attention, but many of them were weeping. The pianist also awoke from his morphia trance and played as though inspired.

I continued to dance until the morning and when I left, they all embraced me, and I felt prouder than in any theatre, for this I knew to be the real proof of my talent, without the help of any impresario or fore-notices engaging public attention.

Soon after this my poet friend and I took the boat to Florida, and landed at Palm Beach. From there I sent a telegram to Lohengrin, who joined us at the Breakers Hotel.

* * *

The most terrible part of a great sorrow is not the beginning, when the shock of grief throws one into a state of exaltation which is almost anæsthetic in its effects, but afterwards, long afterwards, when people say, "Oh, she has gotten over it"—or "She is all right now, she outlived it"; when one is, perhaps, at what might be considered a merry dinner-party to feel Grief with one icy hand oppressing the heart, or clutching at one's throat with the other burning claw. Ice and Fire, Hell, and Despair, overcoming all, and, lifting the glass of champagne, one endeavours to stifle this misery in whatever forgetfulness—possible or impossible.

This was the state I had now reached. All my friends said: "She has forgotten; she has outlived," whereas the sight of any little child who entered the room suddenly, calling "Mother" stabbed my heart, twisted my whole being with such anguish that the brain could only cry out for Lethe, for Oblivion, in one form or another, and from this horrible suffering I aspired to create new life, to create Art. Ah, how I envy the resignation of those nuns who pray with pale lips, murmuring incessant prayers all through the night before the coffins of strangers. Such temperaments are the envy of the artist who revolts, who cries, "I will love, love, create joy, joy." What a Hell!

L. brought with him to Palm Beach the American poet, Percy MacKaye, and sitting all together on the verandah one day, L. sketched out a plan for a future School according to my ideas, and informed me that he had bought the Madison Square Garden as a fitting ground-plan for the School.

Although enthusiastic about the plan as a whole, I was not in favour of starting so vast a project in the middle of the war, and it was this that finally irritated L. to such an extent that, with the same impulsiveness with which he had bought the Garden, he cancelled the sale upon our return to New York.

Percy MacKaye had written a beautiful poem the year before after seeing the children dancing here.

> "*A bomb has fallen over Notre Dame:*
> *Germans have burned another Belgian town:*
> *Russians quelled in the East: England in qualm:*
>
> *I closed my eyes, and laid the paper down.*
> *Grey ledge and moor-grass and pale bloom of light*
> *By pale blue seas:*
> *What laughter of a child world-sprite,*
> *Sweet as the horns of lone October bees,*
> *Shrills the faint shore with mellow, old delight?*
> *What elves are these*

In smocks grey-blue as sea and ledge,
Dancing upon the silvered edge
Of darkness—each ecstatic one
Making a happy orison,
With shining limbs, to the low sunken sun?
See: now they cease
Like nesting birds from flight:
Demure and debonair
They troop beside their hostess' chair
To make their bedtime courtesies:
> *"Spokoini Notchi! Gute Nacht!*
> *Bon soir! Bon soir! Good night!"*
What far-gleaned lives are these
Linked in one Holy Family of Art?
Dreams: Dreams once Christ and Plato dreamed:
How fair their happy shades depart!

Dear God! How simple it all seemed
Till once again
Before my eyes the red type quivered: slain:
Ten thousand of the enemy.
Then laughter! Laughter from the ancient sea
Sang in the gloaming: Athens! Galilee!
And elfin voices called from the extinguished light:
> *"Spokoini Notchi! Gute nacht!*
> *Bon soir! Bon soir! Good night!"*

CHAPTER THIRTY

IN early 1917 I was appearing at the Metropolitan Opera House. At that time I believed, as did many others, that the whole world's hope of liberty, regeneration and civilisation depended on the Allies winning the war, so at the end of each performance I danced the "Marseillaise," with the entire audience standing. This did not prevent me from giving my concerts of Richard Wagner's music, and I think that all intelligent people will agree that the boycotting of German Artists during the War was unjust and stupid.

On the day of the announcement of the Russian Revolution all lovers of freedom were filled with hopeful joy, and that night I danced the "Marseillaise" in the real original Revolutionary spirit in which it was composed, and followed it with my interpretation of the "Marche Slav," in which appears the Hymn to the Tsar, and I pictured the downtrodden serf under the lash of the whip.

This antithesis or dissonance of gesture against music roused some storm in the audience.

It is strange that in all my Art career it has been these movements of despair and revolt that have most attracted me. In my red tunic I have constantly danced the Revolution and the call to arms of the oppressed.

On the night of the Russian Revolution I danced with a terrible fierce joy. My heart was bursting within me at the release of all those who had suffered, been tortured, died in the cause of Humanity. It is no wonder that L., watching me night after night from his box, should in the end have been somewhat perturbed, or that he should ask himself

334

whether this School of grace and beauty of which he was
the patron, might not become a dangerous thing that would
lead him and his millions to annihilation. But my Art
impulse was too strong for me and I could not arrest it even
to please one I loved.

L. gave a fête at Sherry's in my honour. It began with a
dinner, and went on through dancing to an elaborate supper.
Upon this occasion he presented me with a wonderful diamond necklace. I had never wanted jewels, and had never
worn any, but he seemed so delighted that I allowed him to
place the diamonds round my neck. Towards morning, after
gallons of champagne had continually refreshed the guests,
and my own head was more or less light with the pleasures
of the moment and the intoxication of the wine, I had the
unhappy idea of teaching the Apache tango—as I had seen
it danced in Buenos Aires—to a beautiful young boy who
was present. Suddenly I felt my arm wrenched in an iron
grasp, and looked round to find L. storming with rage.

This was the only occasion upon which I ever wore this
unlucky necklace, for shortly after this incident, in another
rage, L. disappeared. I was left with an enormous hotel
bill and all the expenses of my School on my hands. After
appealing to him in vain for help, the famous diamond
necklace was taken to the pawnshop and I never saw it
again.

So I found myself stranded in New York without funds,
at the end of the season when any more activity was practically impossible. Fortunately I had in my possession an
ermine coat and also a wonderful emerald that L. had
bought from the son of a Maharajah, who had lost all his
money at Monte Carlo. It was said to have come from the
head of a famous idol. I sold the coat to one famous
soprano, the emerald to another famous soprano and took a
villa at Long Beach for the summer, installing my pupils

there while I waited for the autumn, when it might again be possible to make money.

With my usual improvidence, once I had the money for the villa, the auto and our daily needs, I recked but little of the future. As I was now practically penniless, it would, no doubt, have been wiser to have invested the proceeds of the furs and jewels in solid stocks and bonds, but of course this never occurred to me and we all spent a pleasant enough summer at Long Beach, entertaining, as usual, many artists. Among the guests who stayed with us there for several weeks was the genial violinist Isaye, who made our little villa glad with the tones of his beautiful violin morning and evening. We had no studio, but danced on the beach and we gave one special festival in honour of Isaye, who was as delighted as a boy.

But, as may be imagined, after the pleasures of this summer, when we returned to New York, I found myself without any funds and after two distracted months accepted a contract for California.

In the course of this tournée I found myself nearing my native town. Just before my arrival I had heard the news, which the papers had brought, of the death of Rodin. The thought that I should never see my great friend again made me weep so much that on seeing the reporters waiting on the platform at Oakland to interview me, not wishing them to notice my swollen eyes, I covered my face with a black lace veil, which caused them to write next day that I had affected an air of mystery.

It was twenty-two years since I had left San Francisco on my great adventure, and you can picture my emotion at returning to my native town, where everything had been completely changed by the earthquake and fire of 1906 so that it was all new to me and I could hardly recognise it.

Although the select and expensive audience at the Columbia Theatre was most kind and appreciative, as were the critics also, I was not satisfied, for I wanted to dance for the people on a great scale. But when I asked for the Greek Theatre for this purpose, it was refused me. I have never known the reason for this refusal, whether it was owing to a want of strategy on the part of my manager or to some ill-will which I could not understand.

In San Francisco I met my mother again, whom I had not seen for some years, as, from an unaccountable feeling of homesickness, she refused to live in Europe. She looked very old and careworn and once, lunching out at the Cliff House, and seeing our two selves in a mirror, I could not help contrasting my sad face and the haggard looks of my mother with the two adventurous spirits who had set out nearly twenty-two years ago with such high hopes to seek fame and fortune. Both had been found—why was the result so tragic? Probably because that is the natural sequel of life on this most unsatisfactory globe, where the very first conditions are hostile to man. I have met many great artists and intelligent and so-called successful people in my life, but never one who could be called a happy being, although some may have made a very good bluff at it. Behind the mask, with any clairvoyance, one can divine the same uneasiness and suffering. Perhaps in this world so-called happiness does not exist. There are only moments.

Such moments I experienced in San Francisco when I met my musical twin-soul—the pianist Harold Bauer. To my amazement and delight he told me that I was more of a musician than a dancer and that my art had taught him the meaning of otherwise inscrutable phrases of Bach, Chopin and Beethoven. For some miraculous weeks we experienced a wonderful collaboration of art, for, just as he assured me that I had opened to him secrets of his art, so he showed me interpretations of my own of which I had not dreamed.

Harold had led a subtle and intellectual life, far above the crowd. Unlike most musicians, his scope was not limited to music alone, but embraced a fine appreciation of all art and a wide intellectual knowledge of poetry and the deepest philosophy. When two lovers of the same high ideal of Art meet, a certain drunkenness possesses them. For days we lived in a high degree of intoxication without wine, through every nerve a trembling, surging hope, and when our eyes met in the realisation of this hope we experienced such vehement delight as would cause us to cry out as if in pain: "Have you felt this phrase of Chopin so?" "Yes, like that, with something more. I will create for you the movement of it." "Ah, what realisation! Now I will play it for you." "Ah, what delight—what highest joy!"

Such were our conversations, continually mounting to a profounder knowledge of that music we both adored.

We gave a performance together at the Columbia Theatre in San Francisco, which I consider was one of the happiest events of my career. Meeting with Harold Bauer placed me once more in that marvellous atmosphere of light and joy which only comes from association with such an illuminated soul. I had hoped that this might continue and that we might discover an entire new domain of musical expression together. But, alas, I had not reckoned on circumstance. Our collaboration ended with a forced and dramatic separation.

While in San Francisco, I formed a friendship with a prominent writer and musical critic, Redfern Mason. After one of Bauer's concerts, when we were all supping together, he asked me what he could do to please me in San Francisco. In reply I made him promise that he would grant me one request, at whatever cost. He promised, and, taking out a pencil, I wrote a long eulogy on Bauer's concert, taking as my text Shakespeare's Sonnet beginning:

> *How oft, when thou, my music, music play'st*
> *Upon that blessed wood whose motion sounds*
> *With thy sweet fingers . . .*
> *Do I envy those jacks that nimble leap*
> *To kiss the tender inward of thy hand. . . .*

and ending:

> *Since saucy jacks so happy are in this,*
> *Give them thy fingers, me thy lips to kiss.*

Redfern was terribly embarrassed, but he had to be a "sport," and when the criticism appeared over his name the next day, all his colleagues teased him unmercifully on his new and sudden passion for Bauer. My kind friend bore their teasing stoically, and when Bauer left San Francisco, he was my best comrade and comforter.

In spite of the enthusiasm of the select audiences who filled the Columbia, I was despondent at the lack of response of my native town to support my ideal of a future School. They had a crowd of my imitators and several imitation schools already, with which they seemed quite satisfied, and they even seemed to think that the sterner stuff of my Art might cause some disaster. My imitators had become all saccharine and sweet syrup, promulgating that part of my work which they were pleased to call the "harmonious and beautiful!" but omitting anything sterner, omitting, in fact, the mainspring and real meaning.

In a moment of prophetic love for America Walt Whitman said: "I hear America singing," and I can imagine the mighty song that Walt heard, from the surge of the Pacific, over the plains, the voices rising of the vast Choral of children, youths, men and women, singing Democracy.

When I read this poem of Whitman's I, too, had a Vision —the Vision of America dancing a dance that would be the worthy expression of the song Walt heard when he heard America singing. This music would have a rhythm as great as the exhilaration, the swing or curves of the Rocky Mountains. It would have nothing to do with the sensual lilt of the jazz rhythm: it would be like the vibration of the American soul striving upward, through labour to harmonious life. Nor had this dance that I visioned any vestige of the Fox Trot or the Charleston—rather was it the living leap of the child springing toward the heights, towards its future accomplishment, towards a new great vision of life that would express America.

It has often made me smile—but somewhat ironically— when people have called my dancing Greek, for I myself count its origin in the stories which my Irish grandmother often told us of crossing the plains with grandfather in '49 in a covered wagon—she eighteen, he twenty-one, and how her child was born in such a wagon during a famous battle with the Redskins, and how, when the Indians were finally defeated, my grandfather put his head in at the door of the wagon, with a smoking gun still in his hand, to greet his newborn child.

When they reached San Francisco, my grandfather built one of the first wooden houses, and I remember visiting this house when I was a little girl, and my grandmother, thinking of Ireland, used often to sing the Irish songs and dance the Irish jigs, only I fancy that into these Irish jigs had crept some of the heroic spirit of the Pioneer and the battle with the Redskins—probably some of the gestures of the Redskins themselves and, again, a bit of Yankee Doodle, when Grandfather Colonel Thomas Gray came marching home from the Civil War. All this grandmother danced in the Irish jig, and I learnt it from her, putting into it my own aspiration of Young America, and, finally, my great spiritual realisation of life from the lines of Walt Whitman. And that is the origin of the so-called Greek Dance with which I have flooded the world.

That was the origin—the root—but afterwards, coming to Europe, I had three great Masters, the three great precursors of the Dance of our century—Beethoven, Nietzsche and Wagner. Beethoven created the Dance in mighty rhythm, Wagner in sculptural form, Nietzsche in Spirit. Nietzsche was the first dancing philosopher.

I often wonder where is the American composer who will hear Walt Whitman's America singing, and who will compose the true music for the American Dance which will contain no Jazz rhythm—no rhythm from the waist down, but from the Solar Plexus, the temporal home of the soul, upwards to the Star-Spangled Banner of the great sky which arches over that stretch of land from the Pacific, over the Plains, over the Sierra Nevadas, over the Rocky Mountains to the Atlantic. I pray you, young American composer, create the music for the dance that shall express the America of Walt Whitman—the America of Abraham Lincoln.

It seems to me monstrous that any one should believe that the Jazz rhythm expresses America. Jazz rhythm expresses the primitive savage. America's music would be something different. It has yet to be written. No composer has yet caught this rhythm of America—it is too mighty for the ears of most. But some day it will gush forth from the great stretches of Earth, rain down from the vast sky spaces, and America will be expressed in some Titanic music that will shape its chaos to harmony, and long-legged, shining boys and girls will dance to this music, not the tottering, ape-like convulsions of the Charleston, but a striking, tremendous upward movement, mounting high above the Pyramids of Egypt, beyond the Parthenon of Greece, an expression of beauty and strength such as no civilisation has ever known.

And this dance will have nothing in it of the inane coquetry of the ballet, or the sensual convulsion of the Negro. It will be clean. I see America dancing, standing with one foot poised on the highest point of the Rockies, her two hands stretched out from the Atlantic to the Pacific, her fine head tossed to the sky, her forehead shining with a Crown of a million stars.

How grotesque that they have encouraged in America Schools of, so-called, bodily culture, of Swedish gymnastics, and the ballet. The real American type can never be a ballet dancer. The legs are too long, the body too supple and the spirit too free for this school of affected grace and toe-walking. It is notorious that all great ballet dancers have been very short women with small frames. A tall, finely made woman could never dance the ballet. The type that expresses America at its best could never dance the ballet. By the wildest trick of the imagination you could not picture the Goddess of Liberty dancing the ballet. Then why accept this school in America?

Henry Ford has expressed the wish that all the children of Ford's City should dance. He does not approve of the modern dances, but says, let them dance the old-fashioned Waltz, Mazurka and Minuet. But the old-fashioned Waltz and Mazurka are an expression of sickly sentimentality and romance, which our youth has outgrown, and the Minuet is the expression of the unctuous servility of courtiers of the time of Louis XIV and hooped skirts. What have these movements to do with the free youth of America? Does not Mr. Ford know that movements are as eloquent as words?

Why should our children bend the knee in that fastidious and servile dance, the Minuet, or twirl in the mazes of the false sentimentality of the Waltz? Rather let them come forth with great strides, leaps and bounds, with lifted forehead and far-spread arms, to dance the language of our Pioneers, the Fortitude of our heroes, the Justice, Kindness, Purity of our statesmen, and all the inspired love and tenderness of our Mothers. When the American children dance in this way, it will make of them beautiful beings, worthy of the name of the Greatest Democracy.

That will be America Dancing.

CHAPTER THIRTY-ONE

JUST as there are days when my life seems to have been a Golden Legend studded with precious jewels, a flowery field with multitudes of blossoms, a radiant morn with love and happiness crowning every hour; when I have found no words to express my ecstasy and joy of life; when the idea of my School seems a ray of genius, or when I actually believe that, although not tangible, my School is a great success; when my Art is a resurrection; so there are other days when, trying to recollect my life, I am filled only with a great disgust and a feeling of utter emptiness. The past seems but a series of catastrophes and the future a certain calamity, and my School the hallucination emanating from the brain of a lunatic.

What is the truth of a human life, and who can find it? God Himself would be puzzled. In the midst of all this anguish and delight; this filth and this luminous purity; this fleshly body filled with hell fire, and this same body alight with heroism and beauty—where is the truth? God knows, or the devil knows—but I suspect they are both puzzled.

So, on some imaginative days, my mind is like a stained-glass window through which I see beautiful and fantastic beauties—marvellous forms and richest colours, and, on other days, I look only through dull, grey-glass windows and view the dull grey rubbish heap called Life.

If we could only dive down within ourselves and bring up thought as the diver brings up pearls—precious pearls from the closed oysters of silence in the depths of our subconsciousness!

After the long struggle to keep my School together, alone,

344

sick at heart, discouraged, my wish was to return to Paris, where it might be possible to realise some money on my property. Then Mary returned from Europe and telephoned me from the Biltmore. I told her of my plight and she said, "My great friend Gordon Selfridge is leaving tomorrow. If I ask him surely he will get you a ticket."

I was so worn out with the struggle and heart-break of my stay in America that I accepted this idea gladly and the next morning sailed from New York. But misfortune followed me, for the first night, walking on deck, where all was dark on account of war conditions, I fell down an opening in the deck, a drop of about fifteen feet and was rather seriously hurt. Gordon Selfridge very gallantly put his cabin at my disposal for the trip, as well as his companionship, and was altogether most kind and charming. I recounted to him my first visit to him, over twenty years before, when a hungry little girl asked him for credit for a frock to dance in.

This was my first contact with a man of action. I was amazed how different an outlook on life he had, after the artists and dreamers I had known—he might almost have been of another sex, for I suppose all my lovers had been decidedly feminine. And I had also always had the companionship of men who were more or less neurasthenic and either sunk in deepest gloom or buoyed up to sudden joy by drink, whereas Selfridge had the most extraordinary, even cheerfulness I have ever met, and as he never touches wine this amazed me, for I had never realised that any one could find life in itself a pleasant thing. It had always seemed to me the future held only now and then glimpses of ephemeral joy through Art or Love, whereas this man found happiness in actual living.

When I arrived in London, still suffering from my fall, I had not the money to go on to Paris, so I took a lodging in

Duke Street, and telegraphed to different friends in Paris, but got no answers, probably owing to the war. I spent some terrible and gloomy weeks in that melancholy lodging, completely stranded. Alone and ill, without a cent, my School destroyed and the war appearing to go on interminably, I used to sit at the dark window at night and watch the air raids, and wish that a bomb might fall on me to end my troubles. Suicide is so tempting. I have often thought of it, but something always holds me back. Certainly if suicide pellets were sold in drug stores as plainly as some preventives, I think the intelligentsia of all countries would doubtless disappear over night in conquered agony.

In despair I cabled to L. but got no reply. A manager had arranged some performances for my pupils, who wanted to seek their careers in America. They afterwards toured as the Isadora Duncan Dancers, but none of the profits of these tours were given to me, and I found myself in a desperate situation, until by chance I met a charming member of the French Embassy, who came to my rescue and took me to Paris. There I engaged a room in the Palais D'Orsay, and resorted to money-lenders for the necessary funds.

Every morning at five o'clock we were awakened by the brutal boom of the Big Bertha, a fitting beginning for the sinister day which went on with frequent terrible news from the Front. Death, Bloodshed, Butchery filled the miserable hours and at night the whistling warning of the air raids.

One bright recollection of this time was meeting with the famous "Ace" Garros at a friend's house one evening, when he played Chopin and I danced, and he brought me home on foot from Passy to the Quai D'Orsay. There was an air raid, which we watched and under which I danced for him on the Place de la Concorde—he sitting on the edge of a fountain-basin applauding me, his melancholy dark eyes lit up by the fire of the rockets that fell and exploded quite near us. He told me that night that he only sought and wished for death. Shortly after, the Angel of Heroes sought and carried him away—away from this life that he did not love.

The days passed in dreary monotony. I would gladly have been a nurse, but I realised the futility of adding what would have been a superfluous force when the applicants for nursing were waiting in rows. So I thought to turn to my Art again, although my heart was so heavy that I wondered if my feet could bear the weight.

There is a song of Wagner's that I love—"The Angel"—which tells of a spirit sitting in utter sadness and desolation, to whom comes an Angel of Light, and such an Angel then came to me, in these dark days, when a friend brought Walter Rummel, the pianist, to see me.

When he entered I thought he was the picture of the youthful Liszt, come out of its frame—so tall, slight, with a burnished lock over the high forehead, and eyes like clear wells of shining light. He played for me. I called him my Archangel. We worked in the foyer of the theatre which Réjane had graciously put at my disposal, and during the booms of the Big Bertha and amidst the echoes of the war news, he played for me Liszt's "Thoughts of God in the Wilderness," St. Francis speaking to the birds, and I composed new dances to the inspiration of his playing, dances all comprised of prayer and sweetness and light, and once more my spirit came to life, drawn back by the heavenly melodies which sang beneath the touch of his fingers. This was the beginning of the most hallowed and ethereal love of my life.

No one has ever played Liszt as my Archangel played him, because he has the vision. He sees beyond the written score what frenzy really means, and frenzy spoken daily with angels.

He was all gentleness and sweetness, and yet passion burned him. He performed with unconsenting frenzy. His nerves consumed him, his soul rebelled. He did not give way to passion with the spontaneous ardour of youth, but, on the contrary, his loathing was as evident as the irresistible feeling which possessed him. He was like a dancing saint on a brazier of live coals. To love such a man is as dangerous as difficult. Loathing of love can easily turn to hatred against the aggressor.

How strange and terrible to approach a human being through the envelope of flesh and find a soul—through its envelope of flesh to find pleasure, sensation, illusion. Ah! above all—illusion of what men call Happiness—through the envelope of flesh, through the appearance, illusion—what men call Love.

The reader must remember that these memories cover many years and that each time a new love came to me, in the form of Demon or Angel or Simple Man, I believed that this was the only one for whom I had waited so long, that this love would be the final resurrection of my life. But I suppose love always brings this conviction. Each love affair in my life would have made a novel, and they all ended badly. I have always waited for that one which would end well, and last for ever and ever—like the optimistic cinemas!

The miracle of Love is the varied themes and keys in which it can be played, and the love of one man compared to another may be as different as hearing the music of Beethoven compared to the music of Puccini, and the instrument that gives the response to these melodious players is Woman. And I suppose a woman who has known but one man is like a person who has heard only one composer.

As the summer progressed we sought a quiet retreat in the South. There, near the Port of St. Jean on Cap Ferrat, in the almost deserted hotel, we made our studio in the empty garage, and all through the days and evenings he played celestial music and I danced.

What a blissful time now came to me, gladdened by my archangel, surrounded by the sea, living only in music. It was like the dream of Catholics dead and gone to Heaven. What a pendulum is Life—the deeper the agony, the higher the ecstasy—each time the lower sinking in sorrow, the higher tossed in joy.

Now and then we issued from our retreat to give a benefit for the unfortunate or a concert for the wounded, but mostly we were alone, and through music and love, through love and music—my soul dwelt in the heights of bliss.

In a villa near by lived a venerable priest and his sister, Madame Giraldy. He had been a White Monk in South Africa. They were our only friends, and I often danced for them the inspired and holy music of Liszt. But as the summer waned we found a studio in Nice, and, when the Armistice was proclaimed, we returned to Paris.

The war was over. We watched the Victory march through the Arc de Triomphe, and we shouted, "The World is saved." For the moment we were all poets, but, alas, as the Poet awoke to find bread and cheese for his Beloved, so the World awoke to its commercial necessities.

My Archangel took me by the hand and we went to Bellevue. We found the house falling into ruins. Still, we thought, why not rebuild it? And we spent some deluded months endeavouring to find the funds for this impossible task.

At last we were persuaded of the impossibility of the task, and accepted a reasonable offer of purchase by the French Government, who were of opinion that this great house would be admirable as a factory for asphyxiating gases for the next war. After having seen my Dionysion transformed into a hospital for the wounded, I was fated to finally abandon it to become a factory of instruments of war. The loss of Bellevue seems a great pity—Bellevue—the view was so beautiful.

When the sale was at last accomplished and the money in the bank, I bought a house in the Rue de la Pompe which had been the former Salle Beethoven, and here I made my studio.

My Archangel had a very sweet sense of compassion. He seemed to feel all the sorrow which made my heart so heavy and which often caused me sleepless and tearful nights. At such hours he would gaze at me with such pitying and luminous eyes that my spirit was comforted.

And in the studio our two arts blended into one in a marvellous manner, while under his influence my dance became etherealised. He was the first to initiate me to the full spiritual meaning of the works of Franz Liszt, of whose music we composed an entire Recital. In the quiet music-room of the Salle Beethoven I also began the studies of some great frescoes in movement and light which I wished to realise from "Parsifal."

There we spent holy hours, our united souls borne up by the mysterious force which possessed us. Often as I danced and he played, as I lifted my arms and my soul went up from my body in the long flight of the silver strains of the Grail, it seemed as if we had created a spiritual entity quite apart from ourselves, and, as sound and gesture flowed up to the Infinite, another answer echoed from above.

I believe that from the psychic force of this musical moment, when our two spirits were so attuned in the holy energy of love, we were on the verge of another world. Our audience felt the force of this combined power and often a curious psychosis existed in the theatre such as I had not known before. If my Archangel and I had pursued these studies further, I have no doubt that we might have arrived at the spontaneous creation of movements of such spiritual force as to bring a new revelation to mankind. How pitiful that earthly passion should have put an end to this holy pursuit of highest beauty. For, just as in the Legend, one is never content but opens the door for the bad fairy, who introduces all sorts of trouble, so I, instead of being content to pursue the happiness I had found, felt returning the old will to remake the School, and, to this end, I cabled to my pupils in America.

When they joined me I gathered together a few faithful friends to whom I said, "Let us all go to Athens and look upon the Acropolis, for we may yet found a School in Greece."

How one's motives are misinterpreted! A writer in *The New Yorker* (1927), spoke of this trip as "her extravagance knew no bounds. She took a house-party and, beginning at Venice, went on to Athens."

Alas for me! My pupils arrived, young and pretty and successful. My Archangel looked upon them—and fell—fell to one.

How describe this journey, which was for me Love's Calvary? How I first noticed their affection at the Hotel Excelsior on the Lido, where we stopped for some weeks, how I was assured of it on the boat going to Greece, and how the assurance finally spoilt for me, for ever, the view of the Acropolis by moonlight—these are the stations of Love's Calvary.

On our arrival in Athens everything seemed propitious for the School. By the kindness of Veniselos, the Zappeion was put at my disposition. Here we had our studio and here I worked every morning with my pupils, endeavouring to inspire them with a dance worthy of the Acropolis. My plan was to have trained a thousand children for great Dionysian festivals in the Stadium.

Every day we went to the Acropolis, and, remembering my first visit there in 1904, it was for me an intensely touch-

ing sight to see the youthful forms of my pupils now in their
dance realising a part, at least, of the dream that I had had
there sixteen years before. And now that everything seemed
to indicate that the war was over, I should be able to form
my long-sought School in Athens.

My pupils, who had arrived from America with certain
affectations and mannerisms which displeased me, lost them
under the glorious sky of Athens and the inspiration of the
magnificent view of mountains and sea and great Art.

The painter Edward Steichen, who was one of our party,
took many lovely pictures in the Acropolis and in the theatre
of Dionysus, which faintly foreshadowed the splendid vision
I longed to create in Greece.

We found Kopanos a ruin, inhabited by shepherds and
their flocks of mountain goats, but, nothing daunted, I decided soon to clear the ground and rebuild the house. The
work began at once. The accumulated rubbish of years was
cleared away and a young architect undertook the task of
putting in doors and windows, and a roof. We laid a dancing carpet in the high living-room and had a grand piano
brought up. Here every afternoon, with the gorgeous view
of the sun setting behind the Acropolis, and diffusing soft
purple and golden rays over the sea, my Archangel played
to us magnificent and inspiring music—Bach, Beethoven,
Wagner, Liszt. In the cool of the evenings we all wreathed
our brows with circlets of the lovely white jasmine flowers
that the Athenian boys sell in the streets, and strolled down
to supper by the sea at Phaleron.

My Archangel, among this bevy of flower-crowned
maidens, resembled Parsifal in Kundry's garden, only I began
to notice a new expression in his eyes, which spoke more of
Earth than of Heaven. I had imagined our love so strong
in its intellectual and spiritual fastness, that it was some
time before the truth dawned on me that his shining wings

had been transformed into two ardent arms which could seize and hold the body of a Dryad. All my experience availed me nothing and this was a terrible shock to me. From then on, an uneasy, terrible pain possessed me, and in spite of myself I began to watch the indications of their growing love with feelings which, to my horror, sometimes awakened a demon akin to murder.

One evening at sunset, when my Archangel—who was more and more rapidly taking on the resemblance of a human being—had just finished the great March of the "Götterdämmerung," and the last notes were dying on the air, seeming to melt into the purple rays, to echo from Hymettus and illumine the sea itself, I suddenly saw a meeting of their eyes, flaming with equal ardour in the scarlet sundown.

On seeing this a spasm of rage seized me with such violence that it frightened me. I turned and walked away and all that night I wandered about the hills near Hymettus, possessed with a frenzy of despair. Certainly I had known before in my life that green-eyed monster whose fangs inspire the worst of sufferings, but never to such a degree had I been possessed by such a terrible passion as I now felt. I loved, and, at the same time, hated them both, and this experience has given me much sympathy with and understanding for those unfortunates who, goaded by unimaginable torture through jealousy, kill the one they love.

To avoid arriving at this calamity, I took a little group of my pupils, and my friend Edward Steichen, and we mounted by the wonderful road passing Ancient Thebes to Chalcis, where I saw the very golden sands on which I had imagined the maidens of Eubœa dancing in honour of Iphigenia's ill-fated wedding.

But, for the moment, all the glories of Hellas could not cast out the infernal demon that possessed me, which constantly filled my mind with the picture of the two left behind

in Athens, gnawing at my vitals and eating like acid into
my brain, and, on our return, the sight of them both on the
balcony which stretched before our bedroom windows, radiant with youth and mutual fire, completed my misery.

I cannot understand such a possession now, but, at the
time, it enmeshed me and was as impossible to escape as
scarlet-fever or small-pox. In spite of this, however, I
taught my pupils each day and continued plans for the
School in Athens, upon which everything seemed to smile.
The Ministry of Veniselos was most amenable to my plans,
and the populace of Athens enthusiastic.

One day we were all invited to a grand demonstration in
honour of Veniselos and the young King, which took place
in the Stadium. Fifty thousand people took part in this
demonstration, as well as the entire Greek Church, and when
the young King and Veniselos entered the Stadium they
received a glorious ovation. The procession of Patriarchs
in their brocade robes, stiff with gold embroidery, glittering
in the sun, was an amazing sight.

When I entered the Stadium in my softly-draped peplum,
followed by a group of living Tanagra figures, the pleasant
Constantine Melas came forward and presented me with a
laurel crown, saying:

"You, Isadora, bring to us again the immortal beauty
of Phidias and the age of Greece's greatness," and I replied:

"Ah, help me to create a thousand magnificent dancers to
dance in this Stadium in such a splendid way that the whole
world will come here to gaze upon them with wonder and
delight."

As I finished these words, I noticed the Archangel rap-
turously holding the hand of his favourite, and for once I
felt reconciled. What do petty passions matter in face of
my Great Vision, I thought, and beamed at them with love
and forgiveness. But that night when, on the balcony, I saw

their two heads together, silhouetted against the moon, I was again a prey to the petty, human feeling, which wrought such havoc that I wandered forth wildly alone, and brooded over a Sapphic leap from the Parthenon's rock.

No words can describe the suffering of the torturous passion which consumed me, and the soft beauty of my surroundings only made my unhappiness more intense. And there seemed to be no outlet for the situation. Could the complication of a mortal passion make us forego the immortal plans for a great musical collaboration? Nor could I send my pupil from the School where she had been brought up, and the alternative of watching their love each day and refraining from expressing the volume of my chagrin, seemed also impossible. It was, in fact, an impasse. There remained the possibility of rising to spiritual heights above all this, but, in spite of my unhappiness, the constant exercise of dancing, the long excursions in the hills, the daily swimming in the sea gave me a keen appetite and an earthly violence of emotion difficult to control.

And so I continued, and while I endeavoured to teach my pupils Beauty, Calm, Philosophy and Harmony, I was inwardly writhing in the clutch of most deadly torment. What the situation would have led to eventually I do not know.

The only resource I had was to assume an armour of exaggerated gaiety and try to drown my sufferings in the heady wines of Greece every night as we supped by the sea. There might certainly have been a nobler way, but I was not then capable of finding it. Anyhow these are only my poor human experiences and I try to put them down here. Whether they be worthy or worthless, they may perhaps serve as a guide to others as "What *not* to do." But probably every one seeks to avoid their own disaster and torment in the only way they can.

This impossible situation was put an end to by a strange

stroke of fate, caused by so slight a thing as the bite of a malicious little monkey, the monkey whose bite proved fatal to the young King.

For some days he hovered between life and death, and then came the sad announcement of his death, causing such a state of upheaval and revolution as to necessitate once more the departure of Veniselos and his party, and, incidentally, our departure also, for when we had been invited to Greece, it was as his guests, and we also fell political victims of the situation. So all the money I had spent in rebuilding Kopanos and arranging the studio was lost, and we were all forced to abandon the dream of a School in Athens and take the boat, returning via Rome to Paris.

What a strange, torturous memory is this last visit to Athens in 1920, and the return to Paris and the renewed agony and final separation and the departure of my Archangel, and my pupil, who was also leaving me for ever. Although I felt I had been the martyr of these happenings, she seemed to think just the opposite, and blamed me very bitterly for my feelings and lack of resignation about it all.

When at length I found myself alone in that house in the Rue de la Pompe, with its Beethoven Salle all prepared for the music of my Archangel, then my despair had no words. I could no longer bear the sight of this house in which I had been so happy, indeed I had a longing to fly from it and from the world, for, at the time, I believed that the world and love were dead for me. How many times in one's life one comes to that conclusion! Whereas, if we could see over the next hill, there is a valley of flowers and happiness awaiting us. Especially do I resent the conclusion formed by so many women that, after the age of forty, a dignified life should exclude all love-making. Ah, how wrong this is!

How mysterious it is to feel the life of the body, all

ISADORA DUNCAN

The Caryatid Porch of Erechtheum (Acropolis)

Photograph by Edward Steichen

through this weird journey on earth. First the timid, shrinking, slight body of the young girl that I was and the change to the hardy Amazon. Then the vine-wreathed Bacchante drenched with wine, falling soft and resistless under the leap of the Satyr, and growing, expanding; the swelling and increase of soft, voluptuous flesh, the breasts grown so sensitive to the slightest love emotion as to communicate a rush of pleasure through the whole nervous system; love now grown to a full blown rose whose fleshly petals close with violence on their prey. I live in my body like a spirit in a cloud—a cloud of rose fire and voluptuous response.

What nonsense to sing always of Love and Spring alone. The colours of autumn are more glorious, more varied and the joys of autumn are a thousandfold more powerful, terrible, beautiful. How I pity those poor women whose pallid, narrow creed precludes them from the magnificent and generous gift of the Autumn of Love. Such was my poor Mother, and to this absurd prejudice she owed the aging and illness of her body at the epoch when it should have been most splendid, and the partial collapse of a brain which had been magnificent. I was once the timid prey, then the aggressive Bacchante, but now I close over my lover as the sea over a bold swimmer, enclosing, swirling, encircling him in waves of cloud and fire.

* * *

In the spring of the year 1921 I received the following telegram from the Soviet Government:

"The Russian Government alone can understand you. Come to us: we will make your School."

From whence did this message come? From Hell? No— but the nearest place to it. What stood for Hell in Europe —from the Soviet Government of Moscow. And looking round my empty house, void of my Archangel, of Hope and of Love, I answered:

"Yes, I will come to Russia, and I will teach your children, on one condition, that you give me a studio and the wherewithal to work."

The answer was "Yes," so one day I found myself on a boat on the Thames, leaving London for Reval, and, eventually, Moscow.

Before leaving London I went to a fortune-teller, who said, "You are bound on a long journey. You will have many strange experiences, you will have troubles, you will marry—"

But at the word "marry," I cut her short with laughter. I, who was always against marriage? I would never marry. The fortune-teller said "Wait and see."

On the way to Russia I had the detached feeling of a soul after death making its way to another sphere. I thought I had left all the forms of European life behind me for ever. I actually believed that the ideal State, such as Plato, Karl Marx and Lenin had dreamed it, had now by some miracle been created on earth. With all the energy of my being, disappointed in the attempts to realise any of my art visions in Europe, I was ready to enter the ideal domain of Communism.

I had brought no dresses along. I pictured myself spending the rest of my life in a red flannel blouse among comrades equally simply dressed and filled with brotherly love.

As the boat proceeded northwards, I looked back with contempt and pity at all the old institutions and habits of bourgeois Europe that I was leaving. Henceforth to be a comrade among comrades, to carry out a vast plan to work for this generation of humanity. Adieu then Inequality, Injustice and the brutality of the Old World which had made my School impossible.

When the boat at last arrived my heart gave a great throb of joy. Now for the beautiful New World that had been created! Now for the World of Comrades. The dream that had been conceived in the head of Buddha; the dream that had resounded through the words of Christ; the dream that has been the ultimate hope of all great artists; the dream that Lenin had by a great magic turned to reality. I was entering now into this dream that my work and life might become a part of its glorious promise.

Adieu Old World! I would hail a New World.